# STUDIES IN RURAL CAPITALISM
# IN WEST AFRICA

# AFRICAN STUDIES SERIES

*General Editor:* DR J. R. GOODY

# STUDIES IN
# RURAL CAPITALISM
# IN WEST AFRICA

*by* POLLY HILL

*Fellow of Clare Hall, Cambridge*

CAMBRIDGE

AT THE UNIVERSITY PRESS, 1970

Published by the Syndics of the Cambridge University Press
Bentley House, 200 Euston Road, London N.W.1
American Branch: 32 East 57th Street, New York, N.Y.10022

© Cambridge University Press 1970

Library of Congress Catalogue Card Number: 77–96093

Standard Book Number: 521 07622 6

Printed in Great Britain
at the University Printing House, Cambridge
(Brooke Crutchley, University Printer)

*To my daughter Susannah Humphreys, who*
*accompanied me on my travels*

The new arrangements on his farm absorbed him as completely as though there would never be anything else in his life. He read the books lent him by Sviazhsky and, having ordered various others that he required, he read political economy and socialistic works on the same subject, but, as he had expected, found nothing in them related to his undertaking. In the political economy books—in Mill, for instance, whom he studied first and with great ardour, hoping every minute to find an answer to the questions that were engrossing him—he found only certain laws deduced from the state of agriculture in Europe; but he could not for the life of him see why these laws, which did not apply to Russia, should be considered universal...Political economy told him that the laws by which Europe had developed and was developing her wealth were universal and absolute. Socialist teaching told him that development along these lines leads to ruin. And neither of them offered the smallest enlightenment as to what he, Levin, and all the Russian peasants and land-owners were to do with their millions of hands and millions of acres, to make them as productive as possible for the common good.

*Anna Karenin* by L. N. Tolstoy,
trans. Rosemary Edmunds, Penguin Books, pp. 366–7

The condition of the native tribes had been investigated [by the official commission of enquiry] in its political, administrative, economic, ethnographic and religious aspects. All these questions had received admirably drafted answers—answers admitting no shade of doubt, since they were not a product of human thought, always liable to error, but were the outcome of official labours. The answers were all based on official data furnished by governors and prelates, founded on reports from district authorities and ecclesiastical superintendents, founded in their turn on the reports of rural administrative officers and parish priests. Consequently these answers left no possible room for doubt. Such questions, for instance, as to why crops failed, or why certain tribes adhered to their own creeds, and so on—questions which without the convenience of the official machine do not and cannot get solved for centuries —received clear and convincing answers.

*ibid.* p. 395

# CONTENTS

# Contents

# TABLES

# GRAPHS

# MAPS

# ACKNOWLEDGEMENTS

Thanks are due to Rosemary Edmunds and Penguin Books Ltd, for permission to include quotations from Rosemary Edmunds's translation of Tolstoy's *Anna Karenin*. Earlier versions of two of the chapters have appeared elsewhere as articles in journals. 'A Plea for Indigenous Economics: the West African Example' appeared in (the *Journal of*) *Economic Development and Cultural Change* in October 1966 and 'Notes on the History of the Northern Katsina Tobacco Trade' appeared in the *Journal of the Historical Association of Nigeria* for October 1968. The author and the publishers would like to thank the editors of the journals concerned for their collaboration in readily agreeing to the republication of the articles.

# PREFACE

This book is an attempt to provide social anthropologists, economists and geographers with *material* relating to the way in which rural people in West Africa order their economic behaviour. Believing in academic division of labour, I have deliberately avoided many theoretical and definitional issues which it would be conventional to discuss in a book with this kind of title and I draw hardly any 'planning' conclusions. But I have tried to avoid remoteness by constantly asking myself the question—'What kinds of things are other people likely to want to know?'

Of course there are numerous reasons why many of the most interesting questions cannot be investigated—how one does wish, for instance, that granaries, like graves, were not private places. But I hope I have demonstrated the academic respectability of pursuing one's fieldwork on the *assumption* that 'economic factors' are sufficiently isolable to justify an economic approach, even when many of the variables are wholly elusive. Anyway, I have found this assumption useful and leave it to others to judge by results.

As an economist turned economic anthropologist, I look for opportunities of placing my detailed field inquiries within a wider statistical framework, this being one way of arguing from the particular to the general. Had I not had access to the Department of Agriculture's farm-maps in their Area Offices, my work on the migrant cocoa-farmers of southern Ghana (chapter 2) would have been impossible. The study of cattle-trading in Northern Ghana (chapter 5) leans wholly upon statistics made available to me by the Animal Health Division. Although I stayed long enough in a Hausa village (chapter 7) to collect a fair amount of statistical data for myself, an air photograph lent to me by the Survey Department at Kaduna was an indispensable aid to mapping the farms. But such a procedure of leaning heavily on pre-existent data is not always possible or necessary, as shown by the examples of the Ewe seine fishermen (chapter 3) and the Hausa tobacco-traders (chapter 6).

If one happens to fall on a large hoard of relevant official statistics, as I did in Northern Ghana, then it may be possible to pursue one's fieldwork with almost improper speed. I was also quick in studying the Ewe seine fishermen —probably mainly because it chanced that my interpreter had been the secretary of a fishing company. But chance plays such a large part in research of this kind, that it is usually difficult to lay down detailed plans in advance. Just as I had not thought that two weeks in Northern Ghana would be so rewarding, so I was astonished by the need to devote as long as 3½ years to studying the migrant cocoa-farmers.

But if one cannot plan one's work in advance, how should it be directed? For myself I depend very much on my naïve feelings of *surprise*—holding that the most surprising 'events' are most worth pursuit. To do *re*search is to search anew for ideas one missed last time when formulating the packet of conscious, pre-conscious and unconscious assumptions one carries to the field. To illustrate this point, I list some specimen 'surprises'.

The basic surprise which triggered my prolonged inquiry on the historical development of southern Ghanaian cocoa-farming, was the observation that this had depended on migrant cocoa-farmers who had bought their land, not on small sedentary farmers. Among numerous other surprises were: the 'nice balance' which was maintained by the matrilineal migrants 'between individual control of newly acquired property and its absorption sooner or later into the common property of the descent group';[1] the persistence and dynamism of the migratory process over many decades; the extent of the farmers' development expenditure on roads and bridges; and the fact that everybody, rich and poor, in many of the Akwapim towns, participated in the migration.

I made an expedition to Anlo country, in south-eastern Ghana, to study the famous shallot-growing industry there—perhaps one of the most intensive examples of agriculture in the world, though developed without any assistance from the Agricultural Department. In the event, I was diverted by the surprise I felt over the elaborate organization (especially the accounting systems) of the seine-fishing companies, as well as by the geographical extent of their migration from the Congo (or even Angola) in the south, to Sierra Leone and beyond in the north. Nylon nets, of up to half a mile long, are very expensive items of capital equipment, which are owned by individual capitalists (net-owners) and sustained by a perpetual capital fund (*agbadoho*) which, unlike most other forms of property in Eweland, is (ideally) indivisible on death. Those who are interested in my preliminary findings may fortunately turn to the later work of M. Albert de Surgy.

Knowing that most of the cattle-owning inhabitants of the western Accra Plains lack any proper tradition of pastoralism, although cattle have been reared there for centuries, I had initially been interested in studying the history of the Fulani herdsmen who are now in charge of most of the cattle there. So I was surprised when I found that the employment of such herdsmen is a recent innovation. One of the more curious aspects of the symbiotic

[1] See 'Is Matriliny Doomed in Africa?' by Mary Douglas, included in *Man in Africa*, ed. Mary Douglas and Phyllis Kaberry (London, 1969), p. 132.

relationship between the kraal-owner and 'his Fulani' is the insistence of the latter on looking after sufficient cattle to enable him to employ a sub-herdsman.

The detailed statistical work on northern Ghanaian cattle-trading resulted from my surprise at finding that there was a very high rate of commercial take-off from the herds in all areas except the north-east. Contrary to popular belief, cattle-rearers (except possibly, though not necessarily, in the north-east) are so little reluctant to sell their stock that premature sale of immature animals is often the real problem. Expecting to study the 'social factors' behind the reluctance to sell, I found myself concluding that, in this context, such factors were irrelevant. The statistics, once assembled, got up their own momentum and led to many further surprises, such as that most cattle-traders comprise a constantly changing section of the population.

My work in Nigerian Hausaland is still in train and I cannot stand back from it sufficiently to report on its numerous major surprises, many of them interrelated. That permanent cultivation of manured farmland is often the preferred agronomic system where land is plentiful, implies that manure is an important scarce factor and that farming is a 'business'. The marked degree of economic inequality in a Katsina village is associated with both permanent cultivation and great seasonal price fluctuations, rather than with 'class stratification'. As for the nineteenth century export trade in tobacco conducted by the farmers of remote Kabakawa, this prompts one to wonder whether most Hausa long-distance trade (*fatauci*) has not always been hamlet-based.

I wish to express my deep gratitude to Professor W. F. Stolper for providing me (through the enlightened agency of the Center for Research on Economic Development, University of Michigan, Ann Arbor) with remarkable opportunities, over four years, both for pursuing my research on rural Hausaland and for writing up other material which I had gathered when a member of the Institute of African Studies, University of Ghana. On this side of the Atlantic my chief intellectual debt is to Mr Ivor Wilks, whose generous friendship did so much to relieve the isolation of my inter-disciplinary plight. To the University of Ghana, which employed me for eleven years in a research capacity (almost free of teaching duties) my gratitude is unbounded and I greatly value my more recent connexion with the Nigerian Institute of Social and Economic Research, University of Ibadan. To my thousands of willing friends and informants in rural Ghana and Nigeria I extend greetings—hoping that the day may come when work of this kind will be of real practical value to them.

*Clare Hall, Cambridge*
*August 1969*

POLLY HILL

FOREWORD

# CAPITAL AND CAPITALISTS
*by* S. HYMER[1]

Polly Hill's approach to the economy of Africa differs from that of most economists in both choice of subject and method of study. As this can lead to unnecessary misunderstandings, perhaps it would be useful for me to set out her theoretical framework more explicitly than she has done and to discuss its relationship to the neo-classical paradigm.[2]

Polly Hill's method is to study intensively small groups of people engaged in specific industries—farming, fishing, cattle raising, marketing, and so forth. This has led her to explore areas of the economic terrain untouched by government and academic economists who, using a different torchlight, ask different questions and focus on different facets of the West African economy. Her approach has already reaped rich rewards. In nearly all her investigations she has discovered features radically different from the conventional wisdom and she has already done much towards her announced goal of destroying the formidable body of folklore on West African economies established by 'reiterations' in books and official publications and responsible in the past and in the present for a number of glaring errors in economic policy. Her discoveries speak for themselves and only a fool would try to formulate economic policy in Ghana without carefully understanding Polly Hill's research on the indigenous economies, namely those sectors of the economy which cover some four-fifths of the population and which historically contained nearly all of its dynamic elements.

The distinguishing feature of Polly Hill's approach is that she focuses on producers rather than on production—on cocoa-farmers rather than on cocoa and, more generally, on capitalists rather than on capital. The econo-

[1] The author is Associate Professor of Economics at Yale University and a member of the Economic Growth Centre.
[2] In writing this foreword I have drawn on some theoretical models of capital and wealth developed in collaboration with Stephen Resnick. (S. Hymer and S. Resnick, *Capital and Wealth in the Industrialization Process*, Yale Economic Growth Center, cyclostyled 1969.) My own contribution to this paper was deeply influenced by my study of Polly Hill's research. The fact that Resnick came to similar views from his study of the Philippines economy suggests that Polly Hill's findings have a greater generality than may at first seem the case.

mist will, therefore, not find in this book the familiar models relating *output* of commodities either to their price or to *inputs* of land, labour and capital. Instead he will find descriptions of farmers, fishermen and cattle owners—their size, their attitudes and their behaviour. Although this approach may give the impression that her research is closer to anthropology and sociology than to economics, it would be very wrong for economists to read the essays in this volume in that light. Whatever the value of this research to anthropologists and sociologists, it is also of central importance to economics proper and contains, I would suggest, extremely important insights into the shortcomings of modern economics as an instrument of development policy as well as some valuable clues to alternative theoretical paths which could be pursued.

The central feature of Polly Hill's framework is the relationship between *capital* and *capitalists*. In economics capital is defined as anything which yields a flow of goods or services through time. As the studies in this book show, the forms of capital, represented by cocoa trees, cattle, fishing nets, manure, lorries, and so forth, play a crucial role in indigenous economies. All economists would agree that this indigenous capital stock is important, requires further study and, contrary to current practice, should be counted in the national capital stock. They have no difficulty in appreciating this part of Polly Hill's findings. But this is only the beginning. Polly Hill's major discovery is that, contrary to the usual view of an amorphous peasantry, the accumulation of capital in indigenous West African economies has been accompanied by the emergence of specialists who own and manage the capital stock—a 'class' of rural capitalists. She has, therefore, concentrated on the behavioural characteristics of these capitalists; on the problems they face and their methods of solving them; on their attitude towards wealth and their notions of the correct ways to invest money, to manage labour, and to preserve capital through time.

Neo-classical economists, in contrast, usually do not study the decision-making processes of capitalists and indeed are somewhat wary of this kind of research. They tend to concentrate their analysis on what are considered to be more fundamental factors—tastes, technology, and the supplies of factors of production—and not on the rules of thumb used by businessmen to make decisions in an environment they only partially understand. This approach stems from the assumption that, independently of their will or knowledge, capitalists are driven by competition to behave in certain ways determined by these fundamental factors, just as water runs down a hill on certain predictable paths. But such an approach is sharply limited in under-developed countries where markets are imperfect and where the primary interest is on how the economy produces capital, technology and organization, rather than on how it allocates factors of production at a given point of time. The analogy is not water running down a hill but mice running through a maze and the peculiar behavioural characteristics of the actors at any point of time cannot be dismissed as deviations from central tendencies but are rather the essential features which determine speed in learning and developing, this being especially true where capital is concerned.

The major problem of capital accumulation in underdeveloped economies is not so much a shortage of savings but a lack of institutions to channel the existing or latent surplus into productive investment. The study of these channels and their development through time lies at the core of the development problem.[1] It is Polly Hill's great contribution to have focused directly on the investment process and to have shown that West African indigenous economies follow laws of capital accumulation very similar to those of other economies including advanced ones.

Consider for example the process of capital accumulation in cocoa. Cocoa trees take from five to seven years to come into bearing and may survive for thirty to forty years or more: accordingly, the cocoa industry is highly capital-intensive, the speed of growth depending not only on the availability of labour in rural Ghana but also on the supply of capital. The essential feature about capital formation in this industry discovered by Polly Hill was that a large part of it was in the hands of a small group of rural capitalists, so that it was their development which determined the development of the industry. Though there are numerous small cocoa-farmers in Ghana who work only land in their native area and who might be described as 'peasant' farmers, they account for a relatively small share of total output. The major part of the crop and the major credit for developing the industry stems from the special group of farmers who expanded their operations beyond the family farm by buying or otherwise acquiring land and by employing strangers. In other words the distribution of ownership of capital in cocoa is highly uneven: there are a large number of small farmers who account for a small share of output and a small number of large farmers who account for a large share. A graph of the distribution of capital would look something like Figure 1 *a* rather than Figure 1 *b*.

This key feature of inequality rather than uniformity in the distribution of wealth is not unique to cocoa but is a fairly prevalent feature in West African indigenous economies. The nets used in Ewe seine fishing, for example, are not owned generally but belong to a few people—a frequency distribution

---

[1] M. Friedman, *A Theory of the Consumption Function*, p. 236, pointed in this direction in an appendix to his study on the consumption function: 'Perhaps the crucial role that has been assigned to the savings ratio in economic development should be assigned instead to the factors determining the form in which wealth is accumulated; to the investment rather than the savings process, as it were.'

such as Figure 1 would show most people as having zero capital and a few as having rather substantial wealth. Similarly, in cattle raising, there are those who work with cattle but do not own them and those who own them but do not work with them. And, as the study of Batagarawa in Northern Nigeria shows, even in a village where living standards are generally low there are significant differences in income based in part on differences in ownership of capital—in this case working capital in the form of manure.

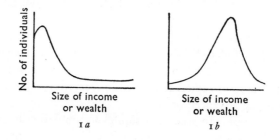

1 a    1 b

The importance of unequal income and wealth based on unequal owner-ship of the capital stock stems from the *qualitative* differences in behaviour between small and large wealth holders.[1] The small cocoa-farmer, for example, works his own land with his own labour. The large cocoa-farmer, on the other hand, must acquire land over and above what he has rights over under the traditional system and he often must hire labour to work his land. He must thus usually develop the organizing and entrepreneurial skills of investing in land, managing labour, and co-ordinating production on a relatively large scale. In learning these techniques he also acquires certain flexibilities and skills which, along with his capital, enable him to diversify into new industries or introduce new techniques. In a word he becomes a capitalist, that is, a man who controls a package of financial and organizational skills and who, therefore, has a certain ability to undertake (*entrepreneur*) productive activities both within his initial industry and outside it. Economic producers in West Africa are, therefore, not *amorphous* but *differentiated*, and analysis of their behaviour must distinguish between the various categories: landless labourers, small capitalists, larger capitalists and, in some cases,

---

[1] The central theme of this paragraph can be stated more formally as follows: Let $a$ be some measure of economic performance, e.g. labour output ratio, capital labour ratio, propensity to save, propensity to diversify, etc.—If $a$ is related to size, then the aggregate value of this parameter will depend upon the size distribution of firms, i.e.

$$a = \Sigma a_i \, x_i,$$

where $a_i$ is the value of the parameter for the $i$th size class and $x_i$ is the share of production made up of enterprises of that size class. The performance of the economy thus depends upon the structure of enterprise (the vector $x = x_1, x_2, \ldots, x_n$) and its change through time. Hence the need to study the values of $a_i$ and the process of change in the vector $x$. Only under very special conditions will the average size of enterprise be a meaningful indicator of the industry's structure.

substantial capitalists who differ in horizons and skills and, therefore, in performance.

No wonder, then, that Polly Hill is so distrustful of *averages* and *aggregates* as used by many researchers in analysis and policy formulation. The concept of the *average* or the *representative* farmer is easy to understand in bell-shaped distribution such as Figure 1 *b*. However, in Figure 1 *a*, the average—whether mean, median or mode—is in no way representative since most production does not occur on 'average' farms. In such cases it is of the utmost importance to be precise about differences and not to disguise them. Similarly, aggregation is extremely dangerous for skewed distributions like those of Figure 1 *a*. Two regions may have the same total production but differ substantially in economic performance if they have different distribution of wealth, since their social, political and economic structures—propensity to save, propensity to diversify, propensity to use capital, and propensity to use land-intensive methods—will depend on the size distribution of production.

If it is granted that the performance of an enterprise depends in some way upon its size and hence that the performance of an industry depends upon the size distribution of its enterprise, the next question becomes one of analysing how a given size distribution arises and how it changes through time. Thus Polly Hill has been concerned with such questions as: where do farmers get their initial capital, how do they acquire land, what system do they use to hire labour, how much can they borrow, what are their investment rules (i.e. rules about savings and re-investment), how do inheritance systems affect the concentration or dispersion of capital. Since the subjects of her investigation do not operate in an environment of perfect markets it is of little help to give standard neo-classical answers to these questions. Economic theory, following Marshall, assumes that each firm borrows capital, hires labour and rents land up to the point where the interest rate, wage rate, and rental rate equals the marginal revenue productivity of the factor involved. All firms are assumed to face the same prices for factors and products and if they differ in size it is due to accidental or irrelevant factors. Whatever its relevance in advanced economies, this model clearly does not apply in under-developed countries where 'markets' are highly imperfect and, in some cases, non-existent. The growth of an enterprise in this context is not merely a problem of maximizing profits subject to known constraints but of exploring the environment and developing systems for concentrating capital, purchasing or renting land, employing labour. The evolution of an industry, therefore, depends upon the ability of its entrepreneurs to learn and adapt, and it is this process of discovery which must be examined in detail in order to derive the laws of motion of the economic system.

In this context, Polly Hill's research can be viewed as a study of capital formation under imperfect capital markets. In economies where financial intermediaries and capital markets are highly developed, saving is allocated amongst various alternatives so as to equalize rates of return on the margin. In underdeveloped countries, and especially in indigenous economies, a highly articulated capital market is not available and most investment is financed from the personal savings of entrepreneurs or from the savings of their close friends or relatives. The national wealth is thus composed of many separate '*capitals*' under the control of specific individuals or families. Since borrowing or lending between these 'capitals' is restricted, the rates of return are not necessarily equalized and there is no general assurance that capital is allocated efficiently.[1] As the strength, ability, and perception of a capitalist depend upon the size of his capital, the capital structure of a country can be defined in terms of the size distribution of 'capitals' and the process of capital accumulation can be described in terms of the evolution of this size structure through time.

Polly Hill is one of the few economists, in West Africa at any rate, who has undertaken serious research within this framework. Her work is thus of great value to economists for the numerous hypotheses it contains on the relationship between size and performance and the process by which capitalists move from one size class to another. The parameters she studies—the propensity to save, the propensity to invest in houses, the propensity to borrow, the propensity to divide estates upon the death of the owner, the method of paying wages, the method of buying land and so forth—are crucial parameters, and far more work is needed, both on empirical estimations of these parameters and on theoretical investigation of their interaction, if we are to understand the development process and to formulate tools for speeding it up.

In summary, I have tried to show in this brief foreword that Polly Hill's research should be viewed in terms of the classical rather than the neo-classical paradigm. Classical writers, concerned with emerging industrial systems, concentrated on how various groups, such as landlords, merchant capitalists, industrial capitalists, behaved and how they were affected by the institutional structure of the economy—by land tenure systems, labour systems, financial institutions, property laws and so forth. These subjects

---

[1] With these basic assumptions, some of the standard procedures of neo-classical analysis become highly suspect. Unless there are capital markets where one can freely borrow or lend it makes little sense to calculate the present discounted value of a stream of earnings and hence it becomes very difficult to measure capital. Similarly, as one cannot assume that the marginal productivity of capital equals the interest rate it is difficult to apply production function analysis. In this context there is something to be said for dropping the notion of a capital stock—i.e. an aggregate of heterogeneous capital goods—and for concentrating on the structure of 'capitals'.

were dropped when economists began to focus on the workings of economies with highly developed self-regulating market systems. As a result many important questions about how systems grow and change have been neglected and now need to be revived. For myself, I find Polly Hill's work valuable not only for the information it contains on West African economies, but for the hypotheses it suggests about the development process in general. It uncovers a whole range of questions and answers (about how economic agents search their environment, concentrate capital, organize labour, and learn about technology and marketing) that are closer to the analytical tools of business administration (information theory, personal relations theory, finance theory, marketing theory and production theory) than to economic theory of market economies, but which appear to be of crucial importance to economists interested in development.

The strength of Polly Hill's research is that she has asked important questions: the weakness is that her sample is small and her categories far from perfectly defined. These are the inevitabilities of working outside the accepted paradigm. Those economists who have the resources for more extensive investigations are interested in different questions, while those that have the time for abstract theory use a different framework. Why this should be so is difficult to understand. Historically, it is certainly tied to political factors. Colonial administrators were not interested in emerging native capitalists and preferred to maintain the economic myths which rationalized their negative policies. Political elements are, no doubt, also present in the current mythologies. Such is the urban bias of development planning that the study of indigenous economies often seems irrelevant—even when such economies are regarded as a source of surplus to be squeezed. Hopefully, the paradigm is changing, and the loneliness of research of the kind found in this book is coming to an end. The future depends on how seriously the problems of promoting West African development and welfare are taken.

# POLEMICS

PART ONE

POLEMICS

# CHAPTER I

# A PLEA FOR INDIGENOUS ECONOMICS: THE WEST AFRICAN EXAMPLE[1]

This chapter is concerned with the need, in underdeveloped regions such as West Africa, to pursue a subject which, for want of a better term, I call 'indigenous economics'—or the study of indigenous economies. I shall start by outlining the general nature of the subject and by discussing the reasons for its neglect, both during the colonial period and today. Although the whole of my discussion relates to West Africa, it has some relevance to certain other newly developing tropical regions.

Indigenous economics is concerned with the *basic fabric* of existent economic life, with such economic activities as the production of export or other cash crops, subsistence farming, cattle raising, fishing (for cash or subsistence), internal trading in foodstuffs, transportation, economically motivated migration, indigenous credit-granting systems, and so forth. Far from being identified with either pre-monetary or subsistence economics, our subject is more concerned with 'cash activities', not because of their greater importance, for here there is much variation, but for the practical reason that the cash sector is easier to study. Nor are we particularly interested in the old-fashioned evolutionary ideas which would identify 'progress' with a shift from subsistence to cash agriculture, for we know that most West African farmers produce both for subsistence ('own consumption') and for cash, and that an increase in the one type of activity may actually enhance a growth in the other; it is the structure of the relationship between the two types of activity which is interesting and important.

If the scope of indigenous economics is so wide, what then distinguishes it from conventional economics? As I hope that the general nature of this distinction will emerge from the later discussion, I make only a few preliminary points. First, although it is true that the indigenous economist stands in some way opposed to the 'development economist', he is as much concerned with processes of change and modernization which he tends to

[1] First published in *Economic Development and Cultural Change* (October 1966), this article has been slightly amended. It was a revised and expanded version of a paper delivered at the March 1962 Conference of NISER (6).

regard from a non-governmental standpoint. Secondly, the distinction between the two types of economics is not hard and fast, but is mainly a matter of approach: while an indigenous economist might find himself very interested in problems of recruiting labour for a new factory, it could happen that he was unconcerned with what that factory produced. Thirdly, the indigenous economist tends to take the broad lines of government economic policy for granted, in that he is not concerned with their formulation, though he may indeed hold strong views on the effects of introducing new measures! Fourthly, the indigenous economist holds that, while his subject is similar, in a general way, to conventional (or Western) economics,[1] the factors which require emphasis in any situation may be unexpected, so that those who guess on the basis of Western experience are apt to go wrong even on fundamentals; he insists that the economic behaviour of individual West Africans is basically 'rational' and responsive, but that the structure of this rationality requires studying in the field.

The study of indigenous economics was neglected during the colonial period and is contemptuously regarded by nearly all economists today. (Those same intellectual, political, and emotional processes associated with the collapse of colonialism, which provided African historians with such glorious new opportunities,[2] hardened the arteries of economists in relation to indigenous studies—and the new history is seldom economic history.)[3] Traditionally, during the brief colonial period, economists were concerned with the point of contact between West African and European economies, with the economic relationship between the metropolitan country and the colony. This led them to concentrate nearly all their attention on external trade, on the acts of exportation and importation as such, rather than on export crop production or indigenous systems of internal distribution. Faced with the question of *how* export production was organized (by whom, on what sort of scale, under what conditions of land tenure, with what capital and labour, etc.), economists were usually obliged to guess. Quite often, as present evidence is beginning to show, they happened to guess wrong, and a formidable body of 'economic folklore', which took strength from its reiteration in books and official publications, established itself during half a century. One of the incidental concerns of the indigenous economist is the destruction of these economic myths, both by means of

---

[1] Some writers assume quite the contrary. Thus W. C. Neale, in *Trade and Markets in the Early Empires* (10), p. 371, states that 'the social scientists writing this volume are at least tentatively committed to the view that self-regulating markets (as distinct from fixed-price markets) are the exception rather than the rule—even to the view that they are unique to the nineteenth and twentieth centuries'. A similar ideology is evident in the Introduction to P. Bohannan and G. Dalton, eds., *Markets in Africa* (2).

[2] See I. Wallerstein, 'The Search for National Identity in West Africa' (14).

[3] This is especially true of modern history.

providing an alternative analysis and by the mere process of calling them in question. Even though he so often lacks the material which would enable him to set up a solid structure in place of any myth, he is encouraged to note that, as his work proceeds, he begins to be able to make judgments, in certain contexts, of the kinds of economic happenings which are likely to make good sense, so that he may be quite an effective critic.

In insisting on the narrow scope of conventional economics in regions such as West Africa, I am not exaggerating. We are all far more ignorant than we are knowledgeable. From Dakar to Cameroon, there is very little systematized knowledge relating to the economic organization of internal trade in West African foodstuffs and raw materials—there is scarcely any literature on this subject fit to be thrust into the hands of the visiting expert.[1] Of course, some anthropologists have ventured into economic fields, but they have seldom been concerned with the kinds of generalization which typify economists. Their example is of profound importance to the indigenous economist—but they have not done his fieldwork for him.

Most British, unlike American, economists are wholly ignorant of agricultural economics, which they regard as a separate discipline. The findings of those few agricultural economists who have worked in the field in Nigeria and Ghana, for instance, have had little influence. Besides, agricultural economists have 'neglected traditional agriculture, leaving it to anthropologists, who have made some useful studies'.[2] Present-day economists are far more ignorant of the rural economies of certain poorer regions, including West Africa, than were their nineteenth-century counterparts of the rural economies of Europe. There has been a retrogression of knowledge:

While agriculture is the oldest production activity of a settled community, surprisingly little is known about the incentives to save and invest where farmers are bound by traditional agriculture. Oddly enough, economics has retrogressed in analysing the savings, investment and production behaviour of farmers in poor countries. The older economist had a better conception than economists now have of the particular type of economic equilibrium relevant under these circumstances.[3]

Growth economists have been producing an abundant crop of macro-models that are, with few exceptions, neither relevant in theorizing about the growth potentials of agriculture nor useful in examining the empirical behaviour of agriculture as a source of growth.[4]

Agricultural economists are themselves, occasionally, very frank about their ignorance:

We hear a lot about this gap between the scientific agriculturalist and the native peasant farmer in the tropics... But I don't think there is a gap. You see, neither

---

[1] [The situation has slightly improved since this article was written in 1965.]
[2] See T. W. Schultz, *Transforming Traditional Agriculture* (13) p. 6.  [3] *Ibid.* p. vii.  [4] *Ibid.* p. 6.

of them knows how to improve agriculture... What do we really know about the effect of the organic matter as compared with the minerals in the dung of cattle on particular savannah soils in Africa? What do we know about the probable results of attempts to integrate livestock and crop production to get more modern farming systems, not only in savannah Africa but in very many other areas?[1]

A great deal of trouble is caused for us and for the natural scientists themselves because, individually and in subject groups, they assume that their pet ideas and results are more fully finished and marketable than in fact they are. They therefore proclaim that much of their knowledge lies unused.[2]

When West African governments announce that the time is ripe for the introduction of large-scale mechanization programmes in agriculture, agricultural scientists lack either the courage or inclination to raise their voices protesting their ignorance of the consequences—but rather offer their services, usually through international specialized agencies,[3] as technical experts. When West African politicians deplore, as they so often do, the backwardness of farm people, they are unaware of the extent to which they are echoing the conventional ignorance of economists. In West Africa, nowadays, the educated urban classes, notably the politicians, increasingly refer to farmers as 'peasants': this is condescending and misleading, for:

The word 'peasant' denotes, among other things, a degree of rusticity, in comparison with his betters, which we do not feel justified in attributing to the African villager...African villagers do not seem to feel the same degree of ambivalence towards the political superstructure that European, Asian and Latin American peasants do...they do not to the same extent feel judged from above by a set of standards which they cannot attain.[4]

The Beatrice Webb tradition of qualitative field observation and experiment[5] has been out of fashion for some half a century, so it is no wonder that field enquiries were neglected in the British colonies. But even had this spirit of scientific enquiry not fallen into desuetude, it is likely that conventional British assumptions about West African economic behaviour would have inhibited field investigation. Typical implicit assumptions were:

(a) That it was the expatriate trader who taught the West African, if only

---

[1] From an article by J. R. Raeburn in *Proceedings of the Ninth International Conference of Agricultural Economists* (11), p. 483.
[2] *Ibid.* p. 484.
[3] Many technical experts are quite deficient in relevant expertise, compared with certain old-style colonial servants. This is especially true of agriculturalists, who seldom remain in any post for more than a couple of years. (Outside technological fields proper, the whole notion of the 'technical expert', whose expertise is applicable anywhere, is apt to be sham.)
[4] From L. A. Fallers, 'Are African Cultivators to be called "Peasants"?' (4), p. 110.
[5] See Beatrice Webb, *My Apprenticeship* (15).

by example, the elementary facts of economic life. (It followed that the economic response of indigenes was essentially Western and familiar and required no study: if it was not familiar it was not economic.)

(*b*) That the basic fabric of economic life was so simple as to be devoid of interest to economists. (Only by assuming that indigenous economics and Western economics were identical did the former become worthy of study—but then assumption (*a*) came to the rescue.)

(*c*) That, given the complexities associated with 'tribalism' (local land tenure, kinship and inheritance, communal work systems, and so forth), indigenous economies operate on too small a scale, or on too local a basis, to be of interest to economists—and are anyway incomprehensible. (Not until social and political systems have been 'modernized' will economic processes become intelligible. By hastening the collapse of 'tribalism', economists hope to move rapidly towards the day when they will understand events.)

Why is each of these implicit beliefs likely to be misleading?

### (*a*) THE WESTERN TRADING EXAMPLE

Of course this was important: West Africans, like everyone else, are apt to be imitative in their economic behaviour. But there were many reasons why the *Western* example was much less important than is commonly assumed, and I select three of these for emphasis:

(1) Other examples were often more important. Thus, it was the North African, or Arabian, example, as demonstrated in the ancient trans-Saharan trade in gold, ivory, slaves, kola, cloth, etc., which set the pattern for long-distance trade within much of West Africa. The principal long-distance traders who linked the northern savannah with the southern forests were the Dioula (who operated mainly in Francophone territory) and the Hausa of northern Nigeria. The northern Muslim example was profound, and many non-Hausa-speaking people in the south employ Hausa trading terms.

(2) In the field of agricultural production, no Western example existed, there being no common basis of agricultural experience and no contact between the farmer and the expatriate trader, who dealt always with African middlemen. Agriculture, unlike trade, was seldom supported or organized by indigenous political authorities, who drew little (if any) revenue from it. This is not to say that agriculture was, in any useful sense, 'inefficient', but rather that it was mainly based on local experimentation and local tradition, adapted to soil, climate, crops, and levels of technology. Recent developments, such as the increased migration of farmers and labourers, which

7

followed the introduction of new export crops, have tended to create more geographical uniformity than existed hitherto—but this should not be exaggerated.

(3) The expatriate trading firms' strength lay in their ability to adapt themselves to indigenous trading methods—rather than *vice versa*. The firms were sophisticated: they learned how to insinuate themselves into the existing trading structure, and they were not afraid of credit. But as buyers of export produce they scarcely ventured inland until after 1900. Thus, the firms which exported Gold Coast cocoa before 1914 knew hardly anything of the organization of cocoa-farming or of methods of bush buying, which increasingly fell into the hands of Nigerian middlemen. Of course, the actual exporting function of the expatriate firms was indispensable; of course, in the end, they established networks of buying stations throughout the cocoa area: but their skill in buying depended on a symbiotic relationship with their bush-buyers. Indigenous methods of marketing kola (a crop which, in several ways, closely resembles cocoa) owe nothing to the Western expatriate example—they are far more ancient, being based on the northern trading influence.

## (b) THE BELIEF THAT INDIGENOUS ECONOMICS IS TOO SIMPLE FOR ECONOMISTS

An alternative version of this doctrine is that it is quite permissible for economists to derive conclusions from general information which has a greater validity than more localized material, despite the admitted variations in basic background circumstances. In the early 1950s it was widely believed that West African cocoa marketing boards had fixed the price to the farmer so far below the world cocoa price that cocoa output was bound to fall catastrophically—although, as the whole world knows, it subsequently rose, as one might say, catastrophically. It was tacitly assumed that the basic socio-economic organization of cocoa-farming had no reference to this belief. When one began to study this organization, in all its diversity, one was struck by the fact, then recorded in none of the books, that rapid cocoa development usually involves migration of farmers, and by the remarkable long-sightedness of the migrant cocoa-farmers, who would not stop planting existing lands, or making future plans for the planting of newly acquired lands, just because the cocoa price seemed low during a run of years—which, in any case, in the early 1950s it did not. No one appreciated the strength of the appeal of the marketing board system of fixed prices for producers which, though introduced by the British at the beginning of the war, was very acceptable to West Africans. The notion of a 'right price'—a price which, ideally, should remain stable indefinitely—is very common in West Africa where economic life is riddled with *attempts* to fix prices on a local (or even wider) basis, usually by implicit agreement, for even among well-organized traders, such as butchers, machinery for centralized price-fixing is non-existent. While short-term price-fixing is often effectively achieved, prices are never stable in the longer run (they *are* determined by supply and demand), and institutions which actually lead to the attainment of this ideal are, therefore, usually welcomed with open arms.

Many economists have visited West Africa in advisory capacities since the war, and much of their advice has been very valuable to governments. But convinced as they have been of the simplicity of indigenous economic organization, few of them, or, indeed, of the growing band of prominent West African economists (most of them Nigerians), have used their influence to urge the need for more 'grass roots research'. Also, some of the expatriate advisers, especially a few who have visited Ghana, have ventured into pastures much wider than those in which they are accustomed to graze—with somewhat unexpected results. It may be that when Sir Arthur Lewis asserted, in a much-read report on industrialization of the Gold Coast,[1] that agriculture was stagnant, he had an over-simplified image of agricultural organization based on the presumption that a simple technology necessarily implies simple socio-economic organization, 'inefficiency' (in some absolute, though undefined, sense), and small-scale production—though none of these notions is necessarily true or meaningful.

In questioning these assumptions, as necessary assumptions, I am making no statement at all about the efficiency of West African agricultural systems, though I would observe that economists are much too prone to make 'efficiency judgments' before they have examined existing mechanisms and alternatives. But I am insistent that an apparently commonsense corollary to the stagnation thesis, to the effect that industrialization cannot proceed until labour is 'released' from the farms as a result of improved agricultural efficiency imposed from outside, happens not to be a corollary. This piece of folklore ignores the special factors, which are summed up in the statement that the supply of labour (mostly of savannah origin) is often best regarded as unlimited in quantity. I am not here referring merely to the magnetic attractive power of industrial employment, but also to the willingness and ability of many West Africans to migrate to rural areas—perhaps even happening to fill the jobs vacated by those who have migrated to the cities. It may well be that, up to the present, food farmers have generally organized themselves so as to keep pace with the vastly expanding demand for marketed food which has resulted from the spectacular increase in West African

[1] *Report on Industrialisation and the Gold Coast*, W. A. Lewis (8).

9

urbanization.[1] So we see how it may come about that economic policies based on apparent economic common sense are more damaging than no policy.

### (c) THE BELIEF THAT INDIGENOUS ECONOMICS IS TOO COMPLEX FOR ECONOMISTS

It is here that the economists are deserving of everyone's sympathy. Where is the social anthropologist, let alone the economist, who has not heaved a sigh at the appearance of yet another detailed study of 'all aspects' of a small society? And yet, lamentably, there is hardly any non-anthropological, non-statistical material fit for the consumption of economists desirous of acquiring local background. My point is that such material might be useful, as well as comprehensible. I am insisting that if economists would persist with detailed studies in the field, they would soon learn to discern a variety of forms of standard economic behaviour amid the diversity—that economic behaviour is often more standardized in West Africa than it is in the West. The difficulty is that the diversity *and* the uniformity require simultaneous emphasis. Thus, taking an actual example, we are the more inclined to insist that *most larger cocoa-farmers* (defined, say, as those with 10 acres of cocoa or more) *employ labourers*, because we know that there are some such farmers who rely solely on family labour and can partially understand why their circumstances are 'different'. As we gain experience, we come to see what 'kinds' of cocoa-farmers employ labourers and to associate various types of work with various systems of employment. Nor do we need to travel everywhere in the cocoa-growing zone before attempting such generalization, as has been shown by the work of Dr Marguerite Dupire[2] among the cocoa-farmers of the south-eastern Ivory Coast.

These and other implicit assumptions have partially accounted for the unwillingness of economists to study the basic fabric of economic life in tropical regions such as West Africa. But there are also many practical difficulties, one of the most troublesome being the compartmentalism of indigenous life, which necessitates studying it in terms of individual industries, occupations, sectors and so on, as well as, all too often, in terms of ethnic groups within these classifications. It is this latter point which tends to break the back of the conventional economist, observing, as he must, the

---

[1] Those who draw up development plans often *assume* the contrary. Thus, on p. 85 of Ghana's *Seven-Year Development Plan* (Accra, 1964), it is asserted that the farmers had failed to keep up with the growing demand for food, though the official published statistical time series relating to prices and quantities of Ghanaian foodstuffs rather indicated the contrary—in so far as one cared to regard them as reliable indicators.

[2] 'Planteurs autochtones et étrangers en Basse-Côte d'Ivoire orientale' (3).

obsessional interest of the 'ethno-economist' in such matters as occupational specialization in relation to ethnic group: how can he learn to think in terms of seventeen (or more) separate (ethnic) labour forces, or fail to be dismayed by the pursuit of ethnic classificatory questions as ends in themselves?

It is this compartmentalism of economic life which partly explains the widespread belief among economists that saving and investment are rare, even as concepts, in indigenous economic life; the economist is so unfamiliar with the forms such saving and investment are apt to take that he does not know where to look for evidence of their existence. (I have heard UN financial experts seriously argue that the admitted unwillingness of individual Ghanaians to buy government securities is evidence of their inability to 'save' in any sense of that word.) The failure of capital to flow between sectors, as in more developed economies, is partly because many farmers, traders, and other business people have such well-developed, even strict, notions of the distinction between capital and spending money and of the proper usages of the former. Though the migrant cocoa-farmers of southern Ghana traditionally invested their savings from cocoa-growing in land-purchase, in the building of houses in the homeland, and in the purchase of lorries (connected with cocoa and food transport), they were usually unconcerned with investing capital in other forms of economic activity. It is only by studying indigenous capital formation sector by sector that the possibilities of inter-sectoral flow may come to be properly appreciated. At present, many of the most important forms of fixed capital, such as cocoa farms, are omitted from all official national accounts, mainly because this reflects traditional accounting practice in developed countries, but also because such farms are wrongly presumed to have come into existence almost accidentally —to be acts of God, rather than man-made capital assets, the creation of which involved much effort, abstention, and planning.

Given this need to study economic life compartmentally (and, alas, ploddingly), should the methods of economists and social anthropologists be distinguished? If the investigator is a social anthropologist, then he must understand the necessity of isolating economic factors; he must also be prepared to use every opportunity of hinging the material he collects either to already existing statistics (or to other broadly based, administratively organized data, such as farm maps, nominal rolls, etc.), or in the last resort (in the absence of existing material) to collect a minimum of simple figures himself. If, however, the investigator is an economist, he should usually discard his traditional procedure of collecting most of his material through field assistants using questionnaires, in favour of a method, learned from anthropologists, which mainly relies on questioning and observing individuals while they are at work. Market women should be interviewed in markets, lorry drivers in lorry parks, farmers on their farms (or at their houses), fishermen on the beach. The procedure should be semi-statistical, in the sense that similar, even identical, questions should be put to many informants independently, with a view to comparing, or even totalling, their replies.

The investigator must adopt an economic point of view. When studying the economic organization of companies of beach-seine fishermen, he may not need to go to the sea in the canoe, but it will be essential to witness the selling of fish to women on the beach and to appreciate that the division of labour between men and women is based on economic good sense—not on mysterious traditional sex roles. It is because he has a point of view that the investigator is able to use his judgment as to what is relevant.

Questionnaires, as I have said, must be discarded by the investigator, for the simple reason that it is impossible to draw up a satisfactory form until after the research has been completed. The indigenous economist studies the *quality* of economic life, a statement which may be made respectable to statisticians by adding that he is concerned rather more with identifying the important variables than with measuring their movements. The conventional type of pilot survey is useless, involved as it is with procedural details rather than with fundamentals. As for the use by the economist of the full-blown questionnaire, this is a far more dangerous implement in West African conditions than is commonly realized—one which should only be handled by the surgeon himself. Not only are the wielders of questionnaires often indulging in a kind of anti-intellectual activity (setting out on a voyage of discovery enclosed in blinkers), but there is also the fact that field assistants have a remarkable capacity to classify recalcitrant material so that it appears to fit neatly into inappropriate boxes, which results in the hardening of prejudices that rather require demolition.

I hasten to insist that I am not denigrating economic statistics as such: of course they are the life-blood of economics, though our dismal science should scarcely be *identified* with statistics, as is happening in some poorer regions. But I am making four assertions about them. Firstly, large-scale statistical enquiries, or even enquiries which are basically much dependent on the collection of statistics, are usually best undertaken by government or other official agencies, which alone command the resources required. Secondly, such 'large-scale statistics' seldom expose the fundamental variables that lie at the 'grass roots' level. Thirdly, it is the duty of social scientists to use such statistics with great discretion in underdeveloped countries, as they are liable to be very misleading. (Official statistics are often assumed to be reliable, just because they are official. Specialized UN agencies, such as FAO and the Economic Commission for Africa are so dependent on these statistics that they feel they must either accept them entirely, or pack up.) Fourthly, statisticians generally, not only expatriate technical experts, usually fail to appreciate the degree of 'geographical diversity' (ecological, economic, and social) which typifies many new under-developed countries, including those of the smaller ones which extend from the coast to the northern savannah. The statistical technique of the UN experts responsible for organizing agricultural censuses in West African countries may be impeccable, so far as concerns the choice of the individuals, or farms, to be counted in any locality; but the whole operation is apt to be invalidated by the failure to select sufficient localities for study, given this great degree of 'geographical diversity'. Such agricultural censuses are wished on the poorer countries by the UN and are a monstrous waste of their financial and manpower resources.

The official statistics of the poorer countries are apt to become in some respects less accurate as, partly in response to outside pressure, they become more detailed. The many published reports on the 1960 Ghana population census are monumentally fascinating sources of huge scope—real landmarks of organization and scholarship. Yet *some* of the statistics are of much worse quality than those collected in previous censuses, and one needs to be an indigenous economist properly to understand this. Certain of the occupational statistics, which appear so accurate because they are so detailed, are very misleading. The traditional prejudices with regard to the relationship between cocoa-farmers and their labourers (the latter usually being presumed to do most of the work, in the absence of the former) led to failure to distinguish labourers from farmers, though they are quite distinct categories. Then, most of the wholesalers of Ghanaian foodstuffs in southern Ghana are women[1]— but the census statistics show them to be nearly all men.[2] In general, the process of demolishing the statistical myths, with the aid of field research, will be a slow one: there is a mystique about official statistics which with-stands much battering.

I have suggested a number of reasons why, as it were traditionally, economists have neglected the study of indigenous economics in West Africa. Nowadays, there is another general and most powerful resistance at work—the whole ideology of those who count themselves under-develop-ment specialists is nearly always actively opposed to indigenous studies. Theoreticians, econometricians, and planners all share a common philosophy of ideological optimism, based on the past success in solving certain economic problems, particularly that of mass unemployment in some industrial countries. The uncritical acceptance of conventional types of official statistics

---

[1] This statement is based on material collected by the present writer which is, as yet, unpublished.

[2] Perhaps the category 'wholesaler', which went undefined in the census, related only to those who handled imported goods or who had office premises. Certainly, in West African conditions, the concept is too difficult to be conveniently handled by census enumerators.

is one consequence of this optimism; while economists know in their hearts that most West African food production figures are guesses (even wild guesses), they hardly ever admit this when quoting and comparing the figures,[1] the idea being, presumably, that some figures are always better than no figures. The theoreticians do not seek to revolutionize their model-building by drawing new ideas from anthropologically oriented material; the econometricians are so much concerned with manipulating their series that they hardly consider the reliability of the statistical data in terms of the humdrum problems of its basic collection in the field;[2] the planners and advisers regard themselves as economic doctors with the duty of making quick diagnoses and judgments on the basis of inadequate knowledge.

This philosophy of optimism would be more justifiable were there more evidence that the economists had met with marked success in solving the economic problems of the poorer countries. Now they are in a hurry, because they had given no thought to such problems (was not the very word 'under-development' coined little more than twenty years ago?) until the under-privileged, expressing themselves politically, left them no choice. It is the politicians and people of the poorer countries who see their salvation in development, who demand assistance from the richer and the better educated. Although economists do their best to keep up with this demand, and although their advice is often ignored, part of the responsibility for the ever-widening gap between the living standards of rich and poor countries is surely theirs. And is there not a sense in which development proceeds, despite the economists?

The future role of the indigenous economist will be a modest one. He will pursue his subject partly for its own sake and partly in the hope that in the longer run he may help to create a more realistic climate of economic thought, especially about rural activities, which will continue to engage most West Africans for many years to come. The present-day planner has no time to read our obscure sources, and we may even sympathize with him when he regards our material as obsolescent, or as an impediment to the ideal with which he is playing. Someone (and I do not know who this should be) should set about digesting our material in a way which would give it some comprehensibility and appeal to those who do not sympathize with our methods and aims.

[1] See Helen C. Farnsworth, 'Defects, Uses and Abuses of National Consumption Data' (5): 'To call such guesses [involving subsistence crops] ''production estimates'' is at best semantic fiction, at worst actual falsehood; to derive residual ''consumption'' estimates from them is farcical . . .' (p. 192).

[2] These problems are apt to be much more pronounced in poorer than in richer countries, both for the general reasons already discussed, and because of such practical difficulties as that of quantifying foodstuffs which are never weighed for trading purposes.

The situation is educationally urgent. On the one hand, there are no respectable textbooks of applied economics appropriate to West African conditions; one certainly need not beg the question of whether basically rural societies, lacking a capitalist landowning class, may become fully socialist without first passing through an industrial stage, before insisting that Marxist textbooks are no more relevant than the capitalist variety. On the other hand, sufficient generalized nonsense is written about African economic conditions, especially by British and American academics, to ensure the hardening of prevailing economic myths.

One of the most fashionable myths is that *shifting cultivation is bad.* Without defining terms, and without considering the possible efficiency of alternative cultivation systems, economists both condemn shifting cultivation out of hand and regard it as usual in sub-Saharan Africa. In point of fact, in West Africa shifting cultivation, properly regarded,[1] is far less common than are systems of 'recurrent cultivation', which commonly involve individual farmers returning to cultivate their portions of land after the restoration of fertility through fallow. Whereas the term shifting cultivation implies a ramshackle, wasteful, obsolete state of affairs, systems of recurrent cultivation, if understood, could often be represented as respectable, even scientific—they usually, of course, involve crop rotation.

Even with systems of continuous (or annual) cultivation of manured farms, which are much commoner in West Africa than is generally realized,[2] it is unjustifiable to assume, as do most economists, that the Malthusian brink is necessarily near by, if only because such systems are often associated with the existence of bush-farms which are 'recurrently' cultivated.[3] However, if the degree of pressure on the land does happen to justify Malthusian despair, the means by which the local population attempts to alleviate the situation (refusing to die off) are often well worthy of study, especially as many population density maps are surprisingly patchy, so that short-distance migration of farmers often presents possibilities.

Tied up with Malthusianism are the presumed dangers of *fragmentation.* (So conflicting are the various definitions of this emotive term that it certainly should be discarded, though it serves well enough for present polemical purposes.) The economists, who are apt to be so much less sophisticated than their subjects, the farmers, presume the latter to be unaware of the dangers of farms becoming smaller and smaller over time— although the fact is that in many instances their socio-economic systems have

---

[1] W. Allan, *The African Husbandman* (1) restricts the use of the term 'shifting cultivation' to circumstances 'in which the whole community of cultivators moves' (p. 6). A typically sophisticated anthropological discussion is to be found in P. C. Lloyd, *Yoruba Land Law* (9), p. 73.

[2] Notably in Northern Nigeria—where they are generally not Malthusian.

[3] Bush-farms are usually less conveniently situated than manured farms.

built-in safeguards against such a process. In many societies a man has a sole heir who inherits all his rights over land; in others, the much-abused 'family system' ensures that, for instance, self-acquired land is divided only between sons and not between grandsons, who are obliged to share their fathers' portions.[1] It is true that fragmentation *may* be a problem; but then so may be the over-consolidation of land in the hands of a sole inheritor.

Most West African farmers in the forest zone (and perhaps also in the savannah) produce much of the food they require for their own consumption —they are *subsistence producers*. But subsistence does not necessarily imply inefficiency, as economists usually assume. There are many reasons why this may be so, and I select the following for mention: (*a*) multi-cropping (the growing of two or more crops simultaneously on the same land) often makes such good agronomic sense in West Africa that specialization on one crop is seldom desirable: (*b*) cocoyam and plantain are necessary cover crops for young cocoa seedlings, so that cocoa-farmers with new farms cannot avoid producing these foodstuffs; (*c*) labour, rather than land, may be the scarce factor, so that to get the maximum output farmers must distribute the available manpower between crops with different growing cycles; (*d*) it is sometimes cheaper to grow food, if need be with hired labour, rather than to buy it, considering the great bulkiness of certain staple West African foodstuffs, especially cassava and plantain; (*e*) it is often economic for labourers who are primarily employed in connexion with the production of a cash crop to produce subsistence crops, both for themselves and their masters; (*f*) given existing technology, there are few obvious advantages in really large-scale production of any crop—nor need there be with mechanization, were tractor-hiring services more often available to the private farmer.

So the problem for economists is that of the right balance, in different circumstances, between subsistence and cash production—the general responsiveness of farmers to the growing demand for marketed food not being in doubt.

Of course, there are many economists who are well aware that economic circumstances in underdeveloped countries are 'different', one of them being Professor W. B. Reddaway, whose experience in India led him to emphasize the need for economists to adopt new sets of instinctive assumptions in underdeveloped countries.[2] But how should the advisory economist set about acquiring such assumptions, given that the civil servants (on whom, presumably, he mainly depends for information) are those most proficient in soaking up, and relaying, prevailing economic folklore, much of it Western in origin? Might not the indigenous economist help?

[1] See *The Migrant Cocoa-Farmers of Southern Ghana* by the present author (7).
[2] 'The Economics of Under-Developed Countries' (12).

The indigenous economist is bound to remain a laughing-stock with governments and mainstream economists alike. As he is not primarily interested in modernization, he will appear to be an intellectual, if not a political, conservative—and perhaps it *is* impossible to study existing institutions unless, with a part of one's mind, one wishes to preserve them, at least for the length of time required for their study. So division of labour must continue to be the rule among economists. But we do ask the planner with whom (so far as we are concerned) all power lies, to agree that a partial return to the Webb tradition of socio-economic observation on crying issues would be a forward, not a backward, step.

# PART TWO

# FIELDWORK

CHAPTER 2

# GHANAIAN CAPITALIST COCOA-FARMERS[1]

It is one of the misfortunes of contemporary Africa that the business of farming is usually referred to so slightingly and contemptuously, especially by economists. Many present-day writers take for granted that the so-called 'small peasants' who produce the food and export crops are invariably, in certain broad and important senses, 'inefficient'. There is much too much of a tendency to consider yield per acre as the measure of efficiency, irrespective of whether land is plentiful. The farmers are often considered to be people who would choose to take up other economic occupations were they better educated or more intelligent. I think it is time that opinions such as these were openly challenged and in order to stimulate further controversy and to emphasize that this 'business of farming' is a business, I have given this chapter a somewhat provocative title. In my opinion the migrant cocoa-farmers of Southern Ghana, with whom I am here concerned, were real economic innovators: people who bent their energy and intelligence to the business of cocoa-farming with supreme success. But, because of the load of condescension showered on farmers as a class, it did not occur to anyone that this might be so and it is only now, with the aid of the Department of Agriculture's maps, compiled for swollen-shoot disease control purposes, that the real account of what happened is being revealed.

The social organization of cocoa-farming in Ghana as a whole is very heterogeneous indeed and the type of farmer with whom I am concerned is only one of many. There is much variation as between different districts, this reflecting differences in population density, customary conditions of land tenure, accessibility of land and so forth. In some districts 'native farmers' (i.e. farmers who were born in the district in question) predominate and some of these farmers may, if one wishes, be referred to as 'peasants'—though, for myself, I prefer to avoid the use of this word with all its emotional overtones, and to refer to 'sedentary' or 'non-migrant' farmers. In certain areas the farms owned by these sedentary farmers are, most of them, of the traditional

[1] Here reprinted, with slight revision, from the *Ghanaian Bulletin of Agricultural Economics*, II, No. 1 (March 1962), this brief article appeared before the publication, in 1963, of my book *The Migrant Cocoa-Farmers of Southern Ghana: A Study in Rural Capitalism*.

size of about one to three acres, this perhaps corresponding (it is a matter which should be investigated by agricultural economists) to the area which could be conveniently cleared and planted by one man in a single season. This type of farmer was described by W. H. Beckett in his famous book *Akokoaso*, which was based on work done while he was a member of the staff of the Department of Agriculture in the 1930s. While in various parts of Ghana, including south-eastern Ashanti, there are many thousands of such farmers (nearly half of whom are women farmers in their own right), they have always accounted for rather a small proportion of Ghana's total cocoa exports, and were certainly not the pioneers responsible for the original development of cocoa growing, as has always been supposed.

In this short chapter I shall not attempt to classify Ghana's cocoa-farmers further. Apart from the sedentary, small-scale farmer and the farmer with which this chapter is concerned, there are many other types, of whom the most important at present are the Ashanti and Brong-Ahafo farmers who have been responsible for the vast expansion of production that has occurred in Ahafo and elsewhere in the west. Unfortunately we know very little, as yet, about the social organization of production in these newer cocoa-growing areas, and there are no Department of Agriculture farm-maps to come to our aid, but I would like to hazard the guess that in West African conditions very rapid expansion of production, such as has occurred in the last 30 years in Ahafo (and which occurred between about 1890 and 1930 in southern Ghana), always involves the large-scale migration of farmers into unin-habited forests. True forest dwellers, residing in their small towns, such as Akokoaso or Asafo-Akim, are not of the stuff of which pioneering farmers are made. The migrant farmer's homelands lie south of the deep forest: they were the farmers behind the spectacular increase in Ghana's cocoa exports from nil in 1890 to about 40,000 tons in 1911—since when Ghana has always been the world's largest cocoa producer. These farmers own most of the cocoa land in Southern Akim Abuakwa south of Kibi, except in the immediate neighbourhood of the old towns such as Apapam, Apedwa, Asafo, Tafo, Kukurantumi and Asamankese. The Department of Agriculture's maps showing farm boundaries, which can be referred to at the various Area Offices, show that this is so.

In this chapter I shall briefly list some of the reasons why it seems justifi-able to regard the migrant cocoa-farmers of southern Ghana as 'capitalists'—a term which I am, of course, employing in a rather general sense. Although my enquiries are based on present-day oral interview in the field, yet my approach is essentially historical so that I often speak of the farmers in the past tense. Nevertheless, I must make it quite clear that most of my findings apply, in general, to the present day, though the situation has been much obscured by swollen shoot disease which destroyed most of the cocoa trees owned by the migrants in southern Ghana. Although since about 1920 the farmers have usually travelled part of the way to their new lands by lorry (in the first twenty years of the migration, before the opening of Pakro railway station in 1911, they always travelled by foot), the migration has continued on traditional lines to the present day and will continue indefinitely, the farmers being committed to this way of life. Contrary to widespread (almost insistent) belief, the poverty resulting from swollen shoot put a brake on the migration: the migration slowed down because the farmers lacked the cash to travel to their new lands.

(1) The most obvious reason for regarding the migrant farmers as capitalists is that they bought their land for the particular purpose of grow- ✓ ing cocoa on it. When the migration first began, in the early 1890s,[1] the land that the travelling farmers bought was situated in western and north-western Akwapim, especially in the Adawso area. (At that time virtually all the migrant farmers were Akwapim, from Aburi, Mampong, Mamfe, Larteh, Akropong and elsewhere.) In about 1897 the westward migration over the river Densu into Akim country began—see map 1. The forests of southern Akim Abuakwa enclosed within the arc of the river Densu were scarcely inhabited, as contemporary maps show, and the chiefs who 'owned' the land, Apapam, Asafo and the rest, were only too glad to sell portions to the stranger-farmers, all of whom lived in areas of south-eastern Ghana where cocoa would not grow or where, as on the Akwapim ridge, there was insuffi- cient land. (The Akwapim migrants were soon joined by Shai, Krobo, Ga and others, including the Anum/Boso who did not start buying land until about 1907.) The main source of money for land-purchase was the oil palm, ✓ which was grown extensively in Akwapim and Krobo countries, oil and kernels being exported to the value of over £200,000 in 1890. The cultivation of one economic crop therefore led directly to the development of another. The Akwapim had a number of other sources of income, including rubber trading, Gold Coast rubber exports having risen from £55,000 in 1889 to £231,000 in 1890; this business also involved travelling, much of the rubber, which was all of natural origin, being collected in distant parts of Akim country and Ashanti. Then there were the travelling craftsmen of Akwapim, such as carpenters, who journeyed widely in West Africa, often returning home to invest their savings in land for cocoa.

(2) The migrant farmers themselves have always regarded cocoa growing as a business, though they have not boasted about this. It cannot be too strongly emphasized that, with the Akwapim at any rate, this business was

---

[1] See Marion Johnson's two remarkable articles 'Migrants' Progress' (5) for the earlier history of land-purchasing.

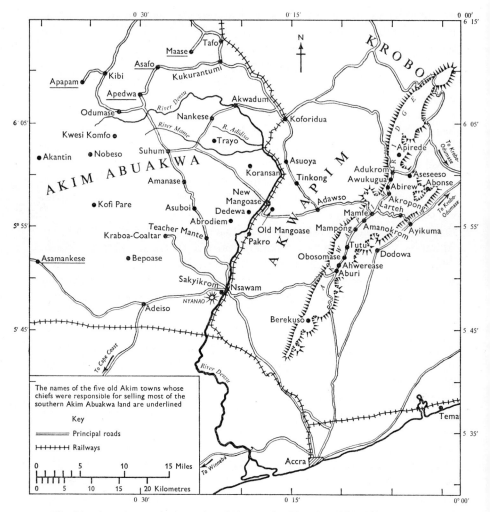

1  The historic cocoa-growing area, in relation to the Akwapim Ridge. This map appeared previously in Hill, *The Migrant Cocoa-Farmers of Southern Ghana*, Cambridge, 1963

not an extension of their general farming activities, for it was women who were responsible for producing, as well as selling, most of the food crops in the homeland, other than yam and the oil palm, while it was the men who, accompanied by their womenfolk, migrated to grow cocoa. Many of the men were literally unemployed (it should be noted that exports of palm produce did not fall significantly until cocoa growing had been established for some 20 years) and were looking for a worthwhile occupation. They were not concerned, as are so many traders and taxi drivers, to 'get rich quick' and then go out of business; all the time they were interested in expansion. From the earliest times it has been conventional for a large part of the profits from growing cocoa on one land (I shall define a land at (4) below), to be invested in the purchase of another. As time went by, nearly all migrant farmers owned several lands acquired at intervals as the cash became available—my enquiries in Akwapim have shown that the typical Akwapim farmer, except in a few of the smaller towns such as Tutu, owns three or four lands, acquired by his forebears and himself. Exceptional migrant farmers, and I have interviewed many of them, acquired long sequences of a dozen lands or more.

With regard to the quite spurious anxieties that are often expressed about an imminent land shortage, it should be noted that when a farmer, or a family, owns more than a small number of lands, it is usual for some of them to lie unplanted for decades: thus, much land that was acquired in the 1930s has never yet been planted, although suitable for cocoa.

(3) For an activity to count as business, it must be conducted on a reasonably large scale, otherwise it more resembles a hobby. Here again, the migrant farmers qualify as businessmen, in terms both of the number of separate lands acquired and their area. This is not to say that all the farms are or were large, and indeed, statistical generalization about farm size is fraught with such dangers that it is very important to understand the structure in qualitative terms before attempting any quantification. The large tracts of a thousand acres or more which were acquired by individuals, especially in the very earliest days when many of the most famous estates were founded, should often be regarded as areas within which farming is undertaken; they are certainly not 'farms'. When an Aburi farmer bought such a large tract (and I would regard the Aburi as the most remarkable of all the early cocoa-farmers), it was not long before many of his matrilineal kin came to settle there, both to help him to establish his own farms and to exert their right to portions of unplanted land for their personal use, and a mosaic, or cellular pattern of farm-ownership or occupation gradually developed. The example of Kofi Pare, an Aburi farmer, should indicate the dangers of statistical generalization about farm size—the first need is classification, not figures. Thus, at Kofi Pare (the place which now bears Kofi Pare's name), present-day farmers may be classified as original farmers, inheritors of original farmers, other members of matrilineages of original farmers, sons of original farmers, outsiders who bought 'secondhand' land and so forth. Kofi Pare bought the land in about 1911; it had an area of more than 2 sq. miles, part of which was resold; in 1959 there were 137 farmers registered by the Department of Agriculture as owning land on this estate, nearly all of whom were close relatives of Kofi Pare himself or of his

six original associates—the latter, it is interesting to note, were all close relatives of Kofi Pare, either by blood or marriage.

(4) Many of the farmers have always had a thoroughly commercial attitude to land-purchase. In order to buy land more cheaply and for numerous other agricultural, economic and social reasons, certain of the land-purchasers formed themselves into groups or clubs, known as companies, for the purpose of acquiring blocks of land which were then divided into strips from a base line, each farmer being allocated a strip of a width proportionate to his cash contribution. (Such a strip, whether planted or not, I refer to as 'a land'—but lands are not necessarily bought through companies.) These companies, which were unimportant until after 1900, were characteristically composed of groups of friends, not relatives, each man being concerned to buy land for his own use. In the early days companies proper were formed only by farmers who belonged to patrilineal societies, such as Larteh and Mamfe, where sons inherit the property of their fathers. Nowadays, farmers from matrilineal societies, such as Aburi, form and join companies—though family lands, with their farms presenting a mosaic pattern, as at Kofi Pare, then develop within the strips. Where strip-farms are shown on the Area Office maps (for the maps to be comprehensible for research purposes, it is desirable for them to be redrawn on a much smaller scale than that used by the Department, which is 40 inches to the mile), it means that the land was originally acquired by a company. There are many districts of southern Akim Abuakwa, such as the Nankese area, where all the land was sold over half a century ago, most of it to companies: in that particular area a typical company land has an area of between about 300 and 1,000 acres.

(5) Contrary to popular belief, the enterprising individual farmer did not find himself unreasonably hampered by the demands made on him by the members of his 'wider family' or lineage. It is very interesting to note that, without doing violence to the traditional structure of society in the various home towns, it was possible for an individual to be accorded full scope to invest 'family money' in the acquisition of cocoa lands which, for some time at any rate, were likely to be regarded as his individual property. The older and less active members of an Aburi *abusua* (matrilineage) were usually clever enough to realize where their interests lay: they urged the younger men on, realizing that only through individual initiative could the wealth of the *abusua* as a whole be increased. On the other hand, the fact that individual property is always in process of conversion to family property has provided individuals with a great incentive to acquire additional lands for their own use.

(6) If an individual is to count as a capitalist, he must operate either on

26

borrowed money or with his own savings. The migrant farmers did both. The original 'pump-priming' savings were those derived from the sale of palm produce, etc., but such sums were far from sufficient. Little progress would have been made had the farmers not ploughed back the proceeds from growing cocoa on one land in the purchase of another land—to the extent that many farmers regarded land as the only reliable 'savings bank'. Then, the land sellers had been willing, from the earliest times, to accept payment for land in instalments—thus enabling those with very small savings to buy land and sometimes to pay for it, in part, from the cocoa grown on it. (I think this idea of paying in instalments has been an important, though theoretically unrecognized, feature of West African economic life for a very long time.) Sometimes, though not for philanthropic reasons, a rich farmer would be prepared to help a poor farmer by reselling him land, from lots acquired earlier, on 'easy terms'. The farm labourers, too, were originally attracted to this work by the prospect of future income from plucking cocoa from the farms which they were helping to establish. And, while on the subject of farm labourers, it must be noted as a most important point of principle (though, again, one that has gone unnoticed) that farmers never 'wasted' their savings on farm labour employment: they never employed labourers until, with the help of their families, they had established sufficient bearing-cocoa to reward their labourers with a share of the cocoa income. (This is why lump sum compensation received for swollen shoot was so seldom used for the finance of labourers.)

(7) The idea of 'branch' businesses is familiar to many capitalists and also to the migrant farmers. The migrant farmer, like the owner of a chain of retail stores or cinemas, both works himself and co-ordinates and directs the activities of others. Although successive Directors of Agriculture, especially around 1914, failed to realize this, it is a fact that earlier-acquired lands (which had proved fruitful) were never abandoned when a new land was acquired. Whether or not labourers were employed (and Akwapim farmers, incidentally, are much more inclined to employ labourers than are Krobo), it was usual for a relative to be installed on each land and for the farmer, while perhaps working primarily at one place, to spend much time travelling about supervising the work on all the lands. I think it is very hard on the farmers that ignorant town-dwellers should so often accuse them of being 'absentees': indeed, I think that the emotive word 'absenteeism', with its suggestion that the farmer is too lazy to perform his proper duty, should be dropped from our vocabulary in this context.

(8) If the word 'capitalist' is to be employed in a respectable sense, and not just as a term of abuse, then I think its creative aspect should be emphasized, and this usually involves the capitalists in taking a long view.

Certainly, the farmers have always been very long-term in their attitude. There is evidence that between the wars, before the swollen shoot destroyed so much of their cocoa, the farmers responded to a higher world cocoa price by buying more land and *vice versa*. Here again, we note, they did not just sit back enjoying their profits. But, like smaller businessmen the world over, they were rather disinclined to invest the profits from one kind of enterprise (cocoa) in establishing another (say, wholesale trading)—though it seems that many of the earliest lorry-owners were migrant cocoa-farmers.

(9) Business is apt to be all-demanding and the farmers' whole way of life was altered by the 'cocoa business'. Although many present-day migrants are of the third generation, their fathers as well as themselves having been born away from home, yet they still insist on regarding themselves as strangers in the farming area, people who are temporarily resident for business purposes in their cottages ('villages') in the forest or in stranger-towns, of which the most notable is Suhum. Ties with the home town are maintained in many ways: the profits from cocoa growing were partially devoted to building houses in the home town and many children are sent back to school there.

(10) The farmers, as businessmen, were unimpressed by the colonial administration and undertook their own development expenditure to provide better links between the cocoa forests and their homeland: before 1914 the Akwapim farmers had hired contractors to build three bridges over the river Densu (being businessmen they recouped their expenses by charging tolls) and a little later they invested at least £50,000 in the building of motorable access roads to Akwapim.

If it be accepted that these migrant cocoa-farmers of Southern Ghana are businessmen (or capitalists), not small 'peasants' who by an unplanned process of trial-and-error happened to create the world's largest cocoa-growing industry, then it is obvious that many stereotyped notions about cocoa-farmers as a group are really misleading. We must study the farmer, not patronize him: we must assume that he knows his business better than we do, until there is evidence to the contrary (here again, I emphasize the word 'business', for this is not to say that the farmer will be unappreciative of skilled technical advice and help); and at all costs we must avoid generalization about different types of farmer, who are as different as chalk from cheese. To illustrate this last point, I will take a practical example. Agricultural economists are often criticized for their failure to agree on the matter of the cost of producing cocoa. But how can they agree when 'it all depends'? With the migrant farmers of southern Ghana an important determinant of costs is the speed with which the farm was established. If two farmers own farms of 25 acres, one of which was fully planted in three years with the help of gangs of daily-paid labourers, the other in 25 years, with the aid of youthful members of the family, then the costs of production, however computed, are likely to work out much higher in the former than in the latter case. This is not an unrealistic example. The migrant farmers were secure within their boundaries, which were established at the time of the purchase of the land, and they did not have to clear and plant their land to assert their rights. Many company farmers had not completed the planting of their strip-farms, acquired perhaps 35 years earlier, when the swollen shoot became serious.

I shall conclude with a further reference to this highly complex question of farm size and scale of production. As most migrant farmers not only own several farms in different areas but are also apt to stand, as it were, in varying relations to these farms (according as to whether they were inherited, self-acquired, usufructuary grants, etc.), the notion of scale of production is fraught with difficulties, such as require rather formal language for their proper expression. While there is usually some tendency for farms to get smaller as time goes by, the process of sub-division tends to peter out in the long run—thus, with patrilineal peoples a son's inherited farms are seldom sub-divided on his death among his sons, the grandsons of the original farmer. With matrilineal migrants the opposite process of consolidation on death (as when the property of three brothers, who each had his own farm, passes to one inheritor), sometimes operates so powerfully as to counteract the sub-division tendency. From the angle of the efficiency of farming, the principal problem may be not 'fragmentation' (and it should be remembered that many of the small farms shown on the maps are no more than kitchen gardens owned by women relatives and others who happen to reside in the farming area), but the fact that, especially with Aburi farmers, too much responsibility is apt to fall on the inheritor, who inherits all the lands formerly owned by his maternal uncle or elder brother. This problem often seems much worse on paper than in fact, owing to the willingness of many inheritors to depute full responsibility to he who happens to be resident on any land even to the extent of raising no objection to his name being registered with the Department as the true owner. The Aburi-style family land (such as Kofi Pare), and a strip-farm acquired through a company, are such different types of organization that the practical agriculturists who work in the field should lose no opportunity of contrasting and comparing them.

# CHAPTER 3

# EWE SEINE FISHERMEN

---

## INTRODUCTION

In May 1963 I spent about a fortnight in Keta, in south-eastern Ghana, studying the Ewe seine fishermen who are based on that coastline.[1] My hope of returning to Keta later that year was dashed by the disastrous floods of October and November when Keta's only road link with the outside world was severed. But I decided to publish my provisional findings, partly as a demonstration that provocative socio-economic fieldwork may sometimes be done very rapidly, even where, as in this case, background anthropological material was scanty and where the investigator (who was obliged to work through an interpreter) had no previous experience of the society in question.

Unfortunately, the book of collected papers by a number of authors which was to have included this contribution was never published. Meanwhile, M. Albert de Surgy, of the Groupe de Chercheurs Africanistes, had completed a splendid survey of traditional fishing on the Ewe and Mina coast, based on fieldwork carried out between May and August 1965, and had issued a provisional report—*La Pêche Traditionnelle sur le Littoral Evhe et Mina* (*De l'embouchure de la Volta au Dahomey*) (22). As M. de Surgy had previously studied sea and lagoon fishermen in the Ivory Coast (21), where he had first encountered the Ewe migrant fishermen, his experience was greatly superior to my own and it seemed that my work had been completely superseded.

However, it has now occurred to me that my original notion of demonstrating the possibilities of 'quick research' has, in a way, been validated by M. de Surgy's work, which shows that my findings had been essentially reliable and that I had laid emphasis on the 'right points'.[2] It is true that M. de Surgy's work was not entirely independent of my own, for I had given

---

[1] I had originally intended to concentrate on studying the remarkable Anloga shallot-growing industry, which is perhaps the most capital-intensive farming in West Africa, but found myself diverted by the seine fishermen. (See p. 33 n. 2.). I wish to express my great gratitude to Mr Felix Hukporti of Keta, a one-time secretary of a seine-company, for his excellent interpretation and for introducing me to many net-owners and others. I am also grateful to Dr Jean Grove for her critical reading of the typescript following her return to Keta in 1966.

[2] Of course the main danger of 'quick research' is that of completely missing the main points: thus, when first studying cocoa-farmers in south-eastern Ghana I failed to distinguish sedentary from migrant farmers. (See *The Gold Coast Cocoa-Farmer*, 1956, by the present writer.)

him a copy of an earlier draft of this article[1] before he went to Keta. But his knowledge of West African fishermen was already so great, his field methods so thorough, that there was no chance of his being over-influenced or biased by my findings—though I hope that the speed of his research was slightly enhanced by my having been in Keta before him.

Although the original article has been condensed and somewhat amended, it is basically unchanged, except for the addition of footnotes (only) on M. de Surgy's work in 1965. I am most grateful to M. de Surgy for permission to refer to his report in my footnotes.[2] This study should be regarded as no more than an English-language introduction to a fascinating subject on which he is the authority.

The seine fishermen to whom this chapter relates belong to the Anlo (or Awuna) branch of the Ewe people and inhabit a coastal district running from the west bank of the estuary of the river Volta in Ghana, eastwards through to Lome, the capital of the Togo republic.[3] They live both on the long sandspit to the south-east of the shallow Keta lagoon—this spit is in places no wider than the road it carries—as well as to the north of the lagoons, mainly in towns such as Afiadenyigba, Anyako and Atiavi.

Cities apart, there are few West African districts as densely populated as the six-mile length of sandspit, centred on Keta, which makes up the Keta Urban Council area: 29,711 people were recorded as living there in 1960, of whom 16,719 were in Keta town, the remainder being in neighbouring Tetevikofe, Dzelukofe, Vodza and Kedzi. If the 1948 census figures were reasonably accurate (and if the 1960 figures were not significantly inflated by the temporary return of those normally living elsewhere, for the loyal purpose of enumeration in the homeland), then the population grew by over 50% between 1948 and 1960. The recorded population of Anloga, the capital of the Anlo state, expanded even more rapidly—from 6,358 in 1948 to 11,038 in 1960, and the towns north of the lagoon also grew fast.

In the Keta Urban Council area there is scarcely any general farming, though coconut palms provide a fringe to the coast.[4] The district north of the lagoon provides some of Keta's food and other supplies and it had been the

[1] Issued by the Institute of African Studies, University of Ghana (1963). See also *Pan-African Fishermen* by Polly Hill (12).

[2] Especially as this may be regarded as raw material for a thesis on the origin, evolution and socio-economic organization of 'la pêche indigène professionnelle le long de l'ancienne Côte de Guinée'. The references to M. de Surgy's work in the *text* relate to his 1965 report; those in the *footnotes* relate to his 1966 report (based on his 1965 research in Eweland).

[3] See 'Some Aspects of the Economy of the Volta Delta (Ghana)' by J. M. Grove (6). (Dr Grove did her fieldwork in 1963.)

[4] Along much of the coast, though not everywhere, the Cape St Paul coconut disease has killed, or is killing, all the palms. (See Grove (6).)

2   The coastline of Ghana from Anloga to Aflao

main Anlo salt-producing area until 1950 when the natural process of crystallization abruptly ceased.[1] Markets in Anlo country are based on a four-day cycle. Keta, as well as Anyako and Afiadenyigba across the lagoon, all hold markets on the same day, and in 1963 there were huge canoes with supplies from the north which berthed at Keta market quay: with their outboard motors, or under sail, they returned home in the evening with up to forty passengers and their loads. That there should be cattle-keepers to the

[1] The Songaw lagoon, west of Ada, Ghana's other major traditional source of salt, also failed. Annual salt production has always been very variable, but there is no local recollection of previous total failure over such a long period. Dr Jean Grove tells me that the failure resulted from abnormally high lagoon-levels; she thinks that salt was again formed in 1967. (See The Volta River Project, *Appendices to the Report of the Preparatory Commission*, II (24), 171, and Grove (6).)

north of the lagoon[1] is important to the remarkable Anloga shallot-growing industry,[2] which draws its supplies of cattle-manure from there as well as from Tongu—other types of manure include local fish, and the droppings of fowl, sheep, goats, bats and swallows. So Anlo country is more of an economic entity than its geography might suggest: facing the sea, it also looks back beyond the lagoons.

Of the total population of 5,324 occupied males in the Keta Urban Council area in 1960, as many as 1,942 (37%) were classified as 'fishermen' (lagoon as well as sea), the corresponding figures for the Anlo South Local Council area (which includes Anloga and the district to the north of the Keta lagoon) having been 4,051 fishermen (31% of total occupied males). Fishing (most of it, presumably, beach-fishing) is much the most important single occupation of men resident in Keta, where there is, presumably, a greater density of beach-seining than anywhere else in West Africa.[3] The Anlo seine fishermen have been migrating[4] in search of richer waters and fish-markets for over seventy years, being found on beaches running from Sierra Leone in the north to the Congo river in the south; during their long sojourns on distant beaches they have taught many others the use of their gear.

On the basis of research in Anlo country only, the number of Anlo companies operating outside Ghana cannot be estimated, partly because net-owners sometimes remain on very distant beaches for many years at a stretch. Certainly there are great concentrations at Lagos, along the Dahomey and Togo coast (Ouidah, Gran-Popo and Anecho were often mentioned) and, as we now know, there were 31 companies[5] on the beaches near Abidjan and Grand-Bassam in the Ivory Coast in 1964. M. de Surgy recorded the existence of seven Anlo companies at Monrovia and eight at Freetown and perhaps there were some elsewhere on the more northerly Guinea coast. As for the southerly coasts, a few informants mentioned earlier migrations to the French Congo—one such adventure being commemorated by a house named 'Congo Villa' in Keta—and possibly to Angola. Distance is no

---

[1] Formerly cattle were kept in the coastal districts. 'Quita [Keta] is the Cincinnati of Guinea. The hogs seem to be as numerous as the people . . . The poultry market is well supplied . . . Cattle are abundant but small'. *Adventures and Observations on the West Coast of Africa and its Islands*, by C. W. Thomas (23), p. 244.

[2] In terms of the annual value of the yield per acre, this is said to be one of the most intensive forms of agriculture in the world. The shallots are grown on specially prepared sand-beds in which many shallow cement wells have been sunk; they are distributed throughout Ghana. (See Grove (6) and Hill (12).)

[3] See de Surgy (22).

[4] The Anlo are not thought to have been freshwater migrants unlike certain other Ewe, of whom there were many colonies on the upper reaches of the river Volta in northern Ghana.

[5] Of the 952 full-time fishermen working with these companies, a few were from Togo or Dahomey, but most were Anlo. According to de Surgy (21) the first Anlo company installed itself in the Ivory Coast as recently as 1935.

obstacle: for half a century, or more, the fishermen have carried their canoes and other gear to the distant beaches by 'steamer', and nowadays the company elders sometimes fly there.

BEACH-SEINING

A sociologist with no knowledge of fishing technology is very much hampered by the scantiness of the literature on West African fishing and, in particular, by the lack of satisfactory technical descriptions of beach-seining.[1] The following notes are partly derived from a number of amateur published sources and partly from untutored observation: they will clearly be of no interest at all to experts on fishing technology.[2]

Beach-seine (or drag-seine) nets are operated, unlike purse-seines, from the shore. When the net is to be cast it is stowed, together with its attached hauling ropes, in a dug-out canoe which is paddled, according to its size, by a crew of up to about 12 men, neither sail nor outboard motor being required for this offshore fishing. The end of the rope attached to one wing of the net is held ashore, while the canoe is paddled out to sea to the full extent of the rope, which may be a mile or more. According to one account,[3] the canoe is then turned parallel to the coast and proceeds against the current paying out the wing; when the end of the wing is reached the bag, which is separate, is either attached by members of the crew, who dive into the sea, or it may be attached later on when the net has been partly hauled towards shore. The other wing of the net is then shot, continuing the line of the first. The canoe then makes for the shore about half a mile or more up-current from the point of departure, paying out the second rope as she goes.

When the second rope is landed, groups of men tail out on each rope, the number required depending mainly on the size of the net, but also on the proportion of small boys, women and other casual helpers. The net is pulled slowly ashore by a disciplined and singing band, which moves rhythmically backward with short stilted steps, often encouraged by the beating of gong-gongs. The end of the rope is carefully coiled on the ground and as each rope-puller reaches the coil, he returns to the head of the line. The hauling may last for four or five hours, or even longer, with some intervals for rest. The work of the two teams requires close co-ordination, by whistling, shouting and waving, for as the net comes in the two wings must be brought

[1] The Gold Coast Fisheries Department did not come into existence until 1949 and until very recently its reports were remarkably brief, as well as out of date by publication date.
[2] See de Surgy (22).
[3] See a chapter by A. P. Brown, in *The Fishes and Fisheries of the Gold Coast* by F. R. Irvine (14). This description relates to nets which are much smaller than most of those in use on the Anlo coast.

closer and closer together, to enclose the fish and drive them into the bag, until when the bag is finally landed they are only a few feet apart.[1]

Such a method of fishing depends on the existence of large groups of well-organized and willing men. Even were power to be used in the hauling of the ropes—and experiments are said to have shown the impracticability of this on the Anlo coast with present gear—many men would still be required for the continuous operation of a net. It is with the socio-economic organization of these groups, with special reference to their leader (the net-owner), that this study is mainly concerned.

### THE BASIC ORGANIZATIONAL SYSTEM SUMMARIZED

The core of the group that operates the beach-seine net, which is always referred to in Eweland as *yevudor*[2] (literally European net), is a so-called 'company' of men, each of whom usually contracts to work with the net-owner for a fixed period, often called a 'season'. On the Anlo coast, seasons are commonly no longer than about six months, but when a company migrates to a distant beach they may be much longer and M. de Surgy reported (21) contract periods of 2, 3 and even 4 years among the Anlo fishermen in the Ivory Coast.

The typical Anlo fishing company, like the typical cocoa-farmers' land-purchasing company in southern Ghana, is composed mainly of non-kinsmen.[3] But there the resemblance ends, for the fishing company, unlike the cocoa company, is not a group of equals. The leader of a cocoa company is concerned, like the company members, with buying land for his own use; but the leader of a fishing-company, the 'net-owner', is different from his men, he being the sole capitalist (the businessman), they being his 'employees'.

It is most unusual for a small group of men, even a set of kin, to combine together to acquire a net. Some nets are owned by the fishermen who originally acquired them, but most by the descendants of such fishermen. Apart from fishermen net-owners (some of whom are also shallot-farmers), there are some business or professional men, such as traders or teachers, who

---

[1] 'The seine net did not catch fish. Even less than most modern types of trawl did it catch fish. It depended for its efficacy on the fish catching themselves. They literally swam into the net in their attempts to swim away from the ropes'. *Living Silver* by Burns Singer (18), p. 167.
[2] The correct orthography is *yevudɔ*, but here it would be pedantic not to use the form which satisfies the ordinary educated Ewe fisherman.
[3] This is confirmed by de Surgy who does, however, note that the net-owner has a moral obligation to employ any 'brothers' who seek work with him; Dr Jean Grove's findings are also confirmatory, though in 1966 she noted the existence of several 'kin-companies', one of them having as many as 80 members.

finance fishing companies, as well as a few women net-owners in their own right.

A net-owner may or may not himself participate in the day-to-day work of his company. If he does not, his authority is always exercised through his 'bos'n' (*omega*)—the head of a group of 'elders'. Many bos'ns are related to their net-owner, being their sons, brother's sons, or younger brothers: they are apt to work permanently with that net-owner. There are also professional types of bos'n who, unrelated to the net-owner, sometimes works with different net-owners. Among the other specialists is a secretary, whose duties include those of keeping records and accounts, though he may sometimes also be an active fisherman: secretaries are seldom related to the net-owner.[1]

The number of regular members in a company is a function of several factors, three of which are net-size, the number of nets operated by the company, and the availability of part-time assistants, including boys. Perhaps in Anlo country a typical company consists of about 40 men, but there are some which are much larger than this, say 80 or more, and some quite small ones.[2] Mainly owing to costs of transport, the companies which travel to distant beaches cut their Anlo manpower down to a minimum.

Most company members are Anlo men, from north as well as south of the lagoons, who are unrelated to the net-owner, though a net-owner's sons, younger brothers, or nephews may work in his company. The individual contracts with the net-owner to work with him for a season, beginning and ending on specified dates. He usually asks for an advance of cash (for which there is a formal written receipt, which binds him to work with the net-owner) which is repayable at the end of the season from his share of the company's proceeds. Typical advances run from about £8 to £15, but very much larger sums are sometimes granted, particularly in respect of experienced men such as bos'ns or for employment for long periods on distant beaches.[3]

Net-owners usually say that the ordinary company member incurs no living expenses during the season, though this (as will be seen) is an assertion which requires qualification. In principle, the company itself pays for, or provides, basic food requirements, and sometimes also provides drinks, tobacco and other extras. Numerous other expenses, such as medical

---

[1] Other 'elders' listed by de Surgy (22), pp. 58–9, include: canoe captains, net repairers and inspectors, 'petty-officers' in charge of net-hauling and other work; several offices may be held by the same man. 'Specialists' include canoe paddlers, divers, rope inspectors, bag-repairers, a whistler (to summon the fishermen) . . .

[2] De Surgy (22), p. 67, noted companies with only 15 members, and others (which operated 2 to 3 seine nets) with 200 members or more.

[3] De Surgy (22), p. 166, regarded £5 to £10 per man as typical for nets working off Ghana or Togo beaches and £20 to £30 as applying to long tours in the Ivory Coast.

expenses, are met as a matter of course. Free accommodation is provided: in Keta this may be in permanent quarters attached to the net-owner's house, or elsewhere in the town; more usually, and this applies to Keta as well as to the rest of the Anlo coast, company members are accommodated in temporary, or semi-permanent, houses on the beach. Keep is thus, in principle, guaranteed throughout the season, at the end of which each man is due to receive a sum of money, the value of which depends partly on the luck of the season's catch, partly on the sharing-formula adopted by the particular company and partly on the individual's special responsibilities, keenness and attention to duty.

Before the season's work starts, the net-owner and the company members may or may not agree on the principle of division of the value of the season's catch—on the sharing-formula. While, as will be discussed below, there are many variations in arithmetical practice and other accountancy details and while statements about practice may represent aspirations rather than facts of past experience (unfortunately no net-owner in Keta volunteered to reveal his full accounts), yet certain generalizations may be made.

All systems of division of the season's catch may be thought of as involving partial accounting: part of the money that is received from selling fish for cash on the beach is deliberately omitted from the accounts of the season's takings, being immediately used by the company to finance living expenses, net-repairs, 'dashes' or advances to certain company members, drinks and so forth. This system does not affect the net sum available for distribution at the end of the season, for the sums that escape accounting would anyway be permissible as expenses, to be deducted before the share-out occurs; but it does mean that, quite apart from the fish consumed by the company members, accountable takings are considerably less than the gross value of the catch.

The sum available for division between the net-owner and his company at the end of the season is determined by deducting certain recorded expenses incurred during the season (which are effectively borne by the company as a whole) from the recorded receipts. These expenses may include such items as food allowances (or food purchases), costs of labour and materials for net repairs, costs of building and repairing houses, transport costs and medical expenses. The net recorded balance is then always divided into a predetermined number of 'parts'—practice is remarkably variable and division into 2, 4, 5, 7, 8 or 9 parts was reported by different companies.[1] Certain fixed numbers of these parts are then allotted to individuals or groups, of whom the net-owner is invariably one, all other company members taken together (including those with special responsibilities who are additionally

[1] These were, also, the partition fractions noted by de Surgy (22).

rewarded) being invariably another. If the proceeds are divided into 9 parts, it may be that 3 parts go to the net-owner;[1] one part to the men who go regularly to sea; one part to other company members with special responsibilities (notably the bos'n); one part to the regular net-menders (provided they are company members); the remaining 3 parts being then divided between all the company members on the basis of some system, or judgment, which takes account of the achievements and skills of individuals. Systems are designed, as it is put, to reward the individual 'according to his activities', and to this end daily attendance registers are kept.

The smooth functioning of the company's work and its general morale depend on the fishermen's 'wives' almost as much as on the men. In cooking and providing for the men, in preserving (usually smoking) and marketing the fish, their services must always be at hand—often far into the night when there happens to be a late catch. Each company member is entitled to bring a woman (or women) with him, and while most women are wives, some unmarried men bring single women, such as sisters, with them. The women, who are always referred to as 'the wives', live with the men in the housing provided, each one usually cooking for herself. The number of women attached to a company, even if it operates from a distant beach, may be almost as great as the number of men—a sign of their indispensability considering that certain of their expenses, such as outward transport, are apt to be borne by the company.[2]

Although, owing to rising hauls and fish prices, the traditional system has been somewhat modified recently, it is still usual for the wives to receive some, if not most, of their fish on credit, records of the value of the fish sold to each of them being kept by the secretary, sometimes in 'pass-books' issued by the net-owner. If fish is also sold to outside women, which it usually is, the wives are normally supplied at a substantial discount.[3] The wives preserve and resell the fish, for whatever price they can get, retaining any profit. Traditionally, they were trusted so completely that they were not asked to pay their debts until the end of the season, though nowadays the money may be called in periodically, perhaps weekly or monthly.[4] If at the end of the season any wife fails to repay all she owes, then the sum outstanding is deducted from her husband's share of the proceeds. Nowadays many of the larger companies bank their money during the course of the season, but

[1] This does not usually mean that the net-owner's 'profit' amounts to one-third of the net proceeds —see p. 49 above.
[2] See de Surgy (22), pp. 62–6.
[3] De Surgy (22), p. 63, states that this discount may vary between one-sixth and one-twelfth (see p. 52 below on the bargaining process). De Surgy adds that half the catch is often reserved for the wives.
[4] De Surgy asserts (22), p. 64, that the wives are expected to repay as soon as possible.

formerly there had always been much to be said for reducing the risk of theft by dispersing the money in many hands, thus effectively using the women as banks.[1]

## THE NET-OWNER

Perhaps there was a time when most Anlo men who lived near the sea, or the lagoon, owned nets of one sort or another, and certainly ownership of lagoon-nets is still widespread. But nowadays the ownership of the main sea-fishing net, the costly *yevudor*, is concentrated in few hands and there are many active seine fishermen, including bos'ns, who are not aspirant owners. In an economic sense a propertied class of net-owner has slowly emerged during the last half-century. While some active fishermen whose fathers were not net-owners invest their savings in nets; while a few professional men and traders become interested in this risky way of making money; while there are even a few women who deliberately acquire nets, the hard core of net-owners consists of the owners of the large contractor-built houses in Keta, Kedzi, Vodza and elsewhere, whose fathers owned *yevudor* before them.

Many net-owners own only one net; many own several, say two, three or four; a few net-owners own large numbers of nets, say ten or even more. This, briefly, is the statistical impression gained. Impressionism is unavoidable, if only because a net-owner does not necessarily know how many complete nets he owns, his proportions of netting being potentially capable of assembly in different ways. Then a man may have a large stock of old netting which is not in use: a Keta net-owner, who had turned over from cotton to nylon, had a roomful of discarded cotton netting, the equivalent of many nets, which he was hoping to sell. Furthermore, if a man has a number of nets which are in constant use, then they are quite likely to be operated from a number of different beaches, which may be widely dispersed.

Although the eldest of a set of fishermen-brothers is most likely to be the inheritor of his father's nets, a junior brother who is in full charge of one of these nets on a distant beach, where he is obliged to take full responsibility, will be regarded by all concerned as effectively a net-owner and he may hold this status indefinitely.

Probably most women net-owners owe their position to the lack of a suitable male inheritor. Sometimes they act as net-owner until the young son of a deceased net-owner is old enough to assume responsibility. If a man dies without sons, a daughter may operate his net during her lifetime, but it is said that her sons may not inherit. Women are occasionally given

---

[1] This is what I was told—see p. 51 below—but de Surgy casts doubt on my findings (22), p. 63.

nets by their husbands. As women are responsible for selling the fish and may make large profits, more of them may be effective net-financiers, if not actual owners, than men care to admit. And there are, certainly, a few women net-owners who deliberately acquire nets for themselves, appointing someone, who may or may not be a relative, to operate them on their behalf.

Some apparent net-owners have hired their nets, on a system known as *mavee* (*ma* to divide, *evi* two), under which the net seasonal proceeds (i.e. the gross value of the fish sold, less certain expenses) are halved, one portion for the net-owner, the other for the hirer and his company. Several informants declared that the *mavee* system is new, perhaps less than twenty years old; it was suggested that in adopting it the fishermen were modelling themselves on the Anloga shallot-farmers[1] who, as simultaneous field enquiries showed,[2] commonly 'rent' shallot-beds on a system known as *damee*, under which the shallots are divided equally between the owner of the beds and the 'tenant'. With both *mavee* and *damee*, operational expenses incurred during the season are deducted, before the proceeds are halved, and refunded to whoever has incurred them. But with *mavee* these expenses do not include the cost of net repairs during the season, which are met by the net-owner himself and not by the company, as is the rule when the net-owner operates his own net.[3] Although the net-owner gets a higher proportion of the seasonal proceeds under *mavee* than he would if he operated the net himself, it does not, of course, follow that his profits will be greater, for much depends on the cost of net repairs: it is the risks that matter and under *mavee* a net-owner may be ruined if his net is severely damaged.

So net-owners seldom decide to let out their nets on *mavee* unless, for some reason, they are prevented from operating them themselves: no one plans to obtain control over a net in order to put it out on *mavee*. If a man is suffering from illness or fatigue he may put out his net on *mavee* for a period; if he lacks capital to raise the advances for company members, *mavee* may be the only alternative; if an elderly man has no suitable son, or paternal nephew, to operate his net for him he may choose *mavee*: women sometimes let out nets on *mavee*. *Mavee* may be on a daily basis, relying on schoolchildren at the weekend, or it may involve the formation of a company proper. If the hirer is not a friend or relative, then it may be necessary for the net-owner to employ a representative to work as a company member, so that he may check the value of the catch.

Net-owners and hirers may be so satisfied with their relationship that it persists indefinitely. An Anlo hirer at Tsokome beach, west of Accra, said

[1] De Surgy (22), p. 95, notes the possibility that the Anlo fishermen were imitating the Fanti, who universally employ this system of division in seine-fishing.　　[2] See Hill (12)

[3] This is confirmed by de Surgy—see summary of partition systems in (22), p. 101.

that he had been working there, on a *mavee* basis, with the same retired net-owner, for as long as sixteen years. Although his net-owner took an active interest in the work, not only travelling from Keta to Tsokome to witness the sharing of the seasonal proceeds but also to receive cash at earlier stages ('if catches are good we send for the net-owner to come for the money'), yet the hirer said that the Anlo company members, whom he recruited with advances made available by his net-owner, regarded him as the net-owner and that the company even bore his name.

## AGBADOHO

There is a widespread belief in West Africa that every businessman, or woman, must have a separate stock of working capital to sustain his business,[1] and the concept of such a fund is well developed in Anlo country. One word for such a fund is *agbadoho* (from *agba* a load, *ho* money or wealth). Although, curiously, educated Anlo people seem to be generally unfamiliar with this word, all the net-owners who were questioned on the matter expatiated further on it, as did Anloga shallot-farmers, who were apt to compare their *agbadoho* with the funds of women traders—to regard it as 'money that is set aside for business'.

The net and the capital fund (the *agbadoho*) are integrally related concepts —for the net is both a concept and a piece of gear. Neither could exist without the other. As nets are constantly undergoing transformation and must be put in good order before the season opens, the net-owner must have capital at his disposal. Capital is required to recruit the company (the main expense being the advances), to meet the costs of the journey and the building of houses for the fishermen.[2]

A man going into business for the first time[3] must have the use of a net and some power of attracting cash: starting, perhaps, with a piece of second-hand net which is operated by schoolboys at the weekend and with some cash lent by his wife,[4] it will be his aspiration to develop both net and fund simultaneously. As the business begins to develop, so the *agbadoho* comes into existence—the process of capital formation is at work. Initially the net-owner may not have a very clear notion of the central fund. So far as he can borrow enough money to sustain the net at its work, he will be an acceptable

---

[1] For a note on the distinction between capital and 'spending money' see Hill (10). See also *Malay Fishermen: their Peasant Economy*, by Raymond Firth (2): 'the concept of capital as a stock of money used to finance production is quite a clear one to the Malay peasant' (p. 128).
[2] See de Surgy (22), pp. 114–17.
[3] The huge cost of modern netting (see p. 45) means that few net-owners nowadays are new-comers to this business—as already noted (p. 39), they are mostly sons of net-owners.
[4] Or borrowed from 'family funds' (see de Surgy (22).)

net-owner to his company. Gradually, he may find himself getting into a position where a company secretary takes a partial hand in sorting out his capital accounts. Gradually, as the funds at his disposal increase, he may find himself regarding part of them as 'separate'—money not to be dissipated on food or other current living expenses.

It is when sons begin to assume full charge of some, or all, of their father's net, or when a net-owner dies, that the notion of *agbadoho* necessarily[1] crystallizes, so that, thereafter, the son will say: 'this money is a central fund for my father's net'. It is when *agbadoho* is considered in relation to inheritance that ideas begin to clarify. Then it is seen that, *ideally*, it represents a perpetual and indivisible fund—that it is as unthinkable that an *agbadoho* should be divided following a net-owner's death as that the net itself should be divided. 'However many canoes a man might own, there would never be more than one *agbadoho* formed after his death.[2]'

During the season the company aims at keeping the money that accrues to it from the sale of fish as intact as possible—if banked it should be kept there until the final payout. When materials such as bundles of net, coils of rope, twine, floats, leads, etc. are required, then ideally it should be the *agbadoho* which disburses in the first instance, being refunded at the end of the season. There is, then, a concept of the company borrowing from the *agbadoho*. Some net-owners hold large stocks of fishing materials and the secretary, or bos'n, may then sometimes act as a kind of storekeeper. One net-owner, when endeavouring to explain the concept of *agbadoho*, said: 'This *agbadoho* is money used for materials so that you always have stock.' But when a net-owner decides to improve his net, to invest new capital in it, it is usually[3] the fund, not the company, which meets the cost. Companies are temporary organizations, never reproducing themselves. Ideally, the net and the *agbadoho* should live for ever.

Information was conflicting as to whether a net-owner who owned nets at several beaches would be likely to have more than one *agbadoho*—presumably 'accounting practices' vary. One net-owner spoke of his son, who was his bos'n, taking a portion of the *agbadoho* away to a distant beach: 'A man who travels for fishing carries part of the *agbadoho* with him.' Another said that when a young man travels he must not take more than £25 of the *agbadoho* with him, 'even if the fund is £200 altogether'. This indivisibility of the fund connects with the fact that fathers seldom give their sons nets

---

[1] See de Surgy (22), pp. 118–21, for an extremely interesting analysis of *agbadoho* in relation to inheritance.

[2] In discussing the transformation of nets de Surgy uses the terms *l'agbadoho-père* and *l'agbadoho-fils*, the latter developing under the protection of the former— (22), p. 120.

[3] De Surgy notes (22), pp. 100, 107, that with long-lived companies which operate on distant beaches there is a growing tendency for the company to meet these capital costs.

during their lifetime. But as the death of the father is the signal to the sons to start being enterprising on their own accounts, so it may be that a few years later several of them have succeeded in establishing their own *agbadoho*.

## INHERITANCE AND THE POSITION OF SONS

Although the authorities[1] insist that with Anlo (and Glidyi) people, individual, as distinct from family, property is transmitted matrilineally, a man's heir being his sister's son, no trace of such a practice was found so far as concerns the inheritance of fishing gear.[2] It became clear that, in practice, the usual inheritor of a man's self-acquired fishing gear is his eldest son, provided he is a fisherman.[3] A son who had taken up some non-fishing occupation, especially one who was living outside Anlo country, would be unlikely to inherit the net (and the *agbadoho*) unless there were no more suitable inheritor.

With the fishing gear of Anlo fishermen the process of inheritance does not begin to operate before death, as it often does with the self-acquired land of certain migrant cocoa-farmers, or with the cattle owned by pastoral Fulani: this is, presumably, associated with the indivisibility of the property. So, however decrepit a father may be, or however actively his sons may work on his behalf, he continues to assert his status as *the* net-owner.

Even if a father has several nets, any kind of final division of them between his sons is frowned on. Brothers who divide their father's gear following his death are considered to be ill-organized from a business standpoint, so that they will not prosper. As for the difficulties which may arise between half-brothers, with different mothers, on their father's death, it is always hoped that, somehow, these will be resolved leaving the property intact.[4] It would be so regrettable for a group of brothers to sell their father's gear on his death, in order to divide the proceeds among themselves, that fishermen can

[1] These authorities are: D. Westermann, *Die Glidyi Ewe in Sud-Togo* (26); Madeline Manoukian, *The Ewe-Speaking People of Togoland and the Gold Coast* (16); and Barbara E. Ward, 'An Example of a "Mixed" System of Descent and Inheritance' (25). So far as concerns their discussion of the matrilineal transmission of individual property among the Anlo, both Manoukian and Ward are, in fact, entirely reliant on Westermann. See also G. K. Nukunya (17) and note 2 below.

[2] Anloga shallot-farmers, unlike Keta net-owners, readily remembered the time when certain types of self-acquired property passed matrilineally. Nukunya (17) has confirmed that fishing nets are inherited only in the male line. On the general issue he writes: 'Westermann's view, later developed by Ward, that personal property among the Anlo is transmitted from a man to his sister's son has no foundation in oral tradition or genealogical history . . . However, I think the term "mixed descent" suggested by Ward is an apt description of the system' (p. 78).

[3] De Surgy (22), pp. 118–21, adds a great deal to this brief analysis.

[4] See de Surgy (22), p. 121.

seldom bring themselves to discuss such a possibility. However, one man did venture to say that, in the last resort, 'if a father decides there is too much trouble, he may become defiant and furiously divide his net between his sons'.

As a father usually continues to exert some control over his net until his death, so his removal may very much affect the attitude of the sons to their father's business and to one another. Rather than dispute with the inheritor, a younger brother who was previously operating one of his father's nets may regard this as the moment for setting up on his own account, perhaps borrowing from the *agbadoho* to do so; but many sons continue to work with their elder brothers.

There are many special circumstances which may prevent the attainment of the ideal of keeping the property intact. Thus, one Kedzi net-owner said that his father, who had died 29 years before and who had been buried under a huge monument in front of his house, had owned six nets, two of which had passed to his (father's) brother's sons, on the grounds that his brother, who had died young, had formerly helped him.

THE NET

Whether the net is called *yevudor* ('European net') because it was first introduced by Europeans or first made from imported twine (as it certainly was at the end of the last century) one does not know.[1] All that is certain is that the great migration of Anlo seine fishermen began before 1900.[2] The earliest reference to the net which has yet been noted occurs in Härtter,[3] who referred to a large net (*yofudo*) worth about 400–500 marks. Gruvel,[4] writing in 1913, noted that beach-seine nets known as *yevonde* were in operation along the Ivory and Gold Coasts, in Dahomey, along the coast near the Congo and in Angola, as they had been earlier in the Dakar area of Senegal where Lebou fishermen operated nets some hundred of metres long.[5]

Traditionally, portions of net were netted by hand and laced together into a whole. That nets still grow and develop, rather than suddenly coming into existence as entire new objects, is a fact of great significance that emerged

[1] In a letter to the author M. de Surgy writes that the net may have been first introduced into Africa by the Portuguese in the region of Congo and Angola. (The seine net is one of the oldest pieces of fishing gear of which there is record in the world.)

[2] See de Surgy (22), pp. 15–19: de Surgy considers that the net began to take its present form in the Keta area about 1860.

[3] 'Der Fischfang in Evheland' by Von G. Härtter, 1906 (9).

[4] *L'Industrie des Pêches sur la Côte occidentale d'Afrique*, by A. Gruvel (8).

[5] *Les Pêcheries des Côtes du Sénégal*, by A. Gruvel (7), p. 94.

from the present fieldwork, though its likelihood should have been foreseen.[1] It was only when the manager of a prosperous fishing materials business in Keta was unable to estimate the price of a *yevudor*, without going behind the scenes to do some arithmetic, that the truth dawned: he could never recollect having sold an entire net. He said that it was unusual for a customer to buy more than £200 worth of netting at a time; that much of it was bought in bundles, costing about £25, for use as required; and that (having done his arithmetic) a long nylon net, with nylon ropes, would cost about £3,000 or nearly three times the cost of the equivalent in cotton.

As a net is a form of 'knitted capital', little cash for its creation may be required initially, especially if secondhand or discarded raw material is available. Thus it is that the physical capital and the fund to sustain it may grow simultaneously from small beginnings. Thus it is, also, that those possessed of significant capital sums (derived, perhaps, in the old days, from rubber trading) could go ahead fast investing the proceeds of one good net in the acquisition of others—even purchasing an entire net, for nowadays this does happen occasionally. Thus it is, finally, that nets are often regarded as a perpetual, non-vanishing form of property, analogous to inherited land.

Nets are very variable in size—a large one might be half a mile long[2] (and require a procession of perhaps twenty men to carry it), a small one might be only 250 yards long and be more readily made from secondhand bits and pieces. Although nowadays nylon has almost entirely displaced cotton, this changeover occurred gradually, for nylon sections could be incorporated in cotton nets. Net-owners sometimes import netting directly from England and elsewhere.

## THE SEINE CANOE

Canoes are made in the forest where the tree is felled, nowadays usually in Fanti country, and are then transported to the coast. Their size varies, a very big canoe being about 30 ft long and about 5 ft wide, the cost, including the local carpentry work of fitting seats, etc., being of the order of £150 to £300. They have a built-up bow to keep out the surf, so that they may be launched and beached where there is no natural protection from the waves. These canoes are always paddled and never sailed.

The canoe is usually, though not always, owned by the net-owner.

---

[1] Firth (2), is very relevant in this connexion. Then G. A. Steven, in his *Report on the Sea Fisheries of Sierra Leone* (1947) (20), noted that all the 50 or so seine nets that he had found in Sierra Leone were hand-made of imported twine and that it had never been the practice to buy ready-made net—presumably some, at least, of these nets were Ewe-owned and operated.

[2] This was confirmed by de Surgy who stated (22), p. 47, that a long net measured 300–400 'fathoms', a typical net 225–300 'fathoms'.

Traditionally, it was acquired after the net had been created—a process which may formerly have taken a year or two. One Kedzi net-owner said that if, after making a net, a man lacked money to buy a canoe, he might ask someone else, who would then take a share of the proceeds, to buy one on his behalf; alternatively he might borrow money to buy one for himself. Sometimes it was possible to pay for canoes in instalments over a period. Whoever may happen to have owned the canoe originally, it was usually not long before it came into the possession of the net-owner.

## THE COMPANY AND ITS WORK

Originally, so it is said, beach-seine companies were organized on a family basis, as certain kinds of lagoon-fishing companies still are today.[1] But nowadays (as already noted) most companies which are formed to operate a net for a 'season' consist basically of non-kin, though family groups may sometimes operate nets casually, at weekends, or during school holidays. The ordinary company member, who is an Anlo man, contracts to work with the net-owner for the 'season' in return for which he receives an advance, which is repayable from his share of the proceeds at the end of the season. All informants were agreed that this advance system is new, probably post-war. Whether its existence reflects a growing scarcity of recruits is not known; perhaps it has become conventional for each of them to demand an advance, as a kind of right, knowing that the greater prosperity of the net-owner (or of those from whom he is obliged to borrow) has made this possible. It is perhaps relevant that many company members are primarily farmers, men who join companies from time to time, but who are not obliged to earn a living this way. While in the old days the net-owner was obliged to disburse relatively small sums, for transport for instance, before the season opened, nowadays he may have in addition, if his company is recruited for work on a distant beach, to find a sum of £1,000 or more as advances.

The system of advances has become so standardized that some net-owners even use printed receipt forms. The usual form of receipt records the sum borrowed, the names of the parties concerned, the dates between which the man agrees to work and the beach from which the net will operate. A specimen receipt for £14 recorded that the sum is an 'advance for the purpose of doing fishing industry with $X$ [the net-owner] at Sorku beach for a period of 3 months [an unusually short period] starting from July 1963'. 'I do faithfully promise and undertake not to desert the fishing industry of the said $X$ while at Sorku beach'. Another specimen paper stated that the sum advanced was

---

[1] But with lagoon netting, or trapping, most company members own their own gear—there is no counterpart to the sole net-owner.

for the purposes of 'fishing labour contract'—'which said amount shall be deducted from share of the proceeds at the end of the fishing season'. A third case related to a Denu man whose advance was £30 in return for the promise of two and a half years' work at Abidjan. A fourth case related to a Kedzi man who was advanced as much as £74 for the promise of two years' work; this man, who was to have been employed as a bos'n, 'bolted away' and had never been heard of since.

While net-owners often discuss the possibility of suing those who fail to turn up, or who leave prematurely, they probably seldom do so. Inspection of recent records of the Keta Local Court revealed that the number of such cases is very small. Perhaps the threat of court proceedings is sometimes found effective, perhaps other courts are sometimes involved. But even when a conviction is secured the police often have difficulty in ascertaining the whereabouts of the guilty man who may have received advances from several net-owners and then taken up entirely different work. Net-owners often sub-contract the recruiting work, asking a bos'n whom they already know and trust, or someone else of influence, to assist them. One net-owner said that he had advanced £117 to a friend of his bos'n-brother, who had promised to recruit 18 company members for him in return for £10 (from the £117); this man had disappeared nine months earlier and the police were still looking for him.

As the company must work as a team and as, for accounting reasons, it is very desirable that each man should work for the same period, so net-owners attach much importance to members working for the whole season. But they appear to be little concerned with continuity of employment between seasons and new companies are not replicas of old ones, though they may include some of the same people. A company is formed and then it disperses, by which time the new members of the successor company will have been recruited. As efficient net-owners aspire, like the owners of aircraft, to operate their nets as continuously as the demands of repair and maintenance permit, there may be scarcely a gap between the seasons—but the men, on the other hand, need a rest or have farming duties elsewhere.

Companies are run very democratically, the net-owner exercising his authority, as already mentioned, through a group of elders, who in turn often consult the men. The members of some companies consider that the secretary is effectively employed by them, to act for them in relation to the net-owner; then, if they do not like or trust him, they can demand that someone else should be appointed. In other cases there is one secretary for the net-owner and another for the members.

That company members are likely to be suspicious unless certain conventions are observed, is well understood by the net-owner and by those who take executive responsibility. The ostentatious way in which the money received from selling fish on the beach is put into a lidded stewpan, which is carefully carried by its handle, is a demonstration to all concerned that it is not disappearing into somebody's pocket. When the net-owner, or bos'n, goes to buy fishing materials, he should be accompanied by a company member on the grounds that it is the company as a whole which finances repairs.

Almost as important as the morale of those who operate the net is that of the women. The women must be treated fairly. The price at which fish is offered to them must be 'reasonable' and each must, as far as possible, receive her share. If market prices fall, then the price at which the women had been supplied may be retrospectively reduced, or there may be a later adjustment. If the catch is very small, then the women may be compensated by cash advances. If, at the beginning of the season, supplies of coconut shells as fish-smoking fuel are inadequate, then they may receive advances for firewood. The women must be given notice of demand for repayment of sums outstanding. If outside women are distressed by the sight of the wives receiving credit or paying lower prices than themselves, then the wives may be privately repaid the sums they have so ostentatiously disbursed on the beach!

It is an almost universal feature of fisheries throughout the world that fishermen should be remunerated, wholly or partly, with a share of the value of the catch. A FAO publication[1] refers to this unusual wage system, for which 'there are few parallels in other branches of activity', and speculates as to whether its existence is related to the 'universal riskiness of fishing' (p.v). The Ewe seine fishermen resemble fishermen elsewhere in the world, in the practice of deducting certain items of expenditure from the gross proceeds of the catch before dividing the rest 'in fixed proportions between the vessel and gear and the crew' (p. 26).

With the Anlo companies, as already noted, there is a remarkable degree of variation[2] over the number of 'parts' into which the net proceeds are divided[3] and this presumably reflects the desire of net-owners to modify traditional systems in the interests of efficiency. This variation partly reflects variation in the categorization of those entitled to a specific share (or part). Some

---

[1] *The Economics of Fisheries*, ed. Turvey and Wiseman (4).
[2] In other sectors of indigenous economic life, systems of remuneration which involve fixed shares such as thirds, are usually rather rigid.
[3] In 3 of the 18 cases for which information was obtained the net was operated on *mavee* (see p. 40) and in 2 cases there were no regular companies—the net-owner relying on casual labour to operate the net spasmodically; in the remaining 13 cases, the initial division of the proceeds was into 9 parts in two cases; into 8 parts in one case; into 7 parts in four cases; into 5 parts in two cases; into 4 parts in two cases; and into 2 parts in two cases—possibly similar to *mavee* in that the net-owner met current costs of net-repair.

companies allocate a part to all their executive members, one such group including the bos'n, the secretary, the second-bos'n, a headman (whose duty it was to check up on damage to net or canoe), a second headman, a 'controller of the company' (regarded as the company's spokesman) and a foreman or general supervisor. Many companies earmark a part for certain of those with special responsibilities, notably the bos'n. (If the bos'n and other very important people do not get a specific part, they will simply receive much more than other members from the company's allotment—there is always an allotment for the company as a whole. Or they may receive certain sums before the formal shareout: one net-owner said that the bos'n might receive £10, the second-bos'n £5, the secretary £5, with £2 for the man in charge of the singing during rope-hauling.)

As for the net-owner's share of the proceeds, it was found that despite the variation in the number of parts this varied only between 20% and 41% of the net total—*mavee* and other cases of division in half being omitted as non-comparable. In as many as 7 of the 9 remaining cases, the net-owner's share lay between one-third (33%) and three-sevenths (41%).[1] It is obviously impossible to indicate the size of the net-owner's profit—i.e. the surplus accruing to his *agbadoho* after he had renewed parts of his gear ready for the start of a new 'season'.[2]

## THE BOS'N

'If a man has an active son he must be a bos'n', said a prominent net-owner in Keta, the owner of some five nylon nets—and also of a vast quantity of used cotton netting which he was desirous of selling. At that moment his son, the bos'n in charge of his two nets at Abidjan, walked into the room, explaining that he had returned to Keta, by air through Lome, to attend a funeral. He spoke of the difficulties imposed by the Ghana exchange control in bringing his money back from Abidjan; of the fact that the Ghana customs were apt to charge import duty on fishing materials which have been in use elsewhere; of the superiority of the nylon netting available in Abidjan; of their efforts to teach others to operate their nets. He said that he had been preparing to travel to a beach near Monrovia, when he had heard that the fishing season was bad there, so that he had changed his plans. Clearly, though he is subject to his father's overriding financial control, the functions of such a bos'n resemble those of a net-owner.

---

[1] In the United States one of the most common agreements between crew and ship-owner is the '40–60 lay', i.e. '40 % of the net proceeds, after deducting the joint expenses, to the vessel and 60% to the crew' (FAO (4), p. 26).

[2] See de Surgy (22), pp. 102–9.

This net-owner's other nets were at Anloga, Keta and Gran Popo—he did not say whether any of his other six fishermen sons were in charge there. In 15 cases in which particulars relating to the bos'n were given, 10 were relatives of the net-owner and 5 were non-relatives; of the 10 relatives, 4 were sons, 3 were brothers' sons and 3 were younger brothers. Certainly the employment of relatives is common, though there are also some professional bos'ns, well recognized as such, some of whom are aspirant net-owners.

### THE WIVES AND THE SYSTEM OF SELLING FISH ON THE BEACH

Very occasionally companies travel to distant beaches, such as Abidjan, without their womenfolk, so that all the fish has to be sold to local women. But it has always been usual for women to accompany their menfolk and now, with improved transport, it has become almost a rule, the total number of women being roughly equal to the number of men, for some wives bring assistants and some men have several wives or bring a relative. Statistics collected by M. de Surgy (21), relating to 389 Anlo seine fishermen in the Ivory Coast showed them to be accompanied by 336 women—as well as by 449 children, some of whom would be old enough to assist the fishermen.

Women are of the company yet not of it.[1] Some net-owners frankly admitted that they had no idea of the number of women attached to their company. The women select their own headwoman (or women)—this is their affair. On the one hand each woman (unlike any man) is a separate economic entity (a fish trader): on the other hand she has strong attachments to her particular man, to the other women and to the company as a whole.

In principle, as already noted, the company itself is responsible for providing all the food required by its members during the season. De Surgy found that it was usual, in the Ivory Coast, for this obligation to be met by giving each man a fixed monthly sum with which to buy food as well as fish, which is always distributed free. This sum always seemed to be inadequate for the man's maintenance and required supplementation by his wife—the company might also supplement it by buying cassava in the ground. Systems are more variable on the Anlo coast, where there may be more distribution of foodstuffs as such, but no doubt the women usually make some contribution.

So valuable are the services provided by the women that the net-owner makes no attempt to limit their number. With the exception of widows of former company members, the only rule is that each woman should be

---

[1] De Surgy (22), p. 63, even noted instances when women received an end-of-season share of the proceeds equal to half that of the ordinary fisherman.

attached to a particular man who effectively guarantees her debts to the company. Neither the headwoman, nor anyone else, has any control over the size or composition of the group—'anyone who wants to come can come'.

Traditionally, as already noted, the wives were supplied with much of their fish on credit and were not required to hand over the sums owing until the end of the season—nowadays there is a growing tendency for wives to be asked to pay up at intervals, which may even be weekly, throughout the season. Two informants described their old accounting systems before secretaries were employed. In one case each woman had had, in effect, her own currency store: at the end of the day, after the distribution of the fish on the beach, she would be shown the number of stones, shells, or grains of corn which represented the value of the fish she had received that day, these being kept by the net-owner in a special pot with a cover; it was up to each woman to keep a corresponding hoard of currency at home so that she should know the size of her debt. In the other case, pebbles of various sizes represented coins of different denominations, for which there were separate compartments in a box. Even though the women were allowed to keep the money until the end of the season, there might be periodic, even weekly, accounting checks. Such systems may now be obsolete, but even today a woman sending fish to Accra, by means of a lorry driver, may wrap up stones in a piece of cloth to signify the price.

This study concludes with a brief description of the system of selling fish on the beach as it was observed several times near Keta.

When the bag is first hauled ashore, the multitude of small fish it so often contains form a living pulsating mass which must quieten before being scooped out with large enamel or aluminium bowls, which are then carried further up shore. Larger fish are sorted out to be disposed of separately. Jellyfish, seaweed and other rubbish is discarded. All those entitled to a free distribution come forward for their share. The fish that is for sale is neatly piled; if it has been decided to sell both to the wives and to outsiders, then two piles, not one, may be made.

A ring of women (say ten to twenty of them) forms round the pile of fish. Within the ring there are usually two members of the company, perhaps the bos'n and the secretary, one concerned to distribute the fish and the other to receive the money, which he puts into an enamel stewpan. Bargaining is conducted with formality. The men evidently have entire responsibility to act for the company without reference to anyone else; the women's side of the bargaining is conducted mainly through one of their number, who is well aware of the general feeling of her sisters from their asides and interventions. The bos'n starts by naming his price for a so-called basket; the women answer by naming their price; bargaining proceeds in familiar fashion, earnestly, anxiously and sometimes passionately. (When passions are expected to run especially high a rope fence may be erected round the women.) In one case, the starting prices were £1 and 12s. respectively, the finally agreed price being 16s.; in another, these first prices were 24s. and 16s., the final price being 18s. To avoid the trouble of distributing small quantities of fish to large numbers of women, a minimum quantity of baskets for supply may be fixed.

The prices having been agreed, the distribution begins. A small battered basket is rather carelessly filled with fish and placed in the basin provided by the purchaser. The bos'n then scoops fish with both his hands on top of this full basket—some bos'ns scooped four times, some five, some six, the original basketful plus the fixed number of scoops constituting the unit of supply. (This very old-fashioned system of quantification is said to be demanded by the women—it certainly imposes much strain on the exhausted, wet bos'n whose hands are pricked by the scaly fish; to an observer it would seem much fairer were some standard basin, or other container, to be used and certainly the women themselves are apt to protest—sometimes successfully—that the handscoops are too small.) No records are kept; although it is often said that the secretary makes notes on the beach, he seems rather to memorize what he witnesses, presumably recording the figures at home at his leisure. Generally, pound notes only are accepted and customers have to return for their change. In one case individuals were obliged to buy either 3, 6 or 7 baskets at a cost of £2, £4 or £5; the price was 13s. a basket and change of 1s., 2s. or 9s. was paid out later in the evening.

The Ewe word for the women who are outsiders, not wives, is derived from the word 'beg'—'those who keep begging and begging and asking'. Certainly in the month of May, when these observations were made, the price often seemed to be fixed at a level such that many women returned home with empty headpans despite their begging.

CHAPTER 4

# CATTLE OWNERSHIP ON THE ACCRA PLAINS

## WITH SPECIAL REFERENCE TO THE FULANI HERDSMEN

CONTENTS

INTRODUCTION

This report on cattle-ownership, with special reference to Fulani herdsmen, in the Ashaiman/Dodowa area of the Accra Plains,[1] is based on fieldwork, undertaken on thirty mornings only, between December 1963 and June 1964, and on a full count of cattle made during that time by Mr J. E. A. Afotey,[2]

[1] The area runs from Ashale Botwe in the west to Mobole in the east and from Dodowa in the north to Ashaiman in the south. See map 3.

[2] I wish to thank Mr Afotey for his painstaking work as an enumerator and for his assistance to myself: my own fieldwork would have been impossible had I not been accompanied by a member of the Animal Health Division, an organization which was held in high esteem by all concerned with cattle-rearing.

3   The Ashaiman/Dodowa area of the Accra Plains

then a Veterinary Guard of the Animal Health Division. I had hoped that my original report, dated October 1964, would have been of practical value to a body set up by the University of Ghana known as The Accra Plains Livestock Development Project, which had been sponsoring preliminary research on a variety of subjects in the Ashaiman/Dodowa area. As the main report on the Project has yet to appear in full, I here summarize some of my material, though it was originally intended to be only a small part of a much wider whole.[1]

The area of open grassland known as the Accra Plains stretches from

---

[1] As was Dr E. N. W. Oppong's work on bovine brucellosis which he later extended to other areas—see (11). (I am grateful to Dr Oppong for comments and criticism.)

Accra on the west to the river Volta on the east, a distance of about 60 miles. It is bounded on the south by the sea, and on the north-west by the edge of the closed forest which coincides with the south-eastern Akwapim scarp. As these plains, as well as the Ho-Keta plains to the east of the Volta river, are relatively tsetse-free, cattle may be reared there, and the total cattle population of the two areas in the early 1960s was of the order of 100,000.[1] Although cattle have been reared on the southern fringe of the Accra Plains for centuries,[2] the local inhabitants in the western section, which is the subject of this study, appear to have no tradition of pastoralism and systems of cattle management have been radically transformed by the advent of Fulani herdsmen some 30 to 40 years ago.[3]

According to R. Rose Innes, who cites H. P. White,[4] 'the combined deterrents of uncertain water supply and low-yielding or intractable soils have served to protect large portions of the coastal savannah from over-grazing and denudation', but an improvement in water supplies (and the construction of small cheap earth-dams *had* proved practicable) might 'mark the beginning of serious depletion of valuable grassland'. In 1958 the stock-ing rate for native herds of mixed Fulani/West African Shorthorn ancestry[5] was conservatively reckoned to be about one adult beast per 9 acres of rough grazing. The cattle population counted for the purposes of this survey is not here related to the survey area, which was clearly much smaller than the grazing area—the latter, indeed, varying according to season and circumstance.

The survey area lies about 15 to 25 miles east of Accra, and there is evidence (see Appendix 1) that cattle traders have roamed over it for centuries. The local inhabitants, who may be regarded as based on the Ga-Adangme coastal towns running from Ningo in the east to Teshi and Labadi on the west (with Kpone, Tema and Nungua lying between), have presumably been commercially motivated cattle-raisers for centuries, which makes it the more surprising that some recent observers have regarded the herds as kept merely for social display.[6] Nor did I find that there was any truth in the widespread myth that the cattle on the Accra Plains were regarded by traders as a mere 'reservoir to be tapped when the supply from the north

[1] Or about a fifth of the total cattle population of Ghana. See Appendix II.
[2] See Appendix I.
[3] Although these herdsmen claim, quite convincingly, that they 'were the first to arrive', it may of course be that 'northerners', if not Fulani, were herding cattle on the plains in earlier centuries—though there is no evidence that the plains supported a large cattle population until recently.
[4] 'Grasslands, Pastures and Fodder Production' by R. Rose Innes, included in Wills (14), p. 418. See also H. P. White (13).
[5] These animals are described by R. A. Hutchinson in Wills (14), p. 425, as 'small, unhumped, of good conformation, generally black and white in colour but sometimes red and white'.
[6] Thus H. P. White ((13), p. 77)—'the herds are kept more for social display than for profit, so the emphasis is always on numbers rather than on quality'. See, however, para. 105 of the citation on p. 89 below.

is cut off for any reason'.[1] As in parts of Northern Ghana, the owners permit many immature bullocks to be culled from their herds, and Mr Afotey told me that during the whole course of his work he had never recollected having seen any bullock in the kraals which would have been ready for selling some time earlier.

SECTION I

## A Glossary

The 13,089 cattle which, according to our census, were kraaled in the survey area, were managed by 111 kraal-owners. The cattle were owned by the kraal-owners themselves, by their close relatives (as defined in the Glossary below) and by those whom we denoted as 'private owners'. Nearly all the cattle were placed by the kraal-owners in the charge of herdsmen, most of whom were Fulani: these herdsmen, in turn, employed assistants, here referred to as sub-Fulani or sub-herdsmen. For ease of reference these various key terms, and a few others, are further defined in the following Glossary.

*family herd.* When a Ga-Adangme cattle-owner dies, his animals may either all be divided between his sons and daughters, who then regard them as their individual property, or part (or even the whole) of the herd may be considered to be the joint property of the siblings—a family herd. Family herds usually bear the name of the father-founder and, although in principle they may be replenished by purchase following sale, it seems that they always run down over time. By no means all of our Ga-Adangme informants were familiar with the concept of the family herd.

*Fulani.* A Fulani (unless otherwise qualified) is a head-herdsman who looks after animals for at least one kraal-owner, this following the usage of kraal-owners themselves who speak of 'my Fulani', 'his Fulani', etc. even when the herdsman is a Northerner who is not of Fulani origin. (The Fulani are the main pastoralists of West Africa, and are scattered over a vast area from Senegal and Mauretania in the west to Cameroon and beyond in the east.)

*herd.* Strictly regarded, a herd is a group of animals which usually graze together. But for reasons of practical convenience the term is sometimes used to denote all the animals in the kraals of one kraal-owner, even though these may be divided into a number of herds (proper) for grazing.

*herdsman.* A herdsman is a man (nearly always of Fulani origin) who is in charge of livestock he does not own. If he is remunerated directly by the cattle-owners (mainly, in practice, in milk), then he is a head-herdsman. If he works under

[1] See R. A. Hutchinson, 'Stock and Methods of Animal Husbandry' in Wills (14), p. 431. This is what I had constantly been told by the butchers themselves in Accra, some of whom owned cattle on the plains! But statistics relating to monthly slaughter of locally reared and imported animals respectively, in the Coastal Veterinary Section, suggested there was no truth in the belief.

another Fulani, by whom he is remunerated, he is a sub-herdsman—usually referred to by the Fulani themselves as a 'boy'. A herdsman does not necessarily take the animals out grazing himself—his sub-herdsman may be responsible for all this work.

*kraal.* Strictly defined as an enclosure for penning cattle, we here use the word in a number of separate senses. In the survey area cattle are invariably kraaled when not out grazing, the ramshackle fence (which encloses an unpaved rectangle covered in dung) nearly always being made of an assortment of upright pieces of wood which have been collected, or cut, on the plains. A kraal-owner often owns several kraals, usually alongside each other, but for reasons of practical convenience these are here usually referred to in the singular. It has been impossible, on occasions, to avoid slipping into the usage 'kraal' in place of 'herd', or to avoid referring to 'the size of the kraal', meaning 'the size of the herd'. (Kraals and kraal-owners are, in fact, our main statistical units, apart from head of cattle.)

*kraal-owner.* The kraal-owner is the person who owns the kraal, regarded as a physical structure. He may have built it himself or he may have inherited it— one hears of the sale of herds, but not of kraals. Alternatively, he may be regarded as the man to whom the Fulani herdsman considers himself responsible. Occasionally there is genuine doubt as to who the kraal-owner is—for instance when a resident son is in charge for his elderly father. There are also cases of one man being in charge of a group of kraals individually owned by himself and a number of close relatives and he is here regarded (or at least as far as possible) as the sole kraal-owner, provided he employs only one head Fulani. Few kraal-owners own all the livestock in their kraal and some own a small proportion or fewer than another individual. There is also the question of family herds. The kraal-owner usually owns the service bull—usually a much more valuable item of property than the fence. Most kraal-owners live in the general neighbourhood of their kraals, but there are some, especially among the Ga-Adangme (see Table 1), who live outside the grazing area, usually in one of the coastal towns.

*private-owner.* A private-owner is here defined as an owner of cattle who is neither a kraal-owner nor a very close relative (such as a wife, brother or son) of the kraal-owner who manages his animals: the unsatisfactory lack of precision in this definition reflects the vagueness of our informants. Basically, perhaps, a private-owner should be regarded as one who pays the kraal-owner for his services rather than joining with him in meeting the expenses—he cannot be regarded by any stretch of the imagination as a joint kraal-owner. But in practice there is so much variation regarding payments and sharing of expenses that this definition, also, is far from satisfactory.

*sub-Fulani.* See sub-herdsman.

*sub-herdsman.* See herdsman. The distinction between head-herdsman and sub-herdsman is very important, the former invariably being employed by the kraal-owner, the latter by the head-herdsman. In the survey area the employment of sub-herdsmen by head-herdsmen is almost universal. Sub-herdsmen are alternatively referred to as sub-Fulani.

SECTION II

The Kraal-owners

Of the 111 kraal-owners with kraals within, or nearly within,[1] the survey area (see Table 4. 1), over three-quarters (76) were 'indigenes'—natives of one of the Ga-Adangme coastal towns south of the Accra Plains or of a settlement in the plains adhering to one of those towns.[2] These 'indigenes', hereafter referred to as the 'Ga etc.' kraal-owners, had more than a half of all the cattle in the survey area in their kraals. Then there were 16 kraal-owners, whom we here regard as the 'immigrants', they being Ada, Agave, Battor or Sokpoe men who had migrated to the survey area from their homelands near the Volta river further east, often bringing their herds with them: unlike the Ga etc. kraal-owners, many of whom have established themselves in remote districts (approachable only by heavy lorry or Land Rover), the 'immigrants'' kraals and homesteads are mainly near the main road from Accra to Ada. Seven of the kraal-owners were Fulani and other northerners, none of whom had previously been herdsmen on the Accra Plains—one of these men had over a thousand cattle in his kraals which were situated in three different districts of the survey area.[3] Five kraal-owners were Fulani who had originally established their own kraals while working as herdsmen for others. All the foregoing kraal-owners were men and there were, in addition, 5 women kraal-owners.

Nearly a half (44%) of all the cattle (5,817 head) were in 16 large herds (see Glossary) containing 200 head or more. At the other end of the scale there were 31 kraal-owners (nearly a third of the total) with fewer than 50 cattle in their herds, of whom 8 had fewer than 30 cattle. Over a half (64) o the kraals contained between 50 and 200 animals.

Some of the kraal-owners themselves own rather few animals—their kraals are small, or their Fulani are mainly engaged in looking after cattle for private-owners. Many kraal-owners, together with their close relatives, own between 50 and 150 head; a few of them own 150 head or more. (It was quite impossible[4] to distinguish those owned by the kraal-owner

---

[1] Some of the Mobole kraals were outside the survey area—lying north of the road.

[2] Each settlement on the plain is attached to one or other of the coastal towns to the south, the various stools' jurisdictional interests over the land having been originally established by those who had first settled there: cattle graze freely, without any reference to 'boundaries' which are anyway somewhat notional. See *Gold Coast Gazette*, 24 March 1955 (7).

[3] In Table 1 this kraal-owner is recorded as the equivalent of three kraal-owners, his kraals being in three different localities.

[4] It was usually Mr Afotey, Veterinary Guard, who sought to obtain the information, though I sometimes made an attempt myself. Detailed questions on ownership were considered as intolerably intrusive, but comical rather than rude. (The concept of the family herd was, of course, part of the trouble.)

TABLE 4. I.   NUMBERS OF CATTLE IN HERDS OF DIFFERENT SIZES
(Numbers of kraal-owners are shown in parentheses)

| Kraal-owners | Under 50 | 50–99 | 100–199 | 100 and over | Total |
|---|---|---|---|---|---|
| A   Ga, Kpone, Ningo and Prampram men: | | | | | |
| (i)   Resident in grazing area | 605(18) | 1,485(20) | 2,128(16) | 2,266(7) | 6,484(61) |
| (ii)   Resident outside grazing area | 198(6) | 408(6) | 239(2) | 206(1) | 1,051(15) |
| | 803(24) | 1,893(26) | 2,367(18) | 2,472(8) | 7,535(76) |
| B   Ada, Agave and Sokpoe men | 111(4) | 445(6) | 549(4) | 1,048(2) | 2,153(16) |
| C   Fulani and other northerners (non-herdsmen) | 33(1) | 146(2) | 486(4) | 983(2) | 1,648(9) |
| D   Fulani herdsmen | — | 67(1) | 112(1) | 1,092(3) | 1,271(5) |
| E   Women | 77(2) | 80(1) | 103(1) | 222(1) | 482(5) |
| Total | 1,024(31) | 2,631(36) | 3,617(28) | 5,817(16) | 13,089(111) |

personally.) As for the numbers owned by the private-owners, very rough estimates[1] relating only to the Ga etc. kraal-owners suggested that the private-owners might own roughly a quarter of all the cattle in those herds.

Only a small proportion of the Ga etc. population is interested in kraal-ownership and, despite the popularity of private-ownership, there are not many newcomers to this business. Most kraal-owners are clearly emulating their fathers, for whom, in some cases, they had herded cattle when they were boys.

The prospects of cattle-raising on the Accra Plains, as elsewhere, have been revolutionized by advances in veterinary science. Most of us tend to take this too much for granted. But not the kraal-owners themselves, many of whom emphasized that their fathers had lost all their cattle as a result of 'outbreaks' (of disease). The Chief of Katamanso, for instance, said that his father's herd had 'vanished' five times, the last time in 1918—always it had been built up again.[2] As many herd-owners commented sadly that their father's herd was 'finished' before he died—sometimes, no doubt, because of sales as well as 'outbreaks'—the extent to which present-day herds are descended from the herds of the forefathers should not be exaggerated.

[1] See p. 67.    [2] See Appendix I.

The Ga etc. kraal-owners

Table 1 shows that 7,535 of the cattle in the survey area were in the kraals owned by 76 male kraal-owners who counted themselves natives of one of the Ga coastal towns (Labadi, Teshi, Nungua or Tema), or of Kpone, Prampram or Ningo—there were also 4 women kraal-owners of Ga etc. origin.[1] Sixty-one of the men were resident in the grazing area, nearly all on land 'owned by' their town, many of them near to their kraals; most of the remaining 15 men lived in one or other of the coastal towns.

A high proportion—perhaps about three-quarters—of the 61 Ga etc. kraal-owners who reside in the grazing area were sons (often also grandsons) of men who had been cattle-owners in the same area.

Although nowadays some herds are partly, or even completely, sold off following a father's death, many remain more intact than might be supposed considering that all children (daughters as well as sons) are entitled to a share, which they may then dispose of as they wish. Many, though by no means all, Ga-Adangme brothers consider it proper, or find it convenient, to retain some of their father's animals in a 'family herd'—and it may be that the ideal of maintaining the size of this herd is occasionally observed. But for most practical purposes the family herd may be regarded as owned by the eldest son, who (provided he is interested in cattle rearing) succeeds his father as kraal-owner; he has a duty to 'help' his relatives with the proceeds and to maintain the family house.

The junior sons may choose to leave their animals in their brother's kraal: alternatively they may be so nervous of trusting their brother that they choose to transfer the cattle elsewhere—thus becoming private-owners.

It is most unusual for the son of a kraal-owner to set up a kraal in the life-time of his father—unless, as sometimes happens, he moves to another district. Few kraal-owners are young men. But sons, especially elder sons, are quite often in effective charge of the kraals owned by elderly fathers, to the extent that the Fulani in charge may even be unaware that it is the father, not the son, who is the real kraal-owner. Continuity of management is thus assured.

All the kraal-owners who reside in the grazing area are food-farmers, and many of them have no opinion on whether cattle rearing or farming is their foremost occupation. However, as hardly anyone in the survey area employs any farm labourers, farming is seldom large-scale.[2] One tended, therefore,

---

[1] Out of the total of 80 kraal-owners, 21 were of Prampram origin, 17 of Nungua origin and another 17 of Kpone origin, the remaining 25 being from the other towns (including 2 from Accra).

[2] Nor is it notably productive; little cattle manure is used—it is usually sold very cheaply to vegetable producers and others who are prepared to remove it by lorry.

to be a little sceptical when one was informed that finance derived from food-farming had been invested in the establishment of a herd. Particularly when the herd had expanded rapidly recently, one wondered whether cattle trading was not the main source of finance.[1]

Most of the Ga etc. kraal-owners who are resident outside the grazing area are farmers and/or fishermen living in their home town, or are people such as teachers, clerks or drivers who inherited cattle from their fathers. Twelve of them, out of a total of 15, had fewer than 100 cattle in their kraals—as compared with 38 out of 61 of those resident in the grazing area.

*Brief notes on individual kraal-owners*[2]

  (i) This Tema kraal-owner, who had 207 cattle in his kraals, lives in a huge 'village' at Ashaiman, where his father had removed as a farmer, later acquiring cattle. There is a family herd, bearing the deceased father's name. The kraal-owner has 6 brothers, nearly all of them resident in Ashaiman, each of whom owns cattle in the kraal. There were also about 10 private-owners who owned about 76 head.

 (ii) Two Nungua brothers, resident outside the grazing area, had respectively 171 and 63 cattle in their kraals at a place where their father had lived. The elder brother has a family herd, estimated at 93 head, in his kraal, this bearing his father's name; he said that the receipts from sales from this herd were deposited with his father's sister (unless money was urgently required for maintenance of the family house or by an individual) and that the costs of medicine for the family herd were met from this fund. He, the elder brother, works in Nungua as a mason: his Fulani, who has worked with him most happily for some 20 years, consults him there as necessary, but he and his brother visit the kraals every Sunday. The younger brother is a goldsmith at Nsawam: he founded his own herd, having formerly boarded animals with a non-relative: he now shares his brother's Fulani. Included in the 63 head in his kraal are cattle owned by a brother, that brother's wife and that brother's daughter (a barkeeper).

(iii) Born in 1906, in the house wher ehe now lives, this well-known Nungua man, who has 493 cattle in 7 kraals, is a third-generation resident in the grazing area. When his father died in 1944 his herd was roughly halved, one half for the children of each of his 2 wives. Each of the 4 children of one of these wives set up a kraal for himself, and 3 of the kraal-owners' 7 kraals are, in fact, owned by 3 brothers. Many private-owners (not all from Nungua) board animals with him—'they are fishermen, clerks, farmers and one minister'.

(iv) This kraal-owner (who has 100 cattle in his kraal), lives in a Prampram village in the plains which had been founded by his grandfather; his grandfather owned cattle but no kraal, his father was a kraal-owner. When his

---

[1] Unfortunately, I had no time to study the cattle trade systematically.

[2] A few details which might lead to the identification of individuals have had to be omitted.

father died the cattle were divided between his sons, a portion being retained as a family herd which bears the father's name and which is used for maintaining his father's houses on the plain and at Prampram.

(v) First we thought the kraal-owner was a certain middle-aged man who was later discovered to be the kraal-owner's eldest son, who managed the kraal (in which there are 132 cattle) on his old father's behalf, he being a fisherman. Among the relatives owning cattle are the father's wife, a fishmonger—'she owns plenty of cattle'—and other Nungua women. The son lives in Nungua and visits the kraal 2 or 3 times weekly.

(vi) A woman kraal-owner, with 113 animals in her kraal; she lives in Accra, where her Fulani visits her. She owns a 'chop-bar', and established the herd herself from the proceeds: she is a real businesswoman. Her husband had a separate herd: he died and his cattle were divided among his children. Originally a private-owner, she bought heifers one by one until, many years later, she became a kraal-owner. When she decides to sell an animal, she approaches a butcher and they go to the kraal together. She claimed that 3 private-owners owned 22 cattle in her kraal.

(vii) A woman kraal-owner, a native of Kpone, who had once been a cocoa carrier at Aburi. Later she was a pig-trader and then a cattle-trader with the assistance of a Fulani, on whose death she turned to cattle-rearing. There are 222 animals in her kraals, about 50 of which are owned by her daughter; if it is true, as she insisted, that only 6 relatives have 17 animals in her herds and that she has given up caring for animals for private-owners, it may be that she herself owns over 100 cattle. (When the Veterinary Guard was visiting her she bought three bottles of terramycin at £2. 6s. 9d. a bottle.)

*The Ada, Agave, Sokpoe and Battor kraal-owners.*[1] These 16 kraal-owners nearly all arrived in the survey area (themselves or their fathers) within the last 30 years or so. Many (though not all) of them brought cattle from their homeland; some originally worked as farmers, only later deciding to remove part, or the whole, of their herd. Asked why they preferred to raise cattle in the survey area rather than in the homeland, all of them said the grazing was 'better', and some spoke of better water supplies. No one mentioned the proximity of Accra as a market for livestock and milk, although this had conceivably prompted some of them to migrate.

Five of the 10 Ada kraal-owners are settled at Ashaiman, a rapidly growing centre north of Tema, on the main road—only 163 of the 1,248 cattle counted at Ashaiman were in non-Ada-owned kraals. Two of the Ada-owned kraals contained over 500 animals. The sample is so small, and the circumstances of the Ada kraal-owners are so variable, that only brief notes on individuals are given here.

[1] Ada is about 50 miles east of the survey area on the delta of the Volta river; Agave and Sokpoe are on the lower reaches of the river, and Battor is some 30 miles upstream.

(i)   The father of the present chief kraal-owner removed to Ashaiman from Ada nearly 30 years ago, bringing cattle with him: his wife's brother also removed at the same time and since he died his son has effectively become a joint kraal-owner, though an absentee as he lives in Akim as a cocoa-farmer. Of the 154 cattle in the kraal about 120 were said to be owned by 35 private-owners (but some of these are brothers of the chief kraal-owner).

(ii)  There are 523 cattle in the kraals of this Ada kraal-owner, whose father, like (i)'s father, removed to Ashaiman nearly 30 years ago, for the reason (so it was stated) that the grazing was better at Ashaiman. It was reliably estimated that about two-thirds of all the cattle are owned by the kraal-owner himself, though some of these are in a family herd bearing the father's name; the remaining 174 cattle are owned by about 36 persons, including 5 wives and 3 mothers-in-law of the kraal-owner, who lives in rather a grand style. The private-owners include 3 Ada men (who own 38, 35 and 18 cattle) and several Tema men.

(iii) There are 525 cattle in the 8 kraals owned by this prosperous Ada cattle-rearer, pig-rearer, food-farmer and cattle trader who claimed that he had removed to the survey area some 30 years before, bringing over 100 cattle with him, most of which had died soon afterwards—presumably of rinderpest in 1931. He refused to give information regarding private-owners, except that there were 'many'. He employs 2 Ada farm labourers and lives in fine style over a mile away from his kraals which are managed for him by his senior son.

(iv)  He removed to Ashaiman from Ada in about 1947 bringing with him the family herd which had belonged to his late father, who had been a salt trader on the river Volta—this herd still bears the father's name. He claimed that of the 179 animals in his kraals, 144 were owned by himself and close relatives, and that 31 of the remaining 35 cattle were owned by a Fulani, the son of the late herdsman for these kraals.

(v)   This Ashaiman kraal (of 86 cattle) was established in 1961 by an Ada man who was already living in the district as a farmer and rearer of small livestock—he is the son of a brother of (iv). He claimed that he owns only 20 cattle himself, the remainder being owned by 3 locally resident Ada men.

The 6 Agave, Sokpoe and Battor kraal-owners were all small cattle-owners compared with the Ada—75, 64, 24 and 16 cattle were in the Agave kraals, 49 in the Sokpoe kraal and 22 in the Battor kraal.

(vi)  This kraal-owner claimed that his late father had removed to the survey area in 1960 owing to over-grazing at Agave. The father's herd, which was not divided on his death, bears his name. He has many brothers each of whom owns a few cattle, and about 6 private-owners own about 20 animals. He and his family make and sell large numbers of grass mattresses.

(vii) This Agave man, whose late father first migrated here, is endeavouring to build a herd: as there are only 24 cattle in his kraal, he is unable to employ a

63

Fulani, his herd being in the charge of an Ada man who lodges with him—this man will receive one animal after working for 5 years, he is not paid in milk. Like (vi) he produces large quantities of grass mattresses.

(viii) There are 49 cattle in the kraal of this Ewe man who removed from Sokpoe in about 1952, bringing cattle with him. His elder sister, a fishmonger in Accra, owns many of the cattle, and she shares the expenses of running the kraal. His herdsman is a young boy from Sokpoe, a non-relative; he reckons he will need to have at least 60 cattle in his kraal before he can attract a Fulani.

(ix) Formerly a sawyer at Battor, he first started rearing cattle in the survey area in 1961, boarding the animals in a herd in the charge of a Fulani who has also assumed charge of his own small kraal (22 cattle) which he has just established. If his present experiment is successful he proposes to transfer his family herd here from Battor.

*The northern kraal-owners who are not herdsmen.* As many as 1,120 of the 1,648 cattle with these 7 kraal-owners are in the kraals of one very well-known man, whose kraals are in three different parts of the survey area—he also owns kraals elsewhere on the Accra Plains and boards some animals with others.

Born in Agomeda, on the northern edge of the Accra Plains, he was the son of a Mossi farmer and sheep-trader. Long prominent in the trade in imported cattle from Lagos, he has many other economic activities, being one of the best-known 'landlords' in Accra where he lives in a house with accommodation for many stranger-traders. He owns a 7-ton lorry and employs 6 farm labourers on a food-farm he has bought west of Accra. He is undoubtedly the owner of many hundreds of cattle—we could make no precise estimate.

The other 6 kraal-owners in this class include: a retired Fulani Mallam living elsewhere in the Accra Plains whose brother (who owns about 8 cattle) is in charge of his herd of 33 head; a Hausa (or Fulani) Alhaji resident in Accra—his herdsman would not reveal his name, address, or occupation; and a Fulani cattle trader, who claimed that 81 of the 96 cattle in his kraal were owned by himself and his wives and children, all being self-acquired.

SECTION III

The 'private-owners'

The term 'private-owner'[1] is defined in the Glossary: briefly he is a cattle-owner who boards his animals, at a fee, in a kraal which is not owned by a close relative. A private-owner, unlike a close relative, pays for services

[1] This curious term is in general use on the Accra Plains and has not been coined.

rendered, and does not share the expenses associated with running the kraal.

Who are the private-owners? The following classification is an attempt to analyse a very heterogeneous group of people, ranging from owners of a single heifer to those with herds of 50 head or more.

(*i*) *Aspirant kraal-owners.* This group includes men (and women) who are in course of building a full herd but who, for one reason or another, do not establish their own kraals: their herds may, as yet, be small[1]; they may own no service bull; they may be so satisfied with their relationship with the kraal-owner, and/or his Fulani, that they see no reason to remove; they may have moved their animals from a family kraal on the death of their father, both as an assertion of independence and because 'you cannot trust a close relative'. Either by preference or by chance, an aspirant kraal-owner may board his animals in a number of different kraals: if the former, this may be an insurance against disease or theft.

(*ii*) *The inheritors of small numbers of cattle.* Many of those who inherit cattle on their father's death prefer to remove them from their elder brother's kraal in order to have more personal control.

(*iii*) *Cattle-traders and others who buy animals and leave them in the seller's kraal.*

(*iv*) *The 'investors' in cattle.* An important source of cattle-raising finance is the small investor, who regards this kind of enterprise as affording him a satisfactory return. Such people do not, usually, aspire to own a herd, as such, but yet enjoy the satisfaction of seeing their capital multiplying spontaneously. Our information[2] shows that most of the private-owners were 'small' men or women—clerks, watchmen, farmers, fishermen, labourers, market-traders and so forth: there are not many higher civil servants, or business or professional people who invest in more than a few cattle. Considering the low rate of reproduction of cattle (resulting from the slow maturation of heifers, and the long interval between the birth of calves), capital invested in a young heifer yields an extremely low rate of interest relative to prevailing high rates in other kinds of enterprise.[3] But even so, and

[1] Of course a man who owns but a few animals may find it worthwhile to open a kraal if he can rely on sufficient private-owners depositing animals in it.

[2] Although we did not think it proper to ask kraal-owners to identify their private-owners by name (as many of them would have refused to do in any case), we sought information on their occupations, ethnic group, etc.

[3] The practice of giving the third calf to the kraal-owner reduces this rate—see below.

despite high cattle mortality-rates, many small men are attracted by the security offered by investment in cattle.

The most important 'rich' investors are probably cattle-traders, butchers, and women traders and fishmongers. The cattle-owning affairs of the cattle-traders and butchers are necessarily shrouded in mystery: their trades are highly competitive, and competition and cunning are equated. No doubt they often buy animals for fattening, leaving them with the kraal-owner. And cattle-traders are often aspirant kraal-owners.

As for the 'rich' women private-owners, their finance may be much more important than it appears, if it is true, as sometimes said, that they often prefer to buy animals in the names of men.

I now turn to the systems by which private-owners remunerate kraal-owners for services rendered. First, it is usual for the private-owner to 'dash' the kraal-owner a sum such as 12s. (or more) on the birth of a calf, as well (perhaps) as a bottle of drink. Secondly, it is common, though not universal, practice for private-owners to give the kraal-owner the third calf born to any cow in his care;[1] thirdly the kraal-owner gets a commission, which is commonly 10%, on animals sold for slaughter[2]—if an animal is removed to another kraal, not sold, a charge is made. All these systems of remuneration are long-term—if a one-year-old heifer is placed in a kraal it may be three years before the first calf is born, at least five years until a bullock is sold to a butcher, and more than nine years before the birth of the 'third calf'. Nor does the Fulani benefit from the milk until after the birth of the first calf. Surely there must also be some short-term advantage to the kraal-owner? I think that the private-owner must be accustomed to giving presents (dashes) to the Fulani when he visits the kraal, and that this is to the advantage of his 'master'.

It was admittedly common practice for the private-owner to 'dash' the Fulani when an animal is sold—though not, I think, when a calf is born. This raises the question of whether some private-owners are accustomed to deal directly with the Fulani to an extent which would justify their being considered his 'master'. I do not know whether the Fulani usually informs the kraal-owner or the private-owner when one of the latter's animals is ill—

[1] Many kraal-owners, of different ethnic origin, spontaneously referred to this practice: one might almost distinguish private-owners from relatives according to whether the third calf was collected, were it not that some kraal-owners say that they never collect calves. Opinion differed on whether the 6th, 9th, etc. calf was also collected—I think there is no standard practice. One kraal-owner said that he collected the 2nd, 4th etc. calves; another said that kraal-owners in his district were discussing such a possible change, owing to rising costs.

[2] This commission of 10% was, at that time, a very common feature of West African economic life, being collected in lorry parks, by traders and others. I do not think that in this connexion the practice was as standardized as many kraal-owners would have wished. One kraal-owner boasted that he negotiated the sale on behalf of his private-owner—perhaps he felt that this justified his commission.

probably practice varies. Even from the beginning the kraal-owner is unlikely to recognize the private-owners' various animals, which puts the Fulani in a very powerful position.[1] I think that most kraal-owners learn not to be jealous of their Fulani, knowing that any outside relationship which keeps him happy is to their advantage.

Another way in which private-owners are apt to 'thank' their kraal-owner in the shorter term is by the provision of medicine such as Gammatox, for the use of the whole herd. Some kraal-owners certainly charge up the private-owner with the cost of treating a particular sick animal.

A very great deal of time was spent[2] in an endeavour to count or, failing this, to estimate the numbers of animals owned by private-owners in the numerous kraals. Although the figures we collected are both incomplete and unreliable,[3] our efforts were not completely fruitless: some kraal-owners were very helpful and we gathered much useful miscellaneous information from those who were not.

We came to the conclusion that a high proportion of all kraal-owners, and nearly all those with large kraals, board some animals for private-owners. Only about a third of all kraal-owners claimed that few animals, or none, were boarded with them—and nearly all these people were 'small' kraal-owners with fewer than 100 cattle in their kraals. Roughly a quarter of all kraal-owners boarded 'many animals'—either absolutely, or as a ratio of all the animals in their kraals.

We found a very strong tendency (see Table 4.3) for private-owners to board animals with fellow-townsmen, whom they knew and trusted. But this does not, of course, apply to the non-southern-Ghanaian kraal-owners who board animals for 'anybody', as do some well-known southerners.

For 59 of the Ga etc. kraal-owners rough estimates were made of the total number of cattle owned by private-owners: this total was roughly one-quarter[4] of the total number of cattle (6,187) in the kraals.

Table 4.2 relates to the estimated number of cattle owned by 59 Ga etc. kraal-owners and their close relatives.

[1] Even if the Fulani is the only one who 'recognizes the animals', it does not follow that he thinks in ownership terms, so that private-owners, *A*, *B*, *C*, etc., are automatically associated in the Fulani's mind with animals *x*, *y*, *z*, etc. When contemplating his herd the Fulani, like the social anthropologist, usually thinks in kinship terms: his natural approach is in terms of (cattle) descent groups.

[2] Most of it by Mr J. E. A. Afotey.

[3] Ideally, the cattle owned by the private-owners should have been counted separately as part of the general enumeration, as the animals were released through the gate of the kraal; but many kraal-owners were unwilling to allow their Fulani to do this, so that it was necessary to proceed by enquiring about each private-owner and the numbers he owned.

[4] As there was a tendency to omit calves and as some kraal-owners were ashamed of admitting to boarding animals, the proportion is likely to be an under-estimate.

TABLE 4.2. *Ga, Kpone, Ningo and Prampram kraal-owners*
Estimated numbers of cattle owned by kraal-owners and their close relatives[a]

| Size of kraal (no. of cattle) | No. of kraal-owners | No. owned by kraal-owners | |
|---|---|---|---|
| | | Total | Average |
| Under 50 | 24 | 668 | 28 |
| 50 to 99 | 21 | 1,404 | 67 |
| 100 to 199 | 10 | 1,202 | 120 |
| 200 and over | 4 | 1,384 | 346 |
| Total | 59 | 4,658 | 79 |

[a] See Glossary. Most 'close relatives' are sons, daughters, wives, brothers or sisters.

TABLE 4.3 *Estimated numbers of cattle owned by private-owners*

| 'Ethnic group' of kraal-owner | Total number of cattle in kraal | Estimated number of cattle owned by private-owners (number of such owners in parentheses) | Notes |
|---|---|---|---|
| Ningo | 107 | 56(18) | Fifteen of the private-owners were said to be from Ningo, many of them being women. |
| Tema | 206 | 118(35) | All the private-owners were said to be from Tema. |
| Teshi | 118 | 50(10) | Two of the private-owners (one a woman) were said to own about 10 cattle each. Only 3 of the owners were from Teshi; the others included the Fulani in charge of the kraal, a Hausa butcher and a Hausa woman. |
| Ada | 523 | 174(36) | Nearly all the private-owners were said to be from Ada. |
| Tema | 158 | 58(10) | All the private-owners were said to be from Tema. |
| Nungua | 101 | 61(16) | The private-owners were from Teshi, Tema and Nungua and included a woman. |
| Nungua | 185 | 85(21) | All the private-owners were said to be from Nungua. |
| Total | 1,398 | 602(146) | |

The estimated average number of cattle owned by the 59 kraal-owners (and their relations) is 79. Over half the cattle are owned by the 14 owners of 100 cattle or more. If the average value of an animal is arbitrarily put at £30 (the range being about £20 to £45), then the stock of each of the 24 smallest owners is worth less than £1,500, the corresponding sum for each of the 14 largest owners being over £3,000.

That many of the private-owners own very few animals is indicated by Table 3 which relates to 7 kraal-owners for whom reasonably reliable figures of private-ownership were obtained: the average number of cattle owned by a private-owner in any one kraal[1] was only 4.

SECTION IV

The Fulani herdsmen

The ordinary kraal-owner is only too well aware that the Fulani understands cattle-management, while he does not. Nowadays in most, if not all, districts within the Accra Plains nearly all kraal-owners employ a Fulani herdsman. It seemed that only 2 of the 111 kraals in the survey area were not in the charge of a Fulani.[2]

But, so far at least as the present generation of kraal-owners in the survey area is concerned, the employment of Fulani herdsmen is an innovation associated with the increasingly commercial attitude towards cattle-raising and the growth of herds. None of the 24 (head-) herdsmen we interviewed had arrived in Ghana much before 1930[3] and only about 6 of them had come before 1939. Only one of those interviewed was himself the son of an Accra Plains herdsman.

Before progressive kraal-owners began to employ Fulani between the wars, the Ga owners had always relied on their sons and other 'small boys'. Their cattle-raising methods must have been extremely unscientific. In 1935 A. Fulton deplored the general condition of the herds, but said that conditions were 'a little better' when Fulani were employed 'as they really tend the cattle, taking them to the best available pasturage, seeing that they are watered and doing some castration and deticking.[4]

Although, following general usage, I refer to all herdsmen as 'Fulani', a few of them belong to other northern ethnic groups: in the sample of 24 there

[1] Some private-owners may have owned cattle in more than one kraal.
[2] One of these (a herd of 24 head) was owned by an Ada man who had an Ada herdsman; the other, a herd of 49, was in the charge of a Sokpoe 'small boy', a relative of the Sokpoe kraal-owner.
[3] Nowhere else in the Accra Plains did I find any evidence of the arrival of Fulani herdsmen before the 1920s—but I did not study the Ada area.
[4] *Report on the Development of the Livestock Industry of the Eastern Province* (6).

was at least one Zabrama (from Niger) and one Gruma (from Upper Volta). The Fulani (proper) hail from many different areas.[1] I think that many of the herdsmen had originally set out from their homeland as long-distance cattle-drovers and that few had had the intention of working as cattle herdsmen or on the Accra Plains. Many of them first worked in Ghana as labourers, market carriers, drovers, cattle traders, etc. before settling down as herdsmen.

Such is the general contentment of the Fulani with their way of life on the Accra Plains that few of them plan to return home permanently; many of them claimed that they had never even returned home on a visit. Many had married after arriving in the south—usually Fulani women, who were commonly the daughters of other herdsmen.[2] Contact with the homeland was mainly made through relatives and friends who visited the south[3]—and also through sons who, though born in the south, are sometimes sent 'home' to work with relatives.

Although a few Fulani herdsmen have so far evolved into full kraal-owners[4] and although some of those who own a few beasts are aspirant kraal-owners, most of the herdsmen seem to be content with the symbiotic relationship with their kraal-owners which gives them many of the responsibilities usually associated with full ownership. So I do not think that the fact of permanent settlement on the Accra Plains is necessarily associated with long-term ambitions of acquisitiveness.

Nearly all head-herdsmen—see the Glossary—are assisted by sub-herdsmen, whom they denote as 'boys'. Out of 23 herdsmen, only one had no sub-herdsman,[5] and the total number of sub-herdsmen employed by 22 herdsmen was reported to be 47.[6] All those with more than 150 animals in their charge employed at least 2 sub-herdsmen. Two of the Fulani kraal-owners, each with some 500 animals in his kraals, claimed that they employed 6 and 8 sub-herdsmen.

The sub-Fulani are real *employees* of their herdsmen who pay them cash

[1] Of the 22 who spoke of themselves as Fulani, 9 were from Niger (Niamey, Tera, Tillabery and Say); 9 were from Upper Volta (2 from Dori to the far north, 3 from Diapaga near northern Dahomey, various others vaguely mentioned 'Ougadougou'); 1 was from Mali (Mopti), 1 was from Dahomey, 1 was from Bawku—where his forebears had settled long ago—and 2 were of unascertained origin.

[2] As many of the herdsmen were not especially young when they first migrated, and as few had subsequently sent for their wives, it was clear that many migrants had 'run away' from former marriages: for this and other reasons, many of them were too embarrassed to refer to their long absence from home.

[3] It seems that nowadays many Fulani visit the south in search of work, and that they often return home disappointed: certainly the 'supply' of Fulani is more than adequate.

[4] See p. 75.

[5] And his was the smallest herd in the sample—only 50 head.

[6] The 23 herdsmen for whom this information was obtained were in charge of 4,034 cattle, or an average of 86 per sub-herdsman.

wages varying between about £2 to £3 monthly[1] and who provide them with full board and lodging—no doubt also meeting other incidental expenses. Although many head-herdsmen had formerly been 'boys', I do not think that all 'boys' are aspirant herdsmen, though some of them do succeed to their master's position on his death. 'Boys' are not necessarily at all young. They are seldom, if ever, relatives of their masters.

Most of the sub-Fulani, other than those mainly concerned with the marketing of milk, are largely occupied in herding the cattle: many head-herdsmen delegate all the daytime[2] work of taking the animals out grazing to their 'boys' and their sons, being apt themselves to herd at night.

In order that he may be able to afford to employ a 'boy', a herdsman must be in charge of a large number of cattle. Our survey showed that hardly any Fulani are in charge of less than 50 animals and that most have 100 or more in their care. Of 60 Fulani for whom reliable information was obtained,[3] only 1 was in charge of less than 50 cattle, only 17 of between 50 and 100; 21 Fulani were in charge of between 100 and 199 beasts, 22 Fulani of 200 or more. As it is unusual, though not unknown, for a large kraal-owner to increase the number of Fulani as his herd grows, some Fulani are in charge of as many as 500 animals.

But many kraal-owners, as we have seen,[4] have fewer than 50 cattle in their kraals. So it is common practice for Fulani to increase the number of animals in their charge by working for more than one kraal-owner, as did 16 of the 60 Fulani in our sample. These 16 Fulani had charge of 45 kraals, 16 of which contained fewer than 50 animals, 33 fewer than 100 animals. In some cases the Fulani was in charge of several kraals simply because these had formerly constituted a single kraal;[5] more often, it appeared that the Fulani had deliberately secured more work for himself by taking on additional kraals, his original master raising no objection. Those who share Fulani are not usually brothers—even though brothers often have neighbouring kraals.

As it is quite unusual in rural West Africa for a man to have more than one 'master'[6]—the sharing of *abusa* cocoa-labourers, for instance, is most uncommon[7]—I was surprised at the extent to which the services of the

---

[1] Those concerned with marketing milk may be wholly, or partially, remunerated on a commission basis.
[2] This meant that most head-herdsmen were to be found near the kraals—they always stopped what they were doing to answer importunate questions with a good grace; unfortunately, it was not found possible to interview any 'boys'.
[3] They were in charge of 87 of the 111 kraals in the survey area.     [4] See Table 4.1.
[5] One or two private owners may, for instance, have hived off.
[6] This requires qualification, especially as men commonly have several distinct occupations. It is not common for a man to work in the same regular occupation, in the same capacity, with more than one master simultaneously.
[7] This is the more remarkable, considering the small quantity of cocoa plucked by many of these labourers. (An *abusa* labourer is rewarded with a third share of the cocoa he plucks.)

Fulani were 'shared'. Probably this reflects the great independence of many Fulani, especially those whose 'masters' seldom visit them, as well as their insistence on having a 'boy' to assist them. Unless a Fulani herdsman is also a cattle-owner or cattle-trader he is usually entirely dependent on his earnings as a herdsman—unlike the *abusa* labourer who is usually also a food farmer.

The Fulani herdsmen, unlike their 'boys', are never rewarded by regular cash payments. Their entitlement to milk the cows (the milking is done by men) and to sell such milk as they do not consume themselves is (rightly) regarded by all concerned, as their main remuneration—though, as will be seen, the total of 'dashes' received from the kraal-owner and buyer, when animals are sold, may be considerable when kraals are large. It is *not* standard practice, as it is in some areas of West Africa,[1] for kraal-owners to give calves, or other animals, to their Fulani, although some of them do this.

Before examining the common, and commonsensical, viewpoint, that the system of rewarding the Fulani with milk deprives the calves of nourishment, thus being very deleterious to the growth of herds, so that it 'ought to be discouraged', I now list the other forms of 'income' of the herdsmen in 1964.[2]

(i) The kraal-owner usually gives money to his Fulani when an animal is sold. Sums mentioned varied between 10s. and £3; evidently the amount partly depended on the price realized, but also on the relationship between the parties and the affluence of the kraal-owner; £1 or £2 seemed to be typical sums.

(ii) It was standard practice for the butcher to give the Fulani 4s. when he was buying an animal—some, but not all informants, said that the sum had recently risen to 5s. after having stood at 4s. for some years.[3]

(iii) The Fulani herdsmen in the survey area did little if any food-farming. Many, but not all, of them said[4] that their 'masters' gave them food when they were in need, especially during the dry season—and this 'security' is certainly an important element in their standard of living. A 'good master' may buy bags of maize and gari for his Fulani, as well as provisioning him from his own farm.

A few Fulani lodge with the kraal-owner, but most are obliged to maintain households of their own in the grazing area. As there are no markets at all

---

[1] Thus when a Fulani pastoralist himself employs a herdsman he might, according to F. W. de St Croix (2), give him a one-year-old male animal for herding up to 30 head for a year, a one-year-old heifer for herding 30 to 50 head, or a three-year-old heifer for herding 100 head. See also Dupire (4).

[2] It may, perhaps, again be emphasized that circumstances were unusual that year owing to the cutting-off of supplies of cattle from Lagos.

[3] From all that informants said it was clear that the Fulani were regarded as entitled, by custom, to a minimum fixed sum, a kind of commission on sale.

[4] From what some of the kraal-owners themselves said, this is probably correct.

in the survey area,[1] many Fulani travel some distance to market to buy their food: it is the men, not the women, who do most of the marketing.

(iv) Practice with regard to the provision of housing by the kraal-owner is very variable, as are housing standards. Some Fulani live in small round huts of traditional style, which they build themselves; some have large compound houses; most live in a few ramshackle rooms, with their families. A 'good master' may provide roofing sheets and other modern building materials. Some Fulani themselves invest considerable sums in materials. One kraal-owner insisted that he had built his Fulani a house so that he might sack him at any time and install another. (In these parched plains, where rainwater should be stored in tanks, fed by gutters, domestic water supplies are almost always lacking.)

According to G. Montsma,[2] whose views presumably find general acceptance among experts on animal husbandry, the milk-yield of lactating cows in Ghana is somewhere between 50 and 100 gallons a year. As during the first six months of its life (when its weight should increase fivefold) a calf needs about 100 gallons of milk (far more than its mother produces), Montsma concluded that the sale of milk should be 'discouraged'.

How much income might a typical well-established Fulani in the survey area derive from the sale of his milk? Such a Fulani might, as we have seen, be reasonably expected to have at least 100 to 200 animals in his charge, about half of them being cows.[3] If it is assumed that the average cow lactates for half of its fecund lifetime,[4] then a Fulani with 200 cattle (say, 100 cows) might expect an annual milk production of no more than about $75 \times 50$ i.e. 3,750 gallons[5]—or about 10 gallons a day. If a half of the milk were consumed by the calves (a near-starvation diet of about 40 gallons a year) and a quarter by the Fulani and his household,[6] an average of only about $2\frac{1}{2}$ gallons would be sold daily. Our information suggested that the net receipts from selling a one-pint bottle of milk in Accra might have been about 6*d*.,[7] or about 10*s*. a

---

[1] Except at Ashaiman and Dodowa on the periphery.

[2] 'Sale of Milk and Rearing of Calves in Ghana' (9).

[3] This was according to our census and was a proportion which varied little as between localities: but see the reservation about the accuracy of the figures in Appendix III, p. 78, n. 8.

[4] According to W. Ferguson (5) 'an intercalving interval of 14 to 15 months' is not unusual in Northern Nigeria and presumably rearing conditions are worse, not better, on the Accra Plains owing to lack of water.

[5] Based on an average of 75 gallons a year from the 50 lactating cows in the herd.

[6] A Fulani with 200 cattle in his charge would be likely to have a large household.

[7] Most of the milk was sold to Lebanese traders in Accra, for cheese-making and other purposes, though at some seasons considerable quantities went to Hausa women traders. The price received in Accra was about 9*d*. to 1*s*. a beer-bottle—slightly more than a pint—and varied seasonally. After allowing for transport costs and the 'boy's' commission, net receipts of 6*d*. per pint seemed a reasonable estimate. (Some of the milk was sold in kerosene tins, not bottles.) The milk is of poor quality and very dirty and as—see (11)—the incidence of bovine brucellosis is very high, human consumers are at serious risk.

day for $2\frac{1}{2}$ gallons.[1] So a well-established Fulani with 200 cattle in his herd might derive about £180 annually from his milk sales. Let us now immediately deduct the cash wages of the 2 sub-Fulani which the head Fulani might be expected to employ—at £2. 10s. per month each, this would be £60 a year: then, net receipts from milk (after deducting cash wages) would be £120.

Whatever assumptions may be made about commercial take-off of bullocks from the herds, and the size of the 'dash' given to the Fulani when an animal is sold, it is clear that net receipts from milk account for the bulk (say three-quarters or more)[2] of the Fulani's cash income, from which he must buy most of the food consumed by his household (including his 2 sub-Fulani)—he will, of course, also have many other outgoings.

I was often told that when cases of cattle stealing[3] were brought to the attention of the police, their stock comment was that the Fulani ought to be paid in cash, not in milk—the implication being that they would then be better off. But if the above estimates are even roughly correct, we see that a Fulani in charge of a large herd would need to receive a cash wage of the order of £15 a month, if the sale of milk were to be prohibited leaving him no worse off. I do not think it conceivable that, in the interests of the better development of calves (and thus of the herd as a whole), kraal-owners, together with private owners, would be prepared to disburse such sums—and to disburse them regularly. In the 'traditional economy' the practice of paying *cash wages* on this scale is quite unknown.[4]

So the police are wrong in supposing that the practice of paying in milk is not acceptable to the Fulani—rather the contrary. As the milk-money has proved more than adequate for his (humble) needs, he has become accustomed to giving away part of it to his sub-herdsmen, whom he now regards as indispensable. When the first Fulani arrived on the plains in the 1920s and 1930s they were strangers, far from home, who had no thought of building a herd, so that remuneration in terms of animals would have been inappropriate. Owing to the proximity of the large Accra milk-market they were, as it happened, glad to be paid in milk. They would have no objection, in prin-

---

[1] An estimate based on statements of the average number of bottles sold per day which were made by a few well established Fulani yielded similar results.

[2] See p. 72.

[3] In 1964, cattle-thieving was causing such serious concern that some kraal-owners said that they were contemplating removing from the survey area to a safer district. Of course when animals disappear, as they often do, the Fulani is nearly always under suspicion, even though it is generally recognized that a butcher, trader, or driver usually receives the animals—and may have taken the initiative. (On the other hand, many kraal-owners trust their Fulani implicitly and are not let down: the relationship may be deeply satisfactory to both parties.)

[4] In all fields it is usual either to reward the employee with a share of the proceeds, or to employ him casually for a short term (such as a day), or to pay him a piece-rate for a non-continuing job, or to offer him part of his wages in terms of board and lodging.

ciple, to being paid in another manner: it is just that their income would nowadays be much lower.

So, in 1964, I came to the conclusion that any total prohibition on the sale of milk would have either been disregarded by the Fulani (usually with the connivance of the kraal-owner) or would have resulted in chaos— including more theft. Which was not to say that nothing should have been done about the scandal of calf-starvation.

I then suggested that a start in the right direction might have been: (*a*) for the Animal Health Division to have fixed maximum figures of milk sales for each herd;[1] (*b*) to have imposed a standard fee of 2s. per head of cattle per month payable to the Fulani by all owners, including private-owners;[2] (*c*) to require all kraal-owners whose Fulani remains with them for (say) more than 3 years to give him a heifer;[3] (*d*) to standardize the commission payable, as of right, by the owner to the Fulani on the sale of a mature animal; (*e*) to encourage more kraal-owners to join with others in sharing the services of a head Fulani, thus ensuring that his organizational capacity is exploited to the full and that he is adequately remunerated.[4]

Such a scheme might have failed at the outset, but might have begun to work in the longer run so that, ultimately, liquid milk sales might have been prohibited.

It was impossible to estimate the number of cattle owned by the Fulani herdsmen, as distinct from the Fulani kraal-owner. Many of them insisted that they owned no animals in their kraal and I am sure that this was some-times true. Although most herdsmen are intentionally elusive on this sub-ject, I think one may assume that the answer 'none' when it means 'some', usually means 'very few'. I note, in this connexion, that many head-herds-men had not been working long with their present 'masters'. It has already been noted that the Fulani, unlike their kraal-owners, do not receive calves from the private-owners as a matter of course. So in the survey area (if our sample is at all representative) I do not think (though I cannot be sure) that there are more than (say) 10% of herdsmen who own more than a few animals or who are aspirant (or actual) kraal-owners. As already noted, there are five kraal-owners in the survey area who were formerly herdsmen there and this section concludes with brief notes on four of them:

[1] The kraal-owner being ultimately responsible for enforcement. (It would be hard to exaggerate the practical difficulties involved in such a proposal, especially as yields are so seasonal.)
[2] Some part of the fee, say 6d., might be paid to the kraal-owner by a private-owner.
[3] The gift to be repeated at shorter intervals thereafter.
[4] But such consolidation ought not to go too far: a few head Fulani already have far too many animals in their care—they appear to have too much responsibility.

(i) We counted 485 cattle in the kraals owned by this kraal-owner who is one of the outstanding personalities in cattle circles, on the plains: he would not provide us with any concrete information on the numbers of cattle owned by the numerous private-owners whose cattle were in his charge, but on the basis of information from others we believe him to be the owner of several hundred head.

He speaks as though he has long been a kraal-owner on his own account, boarding cattle for many Hausa, Fulani, Ga and other private-owners, most of them resident in Accra. His cattle-trading and rearing activities are inter-locked: he rears the 'better animals' that he buys and sells the rest. He is a lorry-owner. He employs about 8 'boys' and one of his young sons also herds for him. He lives in a huge 'village', which is constantly being extended, and is surrounded by numerous relatives, assistants and mis-cellaneous strangers.

He first left his homeland (Diapaga, south-eastern Upper Volta) as a drover. After many vicissitudes, including a spell when he was attached to a government office in Accra, he started work in the 1930s as a cattle-trader, using money borrowed from a 'brother', and later became a herdsman.

(ii) We counted as many as 531 cattle in the kraals of this man, who claimed to have arrived in the Gold Coast in about 1937 when he worked as a labourer on cocoa-farms in the Jasikan area of the Volta Region, whence he had walked from his homeland which, as with (i), was Diapaga. He, too, had been a cattle-trader before he was a herdsman. He employs 6 'boys'. He is in charge of the kraals owned by 2 Ga men who live near by; he probably owns several hundred cattle himself.

(iii) We counted 560 cattle in his 5 kraals, 4 of which were owned by others, one by himself. He originally came to Kumasi, from Niger, as a drover. He later worked as a sub-herdsman: doubtless he was a cattle-trader. The Animal Health Division described him as a man harassed by so many responsibilities that he had 'no time' to give medicine to his animals; had he been able to spare more time for us, we might have been less puzzled by the extent of the trust resided in him by so many kraal-owners and others.

(iv) There are 67 animals in the kraal owned by this young man, who owes his position entirely to the fact that he recently married a daughter of (i). He is from Kandy in Dahomey.

APPENDIX I

## Notes on the History of Cattle-Rearing on the Accra Plains

John Barbot,[1] who was on the Guinea Coast in about 1682, noted that cattle were reared and traded on the Accra Plains: 'what cattle they have at the coast is generally bought from Accra, where they are supplied with them from... the eastward of Acra [Accra], and from the country Aquamboe [Akwamu], which are all stocked with cattle, wherewith the natives of those parts drive a great trade at Accra, and all

[1] *A Description of the Coasts of North and South Guinea* (1).

along the Gold Coast... The said cattle, though brought from thence fat and in good case, soon grows poor on the coast [e.g. to the west of Accra]...(p. 215). At Great Ningo, the country was 'flat and low, populous and fertile and particularly stored with cattle, viz. cows, sheep and swine, besides poultry, which are continually bought up there, to be carried along the Gold Coast' (p. 215).

Over a century later, H. Meredith noted that at Prampram and Ningo there were 'large-sized horn-cattle, which are almost in a wild state'.[1]

But perhaps cattle-rearing did not spread far inland in the Accra Plains until the last half of the nineteenth century. In the 1860s the nearest cattle-rearing centre to Berekuso on the Akwapim scarp was said[2] to be at Asarebodsche (i.e. Ashale Botwe within our survey area) where there was 'one of the few cattle farms [hof] of the Ga plain'. 'The cattle are kept solely as slaughter cattle, not for milking'. Nor were the local inhabitants necessarily much given to consuming meat. In the report on the 1891 population census, reference was made[3] to the 'Mohammedans' who brought cattle south from the interior as a result of which the fish-eating populations along the coast were becoming meat-eaters.

At Katamanso, which lies about 8 miles north of Nungua in the heart of the Accra Plains, the present chief said that his grandfather, a Nungua man, was the first to start cattle-rearing there in 1889.[4] No Fulani herdsmen had arrived there until the inter-war period, and he, the chief, had been a herdboy for his father. The chief spoke dramatically about the five occasions, the last in 1918, on which his father's herd had 'vanished' owing to epidemics: probably the first occasion had been the great rinderpest epidemic which swept through much of West Africa in the late eighteen eighties and in the nineties.

APPENDIX II

## The Recent Growth in the Cattle Population of South-eastern Ghana

According to A. W. Cardinall[5] the cattle population of the (then) Eastern Province in 1931 (this province included the coastal areas east of the Volta) was 36,000, of which only 8,000 were in the Accra and Akwapim Districts of which our survey area forms a small part—this causing Cardinall to comment that the true cattle-raising district of the south was Keta-Ada in which 25,000 of the Eastern Province cattle were counted. The Principal Veterinary Officer considered the figures as 'fairly accurate'—though there must surely have been some under-counting.

Presumably the 1931 count was made before the very serious rinderpest epidemic of that year which, as estimated by A. Fulton,[6] reduced the cattle population of the

---

[1] *An account of the Gold Coast of Africa* (1812) (8), p. 202. I am grateful to Mrs Marion Johnson for this and the following references.

[2] See *Evangelische Missions—Magazin*, (1881), p. 184 (Mrs Johnson's translation).

[3] Report on 1891 census, published 1892.

[4] His grandfather had established the church there in the same year. (Katamanso is now a flourishing village; it had a population of 303 in 1960.)

[5] *The Gold Coast 1931* (3), p. 102.

[6] *Report on the Development of the Livestock Industry of the Eastern Province* (6). It is there stated that rinderpest overshadowed all other diseases until 1934.

Eastern Province by some 10,000, for according to the same source the cattle population of that province in 1935 was only about 26,000. In about 1937 this population had risen to nearly 40,000.[1]

By 1937 the cattle population of the Accra Plains and of the Ho–Keta area had more than doubled, being about 95,000 head,[2] of which about 40,000 were on the Accra Plains.[3]

In 1962–3 about 30,000 cattle were enumerated in the Accra and Dodowa Districts within which our survey area lies.

In 1964–5 the total cattle count for the Accra Plains together with the relatively poorly stocked Winneba-Cape Coast Plains (west of Accra) was 41,615, much the same as in 1937.

APPENDIX III

## The Take-Off from the Herds

In Northern Ghana it was found[4] that the bulls + bullocks:cows ratio, based on the official livestock census, provided a convenient rough measure of the degree of commercialization in any locality. But this was not so in the survey area where, for 1962–3, very great variations in this ratio were found, for different localities within it, variations which could not conceivably reflect differing rates of take-off from the herds.[5] Nor was the ratio for the whole survey area,[6] which was 18 bulls + bullocks per 100 cows, necessarily comparable with those computed for Northern Ghana, given the practice, of private-owners and others, of buying young animals for rearing from outside the survey area,[7] a high proportion of which may be heifers. As has been constantly emphasized, the group of cattle which happens to be in any kraal is seldom a 'balanced herd', a considerable proportion usually consisting of animals boarded out by private-owners.

Using the figures of cattle population which were collected for the purposes of this survey,[8] great variations as between districts were again found in the ratio of

[1] See J. L. Stewart, 'The Cattle of the Gold Coast' (12).
[2] See 'Stock and Methods of Animal Husbandry' by R. A. Hutchinson in Wills, J. B. (14).
[3] Presumably including the Ada District, which in 1931 had been included with Keta, thus making detailed comparison impossible.
[4] See pp. 90 *et seq.*
[5] In Northern Ghana, the ratios were found to be rather constant within districts which were much larger than the survey area.
[6] The ratio relates to localities within the Accra and Dodowa Districts which had a total cattle population of 11,545 in 1962–3, and which very roughly corresponded with the survey area where 13,089 cattle were counted for the purposes of our survey.
[7] It may also be that some young animals that are reared in the survey area are removed elsewhere before they are mature.
[8] Mr Afotey was instructed, for purposes other than my own research, to classify the cattle in each kraal into as many as 9 classes, the 6 official census classes (see p. 90, n. 1) being increased by (a) dividing 'bullocks' into those over and under 1½ years and (b) dividing 'calves' (under 1 year) into 'yearling bulls', 'yearling heifers' and calves (under 6 months). (I am very dubious of the practicability of enumerating animals in 9 classes by quick visual inspection as they pass out of the kraal—though I think our total figures are very accurate, except for the possible omission of some calves which were separately penned.)

male to female animals (other than calves) in the kraals. Again, it did not seem possible to make any estimates of relative rates of take-off from the herds on the basis of such figures.

I was constantly informed, by butchers, traders and others, that the ordinary bullock, which receives no supplementary feeding, is not fat enough for slaughter until it is 3 to 4 years old,[1] but the two sets of census statistics strongly suggest that many bullocks must be sold when they are 2 years old. In nearly all localities our census figures show that the total number of male animals over one year is less than, or equal to, the estimated number of male animals over one year—the latter figure being the sum of half the total number of calves and the number of 'yearling bulls' (6 months to one year). I cannot believe the inaccuracies in our figures are so great as to explain away the apparently small ratio of male animals over one year and I therefore conclude that many bullocks are prematurely sold for slaughter.[2]

APPENDIX IV

## A Note on Cattle Marketing

There are no cattle markets on the Accra Plains or, so far as I know, in the southern cattle-raising areas east of the Volta, and such is the enormous size of most West African specialist cattle markets[3] that it seems very dubious whether the cattle population is sufficient to maintain one. Cattle raisers would appear to benefit from the keen competition that prevails—though they are unnecessarily plagued by the plethora of traders and butchers, many of them know how to resist their blandishments. I found no evidence whatsoever of any buying rings and much evidence, as in northern Ghana, of the rejection of incipient 'regular-customer relationships': it is generally realized that 'strangers give the best price'.

The absence of a market does, however, result in much waste of time on the part of those (both traders and rearers) seeking to buy young stock for rearing.

[1] H. P. White (13), p. 77, put the figure as high as 7 years.
[2] If it is common for female calves under 6 months in age to be bought outside the survey area, this would mean that the number of male animals under 6 months is overestimated.
[3] Although cattle are commonly sold at markets in Northern Nigeria, all save the largest of the livestock markets are mere sections of general markets—of which there is none on the Accra Plains.

# CHAPTER 5

# THE NORTHERN GHANAIAN CATTLE TRADE

CONTENTS

INTRODUCTION

In June 1965 I went to Northern Ghana[1] for two weeks intending to study cattle ownership there. I set out in the spirit of fully accepting the traditional belief that the 'trouble' with Northern Ghanaian cattle-owners was their reluctance to sell their animals unless driven to this by the direst economic extremity. While I had felt critical of Southern Ghanaian condescension to the North on economic matters generally, and had presumed that Northerners had rational socio-economic motives for not selling their stock, yet like other general writers on this subject I had swallowed (hook, line and sinker) the assumption that they did not sell. I knew from experience that livestock owners on the Accra Plains are commercially motivated—that they rear cattle for the purpose of selling them to butchers and traders, not for the honour and glory of building a large herd: but I had supposed that things were wholly different in the North.

In the event, I was astonished by the necessity of writing a report on my findings which was mainly concerned with emphasizing the *irrelevance of social factors*—the irrelevance in relation to economic factors *in this instance*. It seemed that (except possibly, though not necessarily, in the North-east where, as I shall constantly emphasize, things are certainly somewhat 'different'), the degree of take-off from the herds was largely determined, not by social factors affecting the attitude of cattle rearers towards the matter of selling, but by the efficiency, in economic terms, of the cattle traders. The statistics suggest that in the North-west, for instance, where the population is ethnically heterogeneous,[2] there was *everywhere* a very high take-off of

---

[1] The area long designated the 'Northern Territories' had by then been divided into two regions —Northern and Upper: the term 'Northern Ghana', or 'the North', is employed to denote both these regions.

[2] So that, for instance, some peoples use cattle for bride-wealth, others do not. (See pp. 139–40.)

cattle from the herds, to the extent that the real problem was the premature sale of immature stock—as the District organization of the Animal Health Division had been aware for some years. Of course, I am not asserting that social factors (such as types of inheritance system, bride-wealth and so forth) are irrelevant in other connexions: some ethnic groups may excel as cattle raisers while others do not, and the strength of the desire to expand the size of the herd may be largely 'sociologically determined'. All I am insisting on is that among all Northern Ghanaian peoples (with the *possible* exception of those in the North-east) there was evidently a great and universal readiness to sell male animals from their herds to traders or butchers.

The traders, for their part, were found to be almost unbelievably responsive to economic conditions. Cattle are not, like cocoa, a seasonal crop which grows on trees. This being so, I think that the fantastic seasonality of the curve of monthly exports of cattle from Western Dagomba and Wa (only 49 cattle were exported from the latter Section in February 1965, against 1,903 in July 1964) indicates a degree of sensitivity to demand which may be seldom exhibited in developed economies. During the dry season the cattle exist and are there for sale—at that time they are bought for slaughter as meat for local consumption, the demand for which continues at a more or less constant rate: *but they are not bought for export until they are fatter and until the demand in the South has risen.*

Although the North-east (as well as the adjoining Gambaga District) is in many respects 'different' from the rest of the North,[1] it does not follow that the cattle-owners there were less willing than were those elsewhere to sell cattle commercially: it might simply be that they were provided with fewer opportunities of selling their animals satisfactorily. Certainly the statistical material on the North-east is rather interesting and provides tempting opportunities for speculation—unfortunately, I had no time to visit that area in this connexion.

The following statistical analysis is mainly based on official material which I 'collected' in the North and in Kumasi, in a period of just over a fortnight. I collected it only in the sense that it would have been available nowhere else[2]—though a little of it could have been extracted from files in Accra had one previously appreciated the possibilities which, owing to unfamiliarity with Northern circumstances, one had not.

I must warmly thank members of the Animal Health Division for their

---

[1] See pp. 101 *et seq.*

[2] In under-developed countries there are often surprisingly good opportunities of 'collecting' official statistics (or similar material, such as maps of cocoa-farms) from district or area offices; such statistics are the more reliable the greater their usefulness to local officials; they are usually wholly unreliable if, like market price statistics, they have no local practical utility.

great help and kindness, for giving me access to their statistics and for enabling me to meet and talk with so many cattle owners. I must emphasize that the statistics collected by the Division were of remarkable reliability and scope, for this is not generally known. Their annual censuses of the cattle population were conducted by their staff of Veterinary Guards, who knew and were trusted by the cattle owners; who checked the figures for individual owners by inter-censal comparisons; and who took care not to associate their work with that of the taxation authorities, but rather with the annual immunization against contagious pleuro-pneumonia—a fatal endemic disease. Then, the Division collected and collated reliable figures of 'local exports' of cattle from the North to Ashanti and Brong-Ahafo, these being based on the compulsory cattle-movement certificates which were necessary for disease control.

The conventional notion of Northern economic stagnation seems peculiarly inappropriate in relation to cattle. Few Northern Ghanaians are pastoralists proper.[1] Commercial cattle rearing is a new development made possible by disease control. It was not until 1930 that the first mass immunization campaign against rinderpest occurred, with the result that the recorded cattle population of the North rose from 69,000 in 1921 to 170,000 in 1941 and to around 400,000 in 1964. Certainly, in the Wa and the Western Dagomba Districts my enquiries showed that high proportions of the herds, both large and small, were effectively created by their present owners, many of whom invested small sums in the purchase of a few heifers and then waited for them to multiply.

Why, then, were we all labouring under the traditional belief regarding cattle owners' reluctance to sell? Who were the culprits responsible for disseminating false information? A thorough reading of the sources suggests that no such culprits exist. Why then, did all of us in Ghana who were interested in this subject and who lacked practical experience, especially those whose thinking was sociologically oriented, take this myth for granted?[2]

I suggest the following main explanations for our stereotyped approach:

(i) We had misread the anthropological sources, which were few in number, not very explicit on the matter of sales of cattle and not very recent.[3]

---

[1] See the Introduction by R. F. Gray to *The Family Estate in Africa*, ed. R. F. Gray and P. H. Gulliver (1964) (8), in which a useful distinction is made, for East Africa, between predominantly pastoral societies and predominantly agricultural societies in which livestock are important.

[2] Any of us might have been responsible for the following statement relating to the North by a normally impeccable authority: '*Even in those few locations where cattle are kept with a view to their sale for meat*, little or no effort has been made to increase their market value by improving husbandry' (my italics). From a chapter by J. B. Wills in *Agriculture and Land Use in Ghana* (1962) (21), p. 219.

[3] Local exports from the North may, indeed, have been very low in the 1930s: in Pong Tamale I could find no figures earlier than 1954—in the following decade exports nearly tripled.

(ii) Although it was recognized that nearly all Northern Ghanaians were agriculturalists, not pastoralists, the implications of this were not pursued. The fact that in most areas cattle are little milked, except (casually) by herdboys, was wrongly thought to signify a non-commercial attitude on the part of owners.

(iii) The fact that Southern Ghana is largely dependent on imported livestock for her meat supplies had blinded us to the significant and growing contribution of the North.

(iv) Nothing whatsoever was known about the organization of the internal cattle trade.

(v) Official figures of take-off from the herds were based on the total cattle population and not on the male population, exclusive of calves.

(vi) The fact that cattle-owners never slaughter their own stock for consumption had been thought to imply that beef is not a popular food.

(vii) Cattle-owners themselves are prone to insist that they have a strong aversion to selling their beasts.

(viii) The brevity of Annual Reports of the Animal Health Division in the post-war years up to 1954–5, and the total lack of such reports for at least five years thereafter.

(i) The *primary* anthropological sources do not state that cattle are not sold commercially except in times of famine[1]—indeed the opposite is implied in a typical quotation such as the following: 'it is not uncommon for men to instigate a daughter to leave her lawful husband for another man, or to take a daughter away from her husband and give her to another man as a means of raising a cow to repay a pressing debt, or to buy grain for the household ...' (*The Web of Kinship among the Tallensi*, by M. Fortes, 1949 (3), p. 86). Although social anthropologists have been concerned to emphasize the various uses to which livestock are put, in 'acquiring wives, performing sacrifices, celebrating funerals and, to a much lesser extent, competing for certain politico-ritual offices' (Fortes, *ibid*. 1949, p. 82)—yet no conflict between these uses and commercial sale has been implied. In stating that wealth, in the form of cattle, is 'really equivalent to provision for delayed consumption', Professor Fortes was indeed insisting that cattle are not an end in themselves, but realizable assets.[2]

Dr J. R. Goody was mainly concerned to emphasize that among the

---

[1] The only exception I have found is the following, though even this is ambiguous: 'Cattle...are kept principally for slaughter during second burials...*they are not bred for sale* [my italics]. Much of the cash from sales is, without any doubt, buried.' From 'On the Growth of some Konkomba Markets', by D. Tait, 1953 (19), p. 45.

[2] Fascinatingly enough, Professor Fortes worked in the district falling within Tongo in the North-east which, as Table 5.2 shows, is probably far less commercialized than any other in Northern Ghana.

LoWiili of the North-west cattle rearing was 'essentially peripheral to farming'. (*The Social Organisation of the LoWiili*, 1956 (6), p. 30.) He explicitly stated (p. 29) that 'sacrifices and funerals constitute the main occasions for the distribution and consumption of meat', as may have been true nearly 20 years ago when he was in the field. Even today, when it is clear that these peoples are enthusiastic cattle-sellers, like everyone else in the North-west, his statement that 'cattle are regarded as an investment of the gains made by farming rather than as a means of increasing wealth or of maintaining life' might still apply. Certainly, the primary economic activity of most Northern Ghanaians is farming—and this irrespective of whether they happen also to be cattle-owners.

However the use of the word 'primarily' in the following quotation from a *secondary* anthropological source is somewhat misleading: 'Cattle are reared primarily for use in sacrifices and, among many but not all tribes, for marriage-payments, but not for routine food supplies or commercial exchange . . .' (*Tribes of the Northern Territories of the Gold Coast*, by M. Manoukian, 1951 (13), p. 21).

And the following emphatic statement is made in a very recent source which relates to Nangodi in the Frafra District: 'Cattle are reared for sacrificial purposes and for payment of bride-price. They supply manure, which is vital for the maintenance of the agricultural system, but no cattle are ever sold, except in time of dire extremity, such as famine, and none are eaten in the normal course of domestic events.' ('Population pressure in a part of the West African Savannah: A Study of Nangodi, North-east Ghana', by J. M. Hunter, 1967 (11).)

(ii) Few Northern Ghanaian cattle-owners are real pastoralists.[1] Unlike the pastoral Fulani, these owners have been, traditionally, uninterested in arriving at improved methods of husbandry by experimentation. They may not even recognize their animals by sight or know the numbers in their herds. They know little of the treatment of sick animals and nothing of breeding. 'No grown man would consider herding cattle himself unless in very straitened circumstances' (Goody, *ibid*, p. 30). Milk is little consumed.[2] Therefore, the herd is not an end in itself,[3] as it is with the Fulani and other pastoralists, but rather a means to an end. So, no distinction being made

---

[1] There may, however, be some. It is reported, for instance, that 'in Builsa the majority of the cattle are white with black points...These Builsa cattle are homogeneous in size and form... Conformation is good and the milk yield rather better than usual'. Chapter on 'Stock and Methods of Animal Husbandry' by R. A. Hutchinson in *Agriculture and Land Use in Ghana* (21).

[2] Most Ghanaian cattle yield little milk—usually there is barely enough for the calves. See p. 73.

[3] But even the Fulani are much more apt than is commonly supposed to sell surplus male animals from their herds. Mr W. Ferguson in 'Nigerian Livestock Problems' included in *Markets and Marketing in West Africa*, University of Edinburgh (23), argues (p. 83) that 'breeding herds in Northern Nigeria do not contain a large proportion of old animals and surplus males'.

between pastoralists and non-pastoralists, economic generalizations such as the following are apt to be misapplied:[1]

The accumulation of cattle largely to achieve social distinction or to discharge obligations (for example, to pay the bride-price) in parts of Africa poses... questions for the economic statistician. Such an interest in numbers rather than in quality gives rise to a quasi-Malthusian situation in which the cattle population grows to the limit of the carrying capacity of the land unless checked by natural calamities such as disease. (*The Economics of Under-Developed Countries*, by P. T. Bauer and B. S. Yamey, 1957 (1), pp. 28–9.)

The land [in Africa] often cannot provide enough to keep these large herds well fed... to make cattle-keeping into an economic activity which gave a good income, the number of cattle would have to be reduced. People are not willing to do this, because they have the old attitude to cattle keeping. They do not look on cattle as a way of producing an income.[2] (*The Economy of Africa* by Arthur Hazlewood, 1961, p. 82.)

As for the matter of milk, I think that the following citation, which relates to the Voltaic peoples of West Africa generally, is typical of the rather confused thinking on this subject: 'All tribes keep at least a few cattle . . . Generally, however, they use them exclusively for sacrifices, for marriage payments and for their hides and manure, almost never for their milk.' (*Africa: its Peoples and their Culture History*, by G. P. Murdock, 1959 (14), p. 81.)

(iii) Southern Ghanaians are only too well aware of their dependence on cattle imported from other countries and are apt to contrast their situation with that of Southern Nigerians who are usually thought to be largely dependent on supplies from Northern Nigeria. But at least half of Nigeria's population lives in the north, whereas more than three-quarters of Ghana's population is in the south, and there are substantial imports into Nigeria from Niger and Chad.[3] The other consideration under this heading is that figures of 'local exports' of cattle from Northern Ghana were never published: statisticians are conventionally uninterested in the movement of cattle within a country, the figures (where they exist) being a mere artefact of the administrative control over cattle movements by veterinary authorities.

---

[1] Economic writers are all too apt to wax Malthusian over cattle questions. The following quotation from a chapter by the then Chief Veterinary Officer of Ghana is, in this connexion, rather interesting: 'And where the disease challenge is strong it is natural that the owner should prefer a large number of indifferent animals of whom he can expect at least a few to survive, rather than a small high-quality herd...which may disappear entirely in the face of an epizootic'. R. A. Hutchinson in Wills, *op. cit.* (21), p. 429.

[2] Although the author qualifies his general statements, not holding them to be universally applicable to African cattle-keepers, yet the point is that *he makes no other statements*, so that the resultant total impression is quite misleading.

[3] W. Ferguson, *op. cit.* p. 38, estimates that about a third of Nigeria's 'trade cattle' comes from Chad and Niger.

'Exports' of cattle from Northern Ghana southwards nearly tripled in the decade following 1954.

(iv) Nothing whatsoever was recorded about the organization of the internal trade in cattle, though there have been a few who have guessed. Thus, in a brief article 'The Cattle of Ghana', in the Ministry of Agriculture's official publication, *The Ghana Farmer* (February 1959), it was stated that northern cattle traders 'are usually Hausa'—though as will be seen my material shows that hardly any of them are Hausa (see Table 5.13). R. A. Hutchinson's account of cattle marketing in *Agriculture and Land Use in Ghana* (21), p. 432, seems to be wholly misleading and to be based on the situation which obtains where organized cattle markets exist, so that brokers regulate the trade[1]—as they seldom do in Northern Ghana.

(v) The official take-off figures (based on the *total* cattle population) which were formerly published in the annual Ghana *Economic Survey* became misleadingly low, considering that the *male* cattle population had already sunk to such low proportions in many districts.

(vi) All the authorities are agreed that, as elsewhere in the world, slaughter of cattle for 'own consumption', as distinct from sacrificial or ceremonial slaughter, scarely ever occurs. But this has nothing whatsoever to do with a distaste for beef, which is much relished as a food, a large proportion of the cattle traded in the North being destined for local slaughter. Cattle-owners do not slaughter for their own consumption partly because, in tropical conditions, this would be extremely wasteful; however, the meat from cattle which have been ceremonially slaughtered is widely distributed in connexion with the ceremony.

(vii) When making field enquiries in the Dagomba and Wa areas, I found that nearly all cattle-owners are very unwilling to discuss, even in general terms, the matter of the sale of cattle—even if they were not downright misleading (insisting that they 'never sold'), they were always very evasive. I know that several investigators have been seriously misled by informants whose statements they took literally. I think it ought to be better realized that West African farmers usually have a very strong aversion to answering questions relating to monetary transactions and that even when, like cocoa-farmers, they readily do this, they are never able to relate their receipts to any standard time-period. In a Hausa village in 1967 I found a very great reluctance on the part of all those selling grain of their own production to admit to this—and as the farmers were frank and eager on most topics, I think this is connected with a traditional fear of being accused of neglecting their wives and children. (In fact, of course, nearly everyone in the village knew who sold grain.) But in the case of cattle-selling, informants' embarrass-

[1] See p. 113, n. 2. See also para. 103 of the citation on p. 89 below.

ment should not, I think, be equated with any traditional reluctance to part with stock (many of the cattle-owners are, in any case, first-generation rearers), but rather with a deep-seated objection to answering questions relating to such large-scale monetary transactions. There is also the question of the annual cattle tax levied by the local authorities in the North, which are everywhere inclined to raise more and more revenue from this source.[1] There were naturally fears that a stranger's enquiries about sales might be related to the size of the herd for tax purposes. Rearers might also associate such enquiries with the prohibition on the movement of female and young stock.

(viii) The greater informativeness of some *pre-war* reports of the Animal Health Department emphasizes how little the modest Animal Health Division did in post-war years to educate the public on increased commercialization. I am grateful to Dr E. N. W. Oppong for the following citation: 'An increased demand for meat has been responsible for the wholesale castration and sale of young male animals (cattle).'[2]

It is a pleasure to conclude this Introduction with the following citations, the only two of their type which a search through the non-anthropological sources has revealed:

In the north 'cows, sheep and goats have a triple value: first as food; secondly they are used in three important spheres of the life of the people, that is to obtain wives, to acquire rights to farm and as offerings for religious purposes; thirdly they are used increasingly for purposes of trade'. (Pogucki, 1955 (15), p. 53.)

Cattle are exported on the hoof from the Mamprusi area to the South of the Territory and the Gold Coast. Cattle owners from the North readily sell their cattle to traders dealing in the markets of the South. Although the export of immature cattle is prohibited, farmers are tempted to meet the demand of the market by selling bullocks before they are mature. (*Togoland under U.K. Trusteeship: Report for the Year 1952.* HMSO, 1953, Colonial No. 296, p. 79.)

I am most grateful to members of the Animal Health Division at Pong-Tamale, Wa and Kumasi for giving me access to so much official material and for other assistance; I particularly appreciated the help of Mr Mahama

---

[1] In the Wa local council area the rate was as high as £1 per head on beasts immunized against rinderpest—the tax not being levied on young stock. Both the Wa and Nadawli councils appeared to raise nearly a third of their revenue from this source. Rates were generally rising so fast that it seemed that, where premature selling of immature stock was a serious problem, there might be a case for replacing the present tax with an 'export duty'.

[2] From a review of the 1935-6 *Annual Report* of the Gold Coast Animal Health Department in *Veterinary Record*, XLVII, 1434. The review went on to cite the report as follows: 'Thousands of cattle can be inspected in the bad areas without a good mature bull being seen.' See also Appendix.

Imoru who was my interpreter and guide in the Wa area. I must also thank Mr R. Rose Innes, then of the Faculty of Agriculture, University of Ghana, at whose instigation I went to the North. Finally, I am very grateful to Dr E. N. W. Oppong, lecturer in Animal Health, University of Ghana, for reading the typescript and offering valuable comments.

APPENDIX

On p. 88 I noted the greater informativeness of some *pre-war* reports of the Gold Coast Animal Health Department: whilst this book was in the press Dr E. N. W. Oppong sent me an extract from the (rare) 1934–5 Annual Report (signed by J. L. Stewart) from which the following remarkable citation is drawn (pp. 23–4). Thus, at times, does knowledge retrogress.

Indigenous Live-stock Trade

'103. The increase has again been marked as regards bullocks, so much so that speaking generally for the Northern Territories, all available bullocks are being slaughtered in the Protectorate or are being traded and taken to the southern markets. The experience of this department is that it is more difficult to buy bullocks for work or serum-making as all available steers are being bought up by traders. Bullocks are also rising in price... Most of the indigenous cattle trade is in the hands of local people and not the Hausas, who control the import live-stock trade. These local traders travel thoughout the country from place to place and purchase the cattle from the owners at the latter's own villages, gradually collecting animals until a herd is procured. Most of the Northern Territories bullocks avoid Prang, which is the main clearing centre for imported zebu cattle and tend to go [directly] to the smaller [southern] markets such as Kpong, Kintampo, Wenchi. Numerous bullocks are purchased by Wongara [Wangara] traders from north-western Ashanti, who travel then to the Banda country and feed them fat there [sic], eventually selling them during the rains to the Ashanti markets, when prices are high...

'104. It has not been necessary to carry on with the live-stock fairs, which were instituted a few years ago to stimulate trade...

'105. An area where live-stock trade is not well developed is, paradoxically, the Eastern Province plains, the furthest part of which is less than a hundred miles from Accra. In many ways, the coastal plains are much more unknown and un-developed than remote parts of the Northern Territories. The area is poor, cattle and fish being the sole products and hence attracts little or no publicity. A scheme for marketing of bullocks is being prepared by the Veterinary Officer in conjunction with the local owners. With adequate development measures, this area could supply Accra and all its outlying towns with a plentiful supply of home-reared and cheap meat.'

SECTION I

## The ratio of male animals in the herds

On arriving at Pong-Tamale, where the Northern headquarters of the Animal Health Division were situated, I was fortunate enough to be given access to several files containing the results of recent cattle censuses. Cattle were divided into 6 classes (bulls, young bulls, bullocks, cows, heifers and calves),[1] and a mere glance at recent figures was sufficient to establish that in many Northern Veterinary Districts there was a low ratio of male animals in the herds.[2] Such low ratios appeared to be explicable only in terms of high rates of commercial take-off (i.e. of sales to butchers or traders), for it seemed inconceivable that the volume of slaughter for sacrifices, funerals or other ceremonies could account for the 'missing males'. As will be seen, such an assumption was indeed validated when statistics of 'local exports' were analysed.

Assuming, then, that the volume of slaughter for ceremonial purposes was not very variable between different districts, and never accounted in any year for more than a small percentage of the total cattle population; and assuming, also, that cattle rearers were much more inclined to sell male animals than fertile females,[3] the 'degree of commercialization' was conveniently measured by the ratio of the number of bulls + bullocks in the herds to the number of cows.[4] The lower this ratio, the higher the commercial take-off from the herds.

[1] A *bull* was a mature uncastrated male animal over about $3\frac{1}{2}$ years in age. A *young bull* was an immature uncastrated male animal under about $3\frac{1}{2}$ years in age. A *bullock* was any castrated male animal—I was informed that animals as young as 6 months were sometimes castrated. A *cow* was a mature female animal that has given birth. A *heifer* was a female animal that has not given birth. I was not able to discover how barren cows were classified. I believe that a *calf* was usually defined as a young animal under one year—but there seemed to be some doubt about this definition, which was perhaps connected with the difficulty in estimating the age of calves. Mr Hussein, then the Stock Superintendent at Wa, informed me that the first calving normally occurred when the cow was about 4 to $4\frac{1}{2}$ years old. With regard to the control over exports of immature animals he stated that no bullock should be exported unless it had 4 pairs of permanent incisor teeth, which would mean that it was at least 4 years old.

[2] The Animal Health Division divided Northern Ghana into 5 Veterinary Sections, each Section being made up of a number of Districts; the Districts were, in turn, divided into Divisions. See Map 4.

[3] The Animal Health Division endeavoured to prohibit the movement for trade purposes of fertile cows.

[4] The most logical measure of the 'degree of commercialization' would have been the ratio between the number of bullocks and the number of cows, if it could have been assumed that all bulls were service bulls which were not being reared for the meat trade. However, it was clear that such an assumption would have been quite unrealistic, the proportion of mature male animals which had been castrated varying greatly as between districts—most castration is done by the owners, and although the Animal Health Division was prepared to castrate cattle on request, in 1962, for instance, only 2,504 castrations were undertaken by the Division and, presumably, lack of staff would have prevented any great increase in this figure. Another possible measure, given the

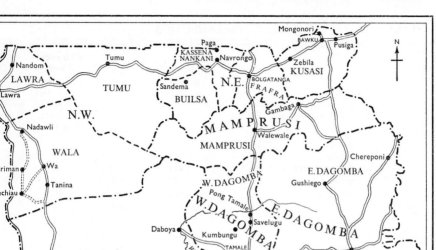

4   Northern Ghana, showing the five Veterinary Sections (N.E., N.W., Gonja, W. Dagomba/
    Mamprusi, E. Dagomba/Nanumba) and certain sub-sections. Many of the place-names mentioned
    in the study are also shown

Table 5.1 shows that, taking the North as a whole, the number of bulls
+ bullocks per 100 cows was only 27. But given the great variations as
between Veterinary Sections, the average for the North as a whole had little
meaning. That the striking variation as between the 5 Veterinary Sections
had much significance was established by the smaller degree of variation

practical difficulty of distinguishing between bulls and young bulls and sometimes between cows
and heifers, would have been the ratio between (bulls + bullocks + young bulls) and (cows +
heifers): this ratio was, in fact, calculated and was found to give a very similar 'order of commercialization' to the simpler ratio which was finally adopted, after experimenting, also, with the
bullocks to cows ratio.

TABLE 5.1. *The bulls + bullocks: cows ratio*, 1964

| Veterinary Sections and Districts | Numbers of bulls + bullocks | Numbers of cows | Numbers of bulls + bullocks per 100 cows |
|---|---|---|---|
| | (1) | (2) | (1) as % of (2) |
| North-east | | | |
| Frafra | 6,641 | 9,802 | 68 |
| Kassena-Nankani | 3,918 | 10,093 | 39 |
| Builsa | 2,845 | 8,276 | 34 |
| Kusai | 8,947 | 13,362 | 67 |
| | 22,351 | 41,533 | 54 |
| North-west | | | |
| Tumu | 633 | 5,034 | 13 |
| Lawra | 728 | 4,952 | 15 |
| Jirapa | 630 | 4,930 | 13 |
| Nandom | 671 | 3,422 | 20 |
| Lambussie | 516 | 2,610 | 20 |
| Nadawli | 579 | 9,295 | 6 |
| Wa | 927 | 13,586 | 7 |
| | 4,684 | 43,829 | 11 |
| Western Dagomba/Mamprusi | | | |
| Tamale | 3,379 | 24,836 | 14 |
| Gambaga | 3,050 | 8,072 | 38 |
| Walewale | 1,686 | 5,867 | 29 |
| | 8,115 | 38,775 | 21 |
| Eastern Dagomba/Nanumba | | | |
| Yendi | 633 | 4,714 | 13 |
| Zabzugu | 550 | 1,966 | 28 |
| Chereponi | 599 | 3,692 | 16 |
| Gushiegu | 1,002 | 4,235 | 24 |
| Saboba | 1,323 | 4,931 | 27 |
| Bimbila | 1,408 | 7,825 | 18 |
| | 5,515 | 27,363 | 21 |
| Gonja | | | |
| Damongo | 505 | 3,059 | 16 |
| Bole | 1,241 | 4,553 | 27 |
| Salaga | 509 | 1,709 | 30 |
| | 2,255 | 9,321 | 24 |
| Total Northern Ghana | 42,920 | 160,821 | 27 |

within Sections. Thus, each of the 4 Districts in the North-east Section had a ratio of 34 or more (as did the Gambaga District which is adjoining), whereas each of the 7 Districts in the North-west section had a ratio of 20 or less. Ratios were notably low (14 and 13) in the Districts based on the large towns of Tamale and Yendi. Nowhere outside the 4 North-eastern Districts and Gambaga did the ratio exceed 30.

Table 5.2 shows that if the statistics for the North-east Veterinary Section are broken down further, considerable uniformity within Districts is found to exist. Thus the variation for 4 sub-divisions of the Frafra District shows a variation between 57 and 83, whereas that for the 5 sub-divisions of the Builsa District was between 29 and 44.

TABLE 5.2. *North-east Veterinary Section*

| | Bulls + bullocks : cows ratio, 1963 | | |
|---|---|---|---|
| | Districts and Main Centres | | |
| Builsa—Total | 36 | Kusasi—Total | 63 |
| Main Centres: | | Main Centres: | |
| Sandema | 33 | Binduri | 79 |
| Chuchiliga | 32 | Bawku | 61 |
| Fumbisi | 44 | Pusiga | 67 |
| Wiaga | 29 | | |
| Kanjaga | 36 | | |
| Kassena-Nankani—Total | 31 | Frafra—Total | 66 |
| Main Centres: | | Main Centres: | |
| Navrongo | 36 | Bolgatanga | 62 |
| Navrompong | 47 | Bongo | 57 |
| Paga | 31 | Tongo | 83 |
| Paga Buru | 37 | Sekoti | 70 |
| Chiana | 29 | | |

Partly as a check on the general reliability of the census classification of cattle by sex and age, the ratio was calculated for 1961 as well as for 1964, so that the 'order of commercialization' for the two years could be compared: the figures (shown in Table 5.3) show remarkably little change in this order, as between the years, and certainly suggest that the statistics are adequate for this limited purpose—as no one had been accustomed to compute this particular ratio, there was no possibility of enumerators having had any incentive to 'cook the figures' to ensure its consistency over time.

Table 5.3 shows that in 1961, as in 1964, Nadawli and Wa were top of the list, with Tumu and Tamale and the District then known as Lawra (later split up into four Districts, Lawra, Jirapa, Nandom and Lambussie) following close behind. The District known as Yendi in 1961 (later Yendi, Zabzugu, Saboba, Chereponi and Gushiegu) was in much the same order in each of the two years, as was Mamprusi (Gambaga and Walewale in 1964). The Districts in the North-east were solidly at the end of the list in each of the years.

TABLE 5.3. *The 'order of commercialization'*

| | Bulls + bullocks : cows ratio | |
|---|---|---|
| District | (1964) *15 and under* | (1961) *17 and under* |
| Nadawli (N.W.) | 6⎫ | 13 |
| Wa (N.W.) | 7⎬ | |
| Tumu (N.W.) | 13 | 17 |
| Jirapa (N.W.) | 13 | a |
| Yendi (E. Dag.) | 13 | a |
| Tamale (W. Dag.) | 14 | 17 |
| Lawra (N.W.) | 15 | a |
| | *16 to 30* | *20 to 30* |
| Chereponi (E. Dag.) | 16 | 20 |
| Damongo (Gonja) | 16 | 25 |
| Bimbila (E. Dag.) | 18 | 29 |
| Nandom (N.W.) | 20 | a |
| Lambussie (N.W.) | 20 | a |
| Gushiegu (E. Dag.) | 24 | a |
| Saboba (E. Dag.) | 27 | a |
| Bole (Gonja) | 27 | 26 |
| Zabzugu (E. Dag.) | 28 | a |
| Walewale (W. Dag.) | 29 | a |
| Salaga (Gonja) | 30 | 30 |
| | *over 30* | *over 30* |
| Builsa (N.E.) | 34 | 36 |
| Gambaga (W. Dag.) | 38 | a |
| Kassena-Nankani (N.E.) | 39 | 35 |
| Kusasi (N.E.) | 67 | 63 |
| Frafra (N.E.) | 68 | 70 |

[a] See below: there were fewer Districts in 1961 than in 1964.

| | | |
|---|---|---|
| Lawra (1961) (divided into Lawra, Jirapa, Nandom and Lambussie, in 1964) | 16 | 19 |
| Yendi (1961) (divided into Yendi, Zabzugu, Saboba and Gushiegu in 1964) | 21 | 28 |
| Mamprusi (1961) (divided into Gambaga and Walewale in 1964) | 34 | 35 |

The table shows that all the 'more commercialized' Districts became increasingly commercialized in the short period 1961 to 1964. On the other hand the 'least commercialized' Districts, namely Gonja (Damongo, Bole, Salaga), Mamprusi (Gambaga, Walewale) and the North-east (Builsa, Kassena-Nankani, Kusasi and Frafra) were 'stagnant'—in two of the North-eastern Districts the percentages even showed a slight rise. The factor (or factors) which had accounted for the increased commercialization in the former Districts were not apparently at work in the latter.

SECTION II

The take-off from the herds

I now proceed to examine the statistical evidence for the presumption, based on Tables 5.1 and 5.3, that commercial 'take-off' from the herds was generally high, except in the North-east and a few other Districts.

As, of course, there are no figures relating to what I shall henceforth refer to as ceremonial slaughter, commercial take-off must be defined as the sum of local exports plus official slaughter (by butchers) in relation to the total stock of animals 'at risk' for sale or slaughter.

Commercial take-off must not be defined (as it has been conventionally in Ghana) as local exports plus official slaughter in relation to the total cattle population.

The convenient term 'local exports' was used by the Animal Health Division to denote the number of cattle for which movement certificates were issued. Such certificates were required by law when cattle were transported from one place to another; although there was, admittedly, some evasion of the control, the statistics were generally considered to be reliable indicators of the movement of 'trade cattle'.

The statistics of official slaughter of cattle (at licensed slaughterhouses) in the North were certainly less reliable than those of local exports and were much less meaningful.[1] They were prepared by the Sanitary Department of the Ministry of Health in connexion with the post-mortem examination of livestock.[2]

Because young bulls, as defined for livestock census purposes,[3] should not have been marketed unless there were special circumstances,[4] I had originally related local exports plus official slaughter to the population of bulls + bullocks only. But this led to the absurd result (see column (7), Table 5.4) that in 3 out of the 5 Veterinary Sections in 1963, take-off was far in excess of 100%—despite the omission of unofficial slaughter. While this was partly to be explained in terms of the take-off of old and barren cows,[5] it was clear that this explanation was inadequate given that only a low proportion of local

---

[1] They are less reliable because for any one month returns are seldom made available from all licensed slaughterhouses; they are less meaningful because much slaughter for both commercial, as well as for ceremonial, purposes occurs in villages where there are no local authority slaughterhouses. Furthermore, much ceremonial slaughter involves widespread distribution of meat and therefore serves the same purpose as commercial slaughter.

[2] The Health authorities made the figures available to the Animal Health Division from whom they were obtained.

[3] See p. 90, n. 1.

[4] Special circumstances, such as an outbreak of contagious pleuro-pneumonia in the herd, might legitimately have led to their slaughter.

[5] Almost all beasts, except those 'found dead', are ultimately slaughtered for meat: Mr Keith Hart tells me that among the Frafra even the 'found dead' are eaten.

exports consists of cows[1]—which as I noticed myself were seldom to be seen in Kumasi Market, the principal outlet. Even if it had been assumed that all the cattle officially slaughtered by butchers in the North-west had been cows (surely an absurd assumption), it would still have been the case that some young bulls had been 'exported'. As the proportion of old and barren cows in the herds was not known, it was therefore necessary to relate local exports plus official slaughter to the recorded population of bulls, bullocks and young bulls.

TABLE 5.4. *Take-off of cattle in relation to male cattle population*

| Veterinary Section | Local exports 1963 (1) | Official slaughter 1963 (2) | Take-off (1)+(2) (3) | Numbers of bulls, bullocks and young bulls[a] 1962 (4) | (3) as % of (4) (5) | Numbers of bulls, bullocks[a] 1962 (6) | (3) as % of (6) (7) |
|---|---|---|---|---|---|---|---|
| North-west | 8,946 | 4,464 | 13,410 | 17,924 | 75 | 6,735 | 199 |
| E. Dagomba | 3,999 | 2,844 | 6,843 | 11,487 | 59 | 4,929 | 139 |
| W. Dagomba | 5,671 | 5,523 | 11,194 | 15,879 | 71 | 8,109 | 138 |
| North-east | 5,630 | 5,909 | 11,539 | 30,723 | 38 | 17,884 | 64 |
| Gonja | 819 | 1,430 | 2,249 | 5,140 | 42 | 2,682 | 84 |
| Total | 25,065 | 20,170 | 45,235 | 81,423 | 55 | 40,339 | 112 |

[a] For definition see p. 90, n. 1.

Table 5.4 shows that in 1963 take-off, thus defined, varied between 75 and 71 in the North-west and Western Dagomba and 42 and 38 in Gonja and the North-east. It was thus confirmed that take-off was generally highest in the areas with the lowest proportions of male animals in the herds.

SECTION III

The seasonality of local exports : introduction

Before examining this general conclusion in more geographical detail it is necessary to consider the matter of the seasonality of local exports of cattle.

Local exports from the North as a whole were very seasonal as is shown by Table 5.5 and Graph 1.[2] Falling to their lowest level during the dry season in the first four months of the year, local exports usually rise suddenly in May,

[1] Licences for the movement of cows were normally not granted by Animal Health unless the animals could be proved to be barren or were being 'exported' as breeding stock.
[2] The earliest year for which I could find monthly figures was 1961.

TABLE 5.5. *Monthly local exports*

| | Number of cattle | | May 1964 to |
| | 1961 | 1962 | April 1965 |
|---|---|---|---|
| January | 855 | 957 | 920 |
| February | 550 | 628 | 841 |
| March | 437 | 563 | 741 |
| April | 489 | 927 | 830 |
| May | 1,395 | 1,433 | 3,053 |
| June | 2,460 | 2,060 | 5,168 |
| July | 3,746 | 3,064 | 5,072 |
| August | 1,771 | 4,101 | 3,784 |
| September | 1,100[a] | 2,215 | 2,648 |
| October | 735[a] | 1,223 | 2,453 |
| November | 779[a] | 1,264 | 1,797 |
| December | 1,187 | 2,217 | 1,535 |
| Total | 15,504[a] | 20,561 | 28,842 |

[a] A very slight element of estimation is involved. See p. 103, n 1.

reaching a peak in June, July or August. They then show a slow decline except for an increase in December connected with the Christmas trade.

But the figures for the North as a whole conceal the fact that local exports from some cattle-buying centres are much more seasonal than from others. As Table 5.6 shows, much the most remarkable degree of seasonality is shown by local exports from the Western Dagomba and North-west Veterinary Sections. In the year May 1964 to April 1965, 83% of total local exports from Western Dagomba was exported in the 5 months May to September—the corresponding percentage for the North-west being 77. On the other hand, the figure for the North-east was only 45%. In the 3 months May to July exports from Western Dagomba were 61% of the annual total.

Average exports from Western Dagomba in the month of March in the 3 years 1961, 1962 (shown in Table 5.7) and 1964–5 (shown in Table 5.6) were 108 cattle (the average of 101, 140 and 84); the corresponding averages for the months of June, July and August were 1,254, 1,445 and 1,000 cattle. The corresponding average figures for the North-west were 42 cattle for March and 1,046, 1,285 and 900 cattle for June, July and August respectively.

At this stage of the analysis it has already become apparent that there was a strong association between the degree of commercialization (as measured in Table 5.1) and the degree of seasonality of local exports—the most commercialized Sections having been the most seasonal and *vice versa*. When this association is examined on the District level it becomes even more striking.

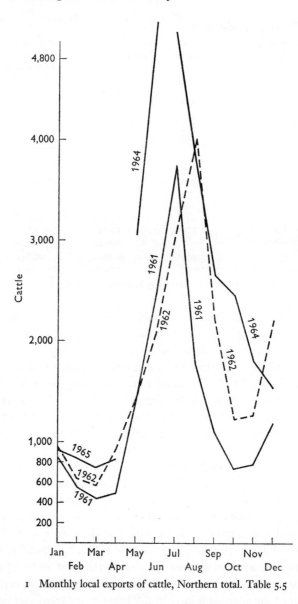

1  Monthly local exports of cattle, Northern total. Table 5.5

The Tamale District was high in the order of commercialization (Table 5.3), while the other two Districts comprising the Mamprusi/Western Dagomba Section, namely Walewale and Gambaga, were respectively average and low. Graph 6 and Table 5.7 show that in 1961 local exports from both Tamale (much the largest urban centre in the North) and Walewale were

98

TABLE 5.6. *Monthly local exports by Veterinary Section*

(Number of cattle)

| | North-west | | Eastern Dagomba | | North-east | | Western Dagomba | | Gonja | Total Northern Ghana | |
|---|---|---|---|---|---|---|---|---|---|---|---|
| May 1964 | 562 | | 516 | | 173 | | 1,722 | | 80 | 3,053 | |
| June | 1,726 | | 708 | | 398 | | 2,227 | | 109 | 5,168 | |
| July | 1,903 | 77% | 574 | 53% | 430 | 45% | 1,780 | 83% | 285 | 5,072 | 68% |
| August | 1,220 | | 647 | | 372 | | 1,292 | | 253 | 3,784 | |
| September | 860 | | 551 | | 466 | | 757 | | 14 | 2,648 | |
| October | 782 | | 484 | | 597 | | 319 | | 271[a] | 2,453 | |
| November | 528 | | 517 | | 178 | | 525 | | 49 | 1,797 | |
| December | 225 | | 534 | | 422 | | 288 | | 66 | 1,535 | |
| January 1965 | 156 | | 278 | | 296 | | 147 | | 43 | 920 | |
| February | 49 | | 325 | | 378 | | 84 | | 5 | 841 | |
| March | 65 | | 278 | | 265 | | 84 | | 49 | 741 | |
| April | 97 | | 225 | | 265 | | 147 | | 96 | 830 | |
| Total | 8,173 | | 5,637 | | 4,340 | | 9,372 | | 1,320 | 28,842 | |

[a] A suspiciously high figure: it has not, however, been omitted as it could have resulted from an outbreak of disease.

very seasonal, with the peak coming about three months after the start of the rains. Given the large volume of local exports from Tamale, the seasonality there is at its most fantastic: as Table 5.8 shows, only 48 cattle were exported from Tamale in the 3 months January to March 1964 compared with 2,204 cattle in the next 3 months.

Although the figures for the three Districts which comprised the North-west District in 1961 were slightly defective (unfortunately, I was unable to find later figures, broken down by District, in the files at Pong-Tamale), Graph 7 shows that Wa exhibited a somewhat greater seasonality than Lawra, the corresponding 'order of commercialization' being measured by the bull + bullock: cow ratios of 13 and 19 (Table 5.3).

The comparative lack of seasonality of local exports from the East Dagomba Section is shown by Graph 4. Graph 8 shows that exports from the Yendi District in 1961 were much more seasonal than those from Chereponi, but 'Yendi' in 1961 included Zabzugu, Saboba and Gushiegu which, as separate Districts in 1964, were lower in the order of commercialization than the new Yendi in that year. It is to be presumed that had the figures for the Yendi District in 1964 been available, the graph would have shown a single marked seasonal peak, corresponding to the high order of commercialization of that District.

For a high degree of commercialization is associated not only with a great degree of seasonality, but also with one marked peak in the curve. The curve

TABLE 5.7. *Monthly local exports by District 1961 and 1962*

(Number of cattle)

| | 1961 | | | | | 1962 | 1961 | | | | 1962 |
|---|---|---|---|---|---|---|---|---|---|---|---|
| | Navrongo | Sandema | Bawku | Bolgatanga | Total North-east | Total North-east | Tamale | Gambaga | Walewale | Total Western Dagomba | Total Western Dagomba |
| January | 200 | 46 | 30 | 161 | 437 | 368 | 17 | 24 | 29 | 70 | 216 |
| February | 36 | 54 | 62 | 30 | 182 | 221 | 79 | 42 | 3 | 124 | 61 |
| March | 78 | 32 | 15 | 38 | 163 | 237 | 45 | 56 | — | 101 | 140 |
| April | 9 | 30 | 41 | 43 | 123 | 220 | 23 | 154 | 13 | 190 | 304 |
| May | 12 | 59 | 6 | 11 | 88 | 119 | 304 | 182 | 28 | 514 | 442 |
| June | 24 | 153 | 57 | 96 | 330 | 241 | 636 | 113 | 44 | 793 | 742 |
| July | 34 | 171 | 29 | 83 | 453 | 548 | 872 | 175 | 240 | 1,287 | 1,267 |
| August | 27 | 82 | 21 | 98 | 328 | 835 | 177 | 163 | 148 | 488 | 1,221 |
| September | 56 | 20 | 42 | 49 | 167 | 345 | 86 | 147 | 34 | 267 | 363 |
| October | 13 | 7 | 26 | 98 | 144 | 388 | 21 | 75 | — | 96 | 218 |
| November | 17 | 7 | 28 | 53 | 105 | 484 | 102 | 77 | 3 | 182 | 110 |
| December | 357 | 44 | 50 | 164 | 615 | 1,103 | 42 | 36 | 1 | 79 | 108 |
| Total | 863 | 705 | 407 | 924 | 3,135 | 5,109 | 2,404 | 1,244 | 543 | 4,191 | 5,192 |

| | 1961 | | | | 1962 | 1961 | | | 1962 | 1961 | 1962 |
|---|---|---|---|---|---|---|---|---|---|---|---|
| | Wa | Lawra | Tumu | Total North-west | Total North-west | Yendi | Chereponi | Total Eastern Dagomba | Total Eastern Dagomba | Gonja Total | Gonja Total |
| January | 76 | 66 | 32 | 174 | 120 | n.a. | n.a. | 170 | 235 | — | 18 |
| February | 55 | 6 | — | 61 | 193 | 92 | 39 | 156 | 146 | 27 | 7 |
| March | 14 | 24 | — | 38 | 24 | 59 | 38 | 113 | 148 | 22 | 14 |
| April | 34 | 4 | 1 | 39 | 59 | 34 | 29 | 79 | 275 | 58 | 69 |
| May | 330 | 127 | 4 | 461 | 324 | 158 | 95 | 261 | 457 | 71 | 91 |
| June | 643 | 118 | 69 | 830 | 581 | 227 | 84 | 375 | 402 | 132 | 94 |
| July | 681 | 476 | 177 | 1,334 | 619 | 421 | 90 | 567 | 482 | 105 | 148 |
| August | 151 | 98 | 89 | 338 | 1,141 | 424 | 111 | 551 | 669 | 66 | 144 |
| September | n.a. | n.a. | n.a. | 653[a] | 922 | 334 | 50 | 434 | 440 | 15 | 145 |
| October | n.a. | n.a. | n.a. | | 187 | 210 | 41 | 273 | 325 | 4 | 105 |
| November | n.a. | n.a. | n.a. | | 298 | 173 | 63 | 274 | 354 | — | 18 |
| December | 55 | 120 | — | 175 | 751 | 286 | 30 | 317 | 227 | 1 | 28 |
| Total | .. | .. | .. | 4,103[a] | 5,219 | .. | .. | 3,570 | 4,160 | 501 | 881 |

[a] A very slight element of estimation is involved.

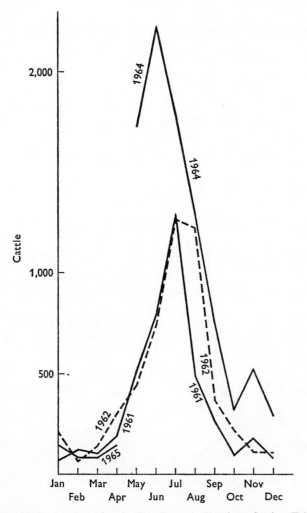

2   Monthly local exports of cattle, West Dagomba Veterinary Section. Tables 5.6 and 5.7

of local exports from the much less commercialized North-east tended to have two peaks, one in July or August (in October in the year 1964) and another at Christmas—see Graph 5. In the North-east local exports fell to their lowest level in May, but they were not then nearly so low relative to peak exports as were exports from Western Dagomba, or the North-west, in January or February compared with mid-year.

When the North-eastern figures are broken down by District, then it is found (see Graph 9) that, at least in 1961, the two least-commercialized

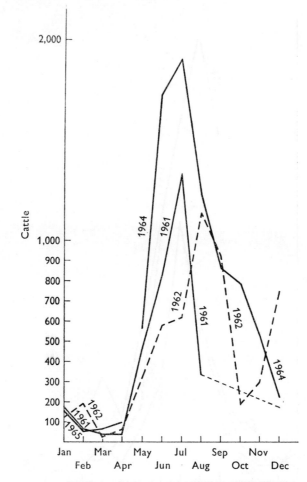

3   Monthly local exports of cattle, North-west Veterinary Section. Tables 5.6 and 5.7

Districts, Frafra (Bolgatanga) and Kusasi (Bawku)—see Table 5.7—have graphs of a shape quite different from those typical of nearly all Northern Districts. The same applies to Kassena-Nankani (Navrongo), with a most pronounced peak at Christmas and another in March. It is interesting to note that the graph for Builsa (Sandema), the most commercialized District in the North-east, is of the standard Northern shape.[1]

The earliest figures of local exports I could find in the files at Pong-Tamale related to 1954, when 10,741 cattle were recorded as 'exported'. The figure

[1] See p. 132, n. 1.

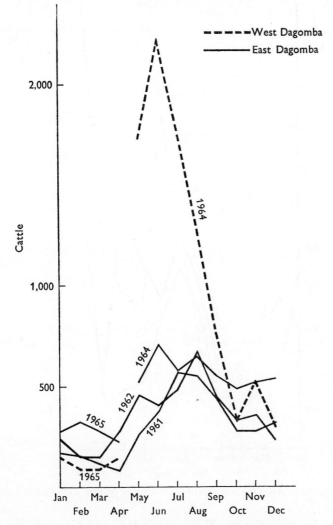

4   Monthly local exports of cattle, East Dagomba (with West Dagomba for comparison).
Tables 5.6 and 5.7.

rose to about 15,500[1] in 1961, to 20,561 in 1962, to 25,065 in 1963 and to 28,842 during the year ending 30 April 1965.

Table 5.9 shows that between 1961 (when statistics on a comparable basis by District were first compiled) and the year May 1964 to April 1965, local

---

[1] There is a very slight element of estimation in this figure, statistics for the North-west for 3 months of the year (Sept. to Nov. when exports were low) having been unavailable. See Table 5.5.

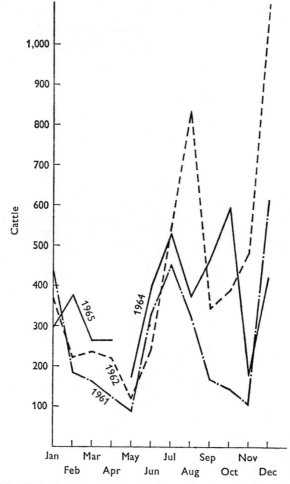

5  Monthly local exports of cattle, North-east Veterinary Section. Tables 5.6 and 5.7

exports rose by 85% for the North as a whole and by 224% for West Dagomba—the Gonja figure is either a freak or inaccurate. The Section which had been least commercialized in 1961—the North-east—shows the lowest rate of increase.[1] In 1953 the North-west, with exports of 8,946 cattle, had accounted for over one-third of the total—but exports from that Section declined somewhat after that, no doubt partly in response to the more stringent control exercised by that branch of the Animal Health Division which had been concerned about the export of immature animals.

---

[1] The decline in exports from the North-east between 1963 (5,630 cattle) and 1964-5 (4,340 cattle) is to be noted, though it cannot be explained.

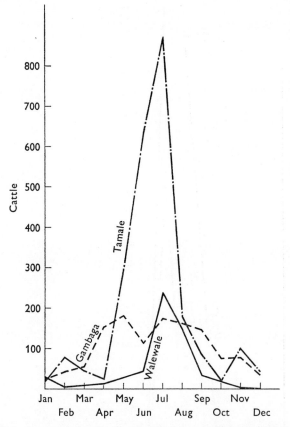

6  Monthly local exports of cattle, Tamale, Gambaga and Walewale Districts, 1961. Table 5.7

TABLE 5.8. *Western Dagomba/Mamprusi Veterinary Section*
*Quarterly local exports*

(Number of cattle)

| 1964 | Tamale (W. Dagomba) | Gambaga (Mamprusi) | Walewale (Mamprusi) | Total |
|---|---|---|---|---|
| January to March | 48 | 234 | 73 | 355 |
| April to June | 2,204 | 994 | 985 | 4,183 |
| July to September | 1,617 | 1,036 | 939 | 3,592 |
| October to December | 793 | 339 | — | 1,132 |
| Total | 4,662 | 2,603 | 1,997 | 9,262 |

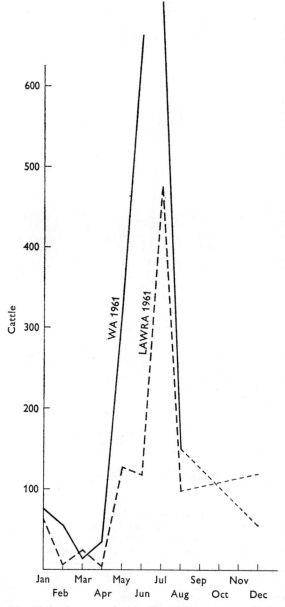

7   Monthly local exports of cattle, Wa and Lawra Districts, 1961. Table 5.7

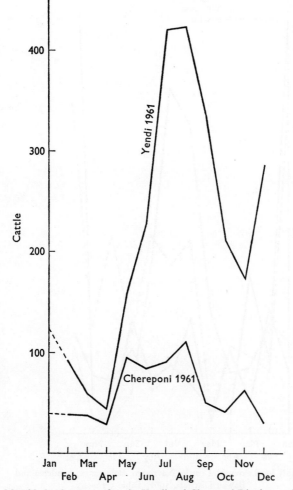

Cattle

400

300

Yendi 1961

200

100

Chereponi 1961

Jan  Mar  May  Jul  Sep  Nov
  Feb  Apr  Jun  Aug  Oct  Dec

8   Monthly local exports of cattle, Yendi and Chereponi Districts, 1961. Table 5.7

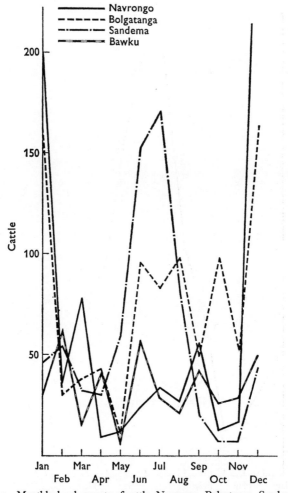

9  Monthly local exports of cattle, Navrongo, Bolgatanga, Sandema and
Bawku Districts, 1961. Table 5.7

TABLE 5.9. *Total local exports 1961, 1962, 1963, 1964–5*

(Number of cattle)

| Veterinary Section | 1961 | 1962 | 1963 | % of 1961 | May 1964 to April 1965 | % of 1961 |
|---|---|---|---|---|---|---|
| North-west | 4,103[a] | 5,219 | 8,946 | 218 | 8,173 | 199 |
| Eastern Dagomba | 3,570 | 4,160 | 3,999 | 112 | 5,637 | 158 |
| Western Dagomba/Mamprusi | 4,191 | 5,192 | 5,671 | 135 | 9,372 | 224 |
| North-east | 3,135 | 5,109 | 5,630 | 180 | 4,340 | 138 |
| Gonja | 501 | 881 | 819 | 163 | 1,320[b] | 263[b] |
| Total | 15,500[a] | 20,561 | 25,065 | 162 | 28,842 | 186 |

[a] A very slight element of estimation is involved.    [b] See the note on Table 5.6.

SECTION IV

The Northern Ghanaian cattle trade with Kumasi

The statistics of local exports will be further considered below, but first it is necessary to analyse the material which was gathered relating to the Northern Ghanaian cattle trade with Kumasi.

The cattle market at Kumasi is one of the greatest institutions of its kind in West Africa.[1] In the three years 1962 to 1964 an average of nearly 70,000 cattle arrived at this market (see Table 5.10), these having certainly been worth more than £2m.[2] In 1964 about a quarter[3] of all the cattle which arrived at the market were of Northern Ghanaian origin, the proportion having risen from about 10% in 1962.

I estimate (see Table 5.11) that in the year ending April 1965 about a half (55%) of total 'local exports' from the North went to Kumasi market,[4] the proportion having risen from 44% in the earlier year. There had been a general tendency for the proportion of total local exports marketed in Kumasi to increase as between the years and this was especially marked for Eastern Dagomba, which had formerly sent most of its cattle elsewhere.

Dr D. Nyarko, then Veterinary Officer, Animal Health Division, Kumasi, most kindly provided me with lists showing for each day of each of two selected years (16 May 1962 to 15 May 1963, and 1 May 1964 to 30 April 1965) the names of all the 'bringers'[5] of Northern Ghanaian (or 'local')

[1] See 'Landlords and Brokers: A West African Trading System' by the present author, 1966 (10).
[2] Accurate valuation is impossible: no price records were kept at the market and the valuations of imports for trade return purposes were purely notional (being too low).
[3] The value of these animals would have been considerably less than a quarter of the total turnover of the market, since Northern Ghanaian cattle were much smaller than imported beasts.
[4] Whence a large proportion was redistributed to other centres in Ghana.
[5] I follow usage in Kumasi cattle market in defining a 'bringer' as one who brings livestock to market in order to sell them. While most bringers in Kumasi market were traders who bought

TABLE 5.10. *Recorded monthly arrivals of cattle at Kumasi market*

(Number of cattle)

| | 1962 | | | 1963 | | | 1964 | | | Average for 3 years | |
| --- | --- | --- | --- | --- | --- | --- | --- | --- | --- | --- | --- |
| | Imported | Northern Ghanaian ('Local') | Total | Imported | Northern Ghanaian ('Local') | Total | Imported | Northern Ghanaian ('Local') | Total | Northern Ghanaian ('Local') | Total |
| January | 6,470 | 21 | 6,491 | 7,120 | 215 | 7,335 | 5,263 | 101 | 5,364 | 112 | 6,397 |
| February | 6,523 | 20 | 6,543 | 7,399 | 68 | 7,467 | 5,900 | 301 | 6,201 | 130 | 6,737 |
| March | 4,926 | 26 | 4,952 | 5,681 | 55 | 5,736 | 7,000 | 68 | 7,068 | 50 | 5,919 |
| April | 2,982 | 150 | 3,132 | 4,448 | 330 | 4,778 | 7,725 | 248 | 7,973 | 243 | 5,294 |
| May | 3,582 | 337 | 3,919 | 2,858 | 1,444 | 4,302 | 4,979 | 2,222 | 7,201 | 1 334 | 5,141 |
| June | 2,471 | 556 | 3,027 | 3,214 | 2,136 | 5,350 | 2,239 | 4,016 | 6,255 | 2,236 | 4,877 |
| July | 2,544 | 2,112 | 4,656 | 3,776 | 2,428 | 6,204 | 3,349 | 3,073 | 6,422 | 2,538 | 5,761 |
| August | 2,939 | 2,833 | 5,772 | 4,006 | 2,000 | 6,006 | 2,199 | 3,214 | 5,413 | 2,682 | 5,730 |
| September | 3,389 | 1,048 | 4,437 | 1,095[a] | 1,200[a] | 2,295[a] | 3,000 | 2,834 | 5,834 | 1,694 | 4,189[a] |
| October | 4,957 | 533 | 5,490 | 3,254 | 459 | 3,713 | 4,462 | 1,600 | 6,062 | 864 | 5,088 |
| November | 5,142 | 514 | 5,656 | 5,743 | 706 | 6,449 | 6,721 | 1,385 | 8,106 | 868 | 6,737 |
| December | 6,112 | 870 | 6,982 | 7,743 | 127 | 7,870 | 7,299 | 800 | 8,099 | 599 | 7,650 |
| Total | 52,037 | 9,020 | 61,057 | 56,337 | 11,168 | 67,505 | 60,136 | 19,862 | 79,998 | 13,350 | 69,520 |

[a] Arrivals affected by floods.

TABLE 5.11. *Local exports to Kumasi and total local exports by Veterinary Section*

| | Local exports to Kumasi[a] | | Total local exports 1962 (2) | Local exports to Kumasi[a] | | Total local exports[b] 1964-5 (4) |
|---|---|---|---|---|---|---|
| | 1962-3 (1) | Col. (1) as % of Col. (2) | | 1964-5 (3) | Col. (3) as % of Col. (4) | |
| Veterinary Section | | | | | | |
| North-east | 2,787 (183) | 55% | 5,109 | 2,857 (145) | 66% | 4,340 |
| North-west | 2,538 (115) | 49% | 5,219 | 4,008 (174) | 49% | 8,173 |
| Eastern Dagomba | 490 (31) | 12% | 4,160 | 1,818 (52) | 32% | 5,637 |
| Western Dagomba | 3,086 (96) | 59% | 5,192 | 6,694 (195) | 71% | 9,372 |
| Gonja | 245 (23) | 28% | 881 | 423 (34) | 32% | 1,320 |
| N.A. | — | — | — | 94 (7) | — | — |
| Total | 9,146 (448) | 44% | 20,561[c] | 15,894 (607) | 55% | 28,842 |

[a] As shown in Table 5.12.     [b] As shown in Table 5.6.
[c] As shown in Table 5.5.

NOTE. The figures in brackets in columns (1) and (3) are the numbers of bringers of cattle to Kumasi.

cattle to Kumasi cattle market, with the number of cattle and place of origin recorded for each consignment. These records were based on Veterinary Movement Permits (Local Export) received by the Animal Health Division at the cattle market: while the statistics were generally very reliable, they were not necessarily quite complete.[1] The following conclusions, relating to the structure and organization of the trade, are based on an analysis of these valuable records,[2] which had never hitherto been used by a research worker.

It was a peculiarity of the Northern Ghanaian trade, at least in 1965, that

the cattle for resale, use of this convenient word avoids begging the question as to whether, in some cases, they were cattle rearers.

[1] There are slight discrepancies between the total derived from these statistics and the official figures of total arrivals of Northern Ghanaian cattle at Kumasi cattle market.

[2] This bulky statistical material was analysed with the aid of a slide rule only, so that simple methods of handling had to be devised. The chief difficulty lay in 'editing' the names of the bringers, many of which were somewhat incorrectly recorded. As most of the bringers were Muslims, many of whom bore popular names such as Mohammad, Alassan, Iddrissu, and as the same man might be referred to by a large number of different variants of the same popular name, the task of sorting out the names of the bringers, with any degree of reliability, would have been impossible had it not fortunately been common practice to record each man's ethnic origin after his name—Alhaji Alhassan Mamprusi thus being distinguishable from Alhaji Alhassan Dagomba. (It was this practice which enables one to classify bringers ethnically—at least to a considerable extent.) The statistics are, therefore, somewhat defective: their analysis has involved the exercise of some degree of judgment: but on such matters as the numbers of cattle brought by a bringer from any buying centre, or the number of large traders, it is believed that they are essentially correct, on the assumption that when one man brings cattle to market on behalf of another, *it is usual for the principal's name to be recorded as the bringer*. With regard to this assumption, which unfortunately could not be checked, I can only say that the general evidence is that actual partnerships among cattle traders are very rare in West Africa, so that there is little chance of confusing the principal and his assistants.

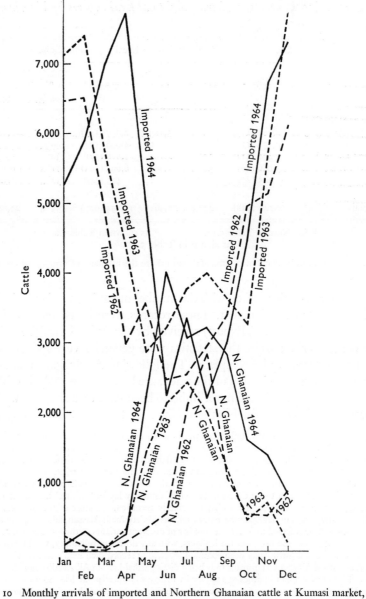

10   Monthly arrivals of imported and Northern Ghanaian cattle at Kumasi market,
1962, 1963, 1964. Table 5.10

nearly all trade cattle were bought directly from rearers and did not pass through a market. In the South I had been repeatedly told that there were no cattle markets in the North (just as there were none in the other main Ghanaian cattle-rearing area, the Accra Plains), but I found that this was not strictly true, though I think it was correct to say that there were *hardly any organized cattle markets* in the North, such that a potential seller could be sure of selling his stock on a certain day at a reasonable price.[1] There were no *mai gida* (landlords) or *dillali* (brokers) in such few Northern cattle markets as existed—and business was casually conducted and on a small scale.[2] The Northern Ghanaian cattle rearer was, therefore, usually dependent on the cattle trader (or on people, such as butchers, who acted on his behalf), unless he had the time, inclination or financial capacity to proceed to a southern market himself.

During the course of my brief fieldwork among cattle rearers in Western Dagomba and Wa (in the North-west) I formed the opinion[3] that individual rearers tried to avoid having any kind of regular relationship with a trader, there having been a general belief that 'you get a better price from a stranger'. I was also convinced that rearers always insisted, like those on the Accra Plains, on receiving 'cash down' at the moment they parted with their animals. These two considerations imply that anyone with capital was usually[4] likely to be able to buy animals, and that a man had to have much capital if he was to buy more than a few animals at a time.

The analysis of the Kumasi cattle market statistics shows that many different men tried their hand at cattle-trading from time to time. I estimate (see Table 5.12) that the number of bringers involved in the Northern

---

[1] It may be that Gushiego, north of Yendi (which I had no time to visit), was the largest cattle market in the North—though it was not a specialist market, only a section of a general periodic market. I was told that up to 100 cattle might be on sale there on market day, that it was an old cattle market, and that Dagomba, Bimbila, Konkomba and Mamprusi rearers sent their cattle there. I observed for myself cattle being sold in the general market at Tangasia near Nadawli, in the North-west; traders travelled there from Wa and invited local rearers to show them their stock in the market.

[2] This is in great contrast to the position in Hausaland (Northern Nigeria) where cattle are on sale at almost all sizeable markets and where cattle *dillali* (brokers) abound. However, with the aim of preventing theft and illegal movement of cattle (as well as of preserving the position of local dealers) the Wala Local Council had introduced a system of licensing cattle dealers, such that only those licensed might buy cattle intended for local export. In June 1965 there were 22 men on the Register of Cattle Dealers, all of them Wala except for one Ashanti resident in Wa—37 men had had their applications refused. I denote these men as 'dealers', as this was the term used both by the Council and the men themselves and as such usage corresponded with the distinction made between dealers and traders in Kumasi cattle market—see Hill, *op. cit.* (10). However, in so far as the dealers themselves took the cattle to Kumasi and other places to sell, they were also cattle traders—though most Wa cattle traders were not dealers. Some, though not all, of the 22 dealers were also cattle *mai gida* (landlords) for stranger cattle-traders.

[3] Owing to the rearers' reticence about selling I formed this opinion on the basis of indirect evidence. See also, p. 79.

[4] For all one knows this *may* have been as true in the North-east as elsewhere—see pp. 130–1 below.

TABLE 5.12. *'Exports' of cattle to Kumasi by buying centre*

| Buying centre[a] | Year 1962-3 | | | | | Year 1964-5 | | | | | |
|---|---|---|---|---|---|---|---|---|---|---|---|
| | Number of cattle | Number of bringers[b] | Number of cattle per bringer | Large bringers[c] No. of cattle | % of total | Number of cattle | Number of bringers[b] | Number of cattle per bringer | Large bringers[c] No. of cattle | % of total | Smaller bringers[e] |
| Bawku (N.E.) | 403 | 33 (2) | 12 | 89 | 22 | 362 | 20 (3) | 18 | 149 | 41 | 12 |
| Bimbila (E. Dag.) | 10 | 1 (—) | d | — | — | 90 | 3 (1) | d | 65 | d | 2 |
| Bole (Gonja) | 150 | 14 (—) | 11 | — | — | 384 | 31 (—) | 12 | — | — | 25 |
| Bolgatanga (N.E.) | 692 | 43 (4) | 16 | 225 | 32 | 572 | 25 (6) | 23 | 280 | 49 | 17 |
| Chereponi (E. Dag.) | 48 | 2 (—) | d | — | — | 182 | 10 (1) | 18 | 39 | — | 10 |
| Gambaga (W. Dag.) | 323 | 14 (2) | 23 | 130 | 40 | 790 | 31 (7) | 25 | 425 | 54 | 23 |
| Gushiego (E. Dag.) | 23 | 2 (—) | d | — | — | 293 | 15 (2) | 30 | 102 | 35 | 10 |
| Kumbungu (W. Dag.) | 169 | 7 (—) | 24 | — | — | 182 | 6 (3) | 30 | 132 | 73 | 2 |
| Lambussie (N.W.) | 93 | 4 (1) | 23 | 52 | 56 | — | — | — | — | — | — |
| Lawra (N.W.) | 853 | 37 (10) | 23 | 463 | 54 | 936 | 47 (6) | 20 | 353 | 38 | 28 |
| Mogonori (N.E.) | 404 | 28 (2) | 14 | 63 | 16 | 70 | 4 (—) | 17 | — | — | 4 |
| Nandom (N.W.) | — | — | d | — | — | 903 | 41 (9) | 21 | 428 | 47 | 24 |
| Navrongo (N.E.) | 77 | 6 (—) | 14 | 43 | 15 | 536 | 20 (6) | 27 | 351 | 65 | 12 |
| Paga (N.E.) | 287 | 20 (1) | 14 | — | — | 204 | 14 (—) | 15 | — | — | 13 |
| Pong-Tamale (W. Dag.) | — | — | — | — | — | 193 | 11 (—) | 18 | — | — | 9 |
| Pusiga (N.E.) | 328 | 22 (1) | 15 | 40 | 12 | 210 | 13 (2) | 16 | 72 | 34 | 11 |
| Salaga (Gonja) | 95 | 9 (1) | 10 | — | — | 6 | 1 (—) | d | — | — | 1 |
| Sandema (N.E.) | 584 | 29 (4) | 20 | 236 | 40 | 565 | 24 (4) | 19 | 286 | 51 | 18 |
| Savelugu (W. Dag.) | 158 | 12 (—) | 13 | — | — | 860 | 28 (10) | 31 | 545 | 63 | 15 |
| Tamale (W. Dag.) | 1,928 | 44 (15) | 44 | 1,249 | 65 | 3,164 | 64 (23) | 49 | 2,392 | 76 | 32 |
| Tumu (N.W.) | 515 | 26 (5) | 20 | 214 | 42 | 357 | 16 (3) | 22 | 114 | 32 | 9 |
| Wa (N.W.) | 1,031 | 45 (9) | 23 | 598 | 58 | 1,724 | 63 (14) | 27 | 955 | 55 | 37 |
| Walewale (W. Dag.) | 464 | 16 (7) | 29 | 341 | 73 | 1,380 | 45 (16) | 31 | 915 | 66 | 25 |
| Yendi (E. Dag.) | 409 | 26 (3) | 16 | 142 | 35 | 1,192 | 21 (5) | 57 | 996 | 84 | 14 |
| Zebilla (N.E.) | 12 | 2 (—) | d | — | — | 298 | 22 (2) | 14 | 87 | 29 | 15 |
| Other | 90 | 6 (—) | d | — | — | 441 | 32 (—) | 14 | — | — | 29 |
| Total | 9,146 | 448 (67) | 20 | 3,885 | 42 | 15,894 | 607 (123) | 26 | 8,686 | 55 | 397 |

a  Veterinary Section in brackets.
b  The number of large bringers who handled more than 30 cattle at any buying centre is shown in brackets.
c  The number of cattle handled by the large bringers who handled more than 30 cattle. The percentage is that of the total cattle from the buying centre handled by the large bringers.
d  Figure too small to be significant.
e  Small bringers are defined as those who made no more than one delivery of cattle to Kumasi during the year from any one buying centre

Ghanaian trade with Kumasi in the year 1962–3 might have been as high as 400 and that the figure might have risen to nearly 600 in 1964–5.[1]

As most cattle-traders lacked the capital to operate on more than a very small scale, and as there were some large-scale traders, the average number of cattle per bringer per year is a figure of little significance—it was about 20 cattle in 1962–3, compared with about 26 cattle in 1964–5. The striking fact was that about two-thirds (397) of all the bringers in 1964–5 (see Table 5.15) brought no more than one consignment to Kumasi, from any buying centre, during the whole course of the year—few consignments consisted of more than 11 beasts, most of less.[2] As the number of bringers who had bought in more than one buying centre was certainly a small proportion of the total, it would seem probable that at least a half of all bringers had brought in a single consignment from one centre only. Although the proportion of small bringers was somewhat higher in the less-commercialized than in the more-commercialized Sections (72%, 73% and 78% in the North-east, Eastern Dagomba and Gonja respectively, compared with 57% and 59% in Western Dagomba and the North-west), there had still clearly been much scope for small bringers in the latter areas. The fieldwork in Western Dagomba and Wa had suggested that most of the small bringers there were traders—i.e. men who bought some (at least) of the cattle they sold at Kumasi—but there may have been a higher proportion of rearer-bringers in some other Districts.

If a 'large bringer' is defined as a man who had brought more than 30 cattle (the equivalent of about $2\frac{1}{2}$ lorry loads) to Kumasi in a year, from any one buying centre, then, as Table 5.12 shows, the proportion of large bringers was about one-seventh of the total number of bringers in 1962–3 and about one-fifth in 1964–5. Western Dagomba was the section with the highest proportion of large bringers—about a third of all bringers from that Section in 1964–5 were 'large'.[3] The detailed figures show that the larger the number

[1] All those bringers who had consigned cattle *from more than one buying centre* in the year are included more than once in the list, which therefore somewhat exaggerates the number of individuals involved. However, inspection of the lists of names for different buying centres clearly establishes that the proportion of bringers who bought in more than one centre is small. (Such an inspection was to some extent facilitated by the possibility of identifying certain names with certain ethnic groups.) It is doubtful whether an analysis of purchases by individuals in all centres would have been reliable enough to be useful, partly because of the incorrect recording of names (see p. 111, n. 2) and also because numbers of different individuals bore the same name.

[2] Such number of cattle as was shown as a single entry against the bringer's name in the records represented a *consignment*. Most of the cattle arrived at the market by lorry, though a few came on foot; the use of trailers being then prohibited, a normal full lorry load consisted of only about 11 beasts (all the large lorries were used for imported cattle only). As most bringers brought less than a full lorry load (lorries might have been shared with other bringers or partially filled with other loads), the average consignment was considerably less than 11 cattle.

[3] There was not much variation in this percentage as between other Sections. As for the proportion of cattle handled by the 'large bringers', this was about two-thirds of the total for Western and Eastern Dagomba and about 45% for the North-east and the North-west.

of cattle which had been bought in any centre, the higher the proportion of large bringers was apt to have been.

The proportion of cattle handled by the large bringers rose (Table 5.12) from 42% in 1962–3 to 55% in 1964–5. The latter percentage was as high as 84 in Yendi and 76 in Tamale, both urban centres.

Most interestingly, the number of large bringers who consigned more than 30 cattle from any one centre in *each* of the two years was almost negligible, except in Tamale—being (exclusive of Tamale) 7 only (3 of them from Walewale, 2 from Sandema). It seems that, except in Tamale, there were few cattle traders who specialized in buying on a large scale in the same centre from year to year. This was associated with the fact that many large cattle-traders are non-resident in the buying area, but travel there to buy—this question will be further examined below.

During the short period covered by the statistics, there was a remarkable increase in the proportion of the trade handled by the largest bringers. In 1964–5 there were about[1] 22 bringers[2] who brought 100 cattle or more to Kumasi in 1964–5, compared with only about 6 such bringers in 1962–3; these 22 bringers handled nearly a third of all the Northern Ghanaian cattle brought to Kumasi. The largest of the 22 traders was a Dagomba man who had brought at least 592 cattle from 4 different centres, 444 of them from Yendi. There were altogether 8 traders who had brought 200 cattle or more—they were all Dagomba or Mamprusi men: if it is assumed that the average head of cattle sold for £30—a sum which was certainly on the low side, as prices were very high in 1965—then the turnover of each of these 8 bringers was at least £6,000 annually.

Reference has already been made to the myth that most cattle-traders are Hausa. In fact, as Table 5.13 shows, hardly any of them were Hausa and the group of bringers was ethnically very mixed.[3] The largest group consisted of Dagomba and Mamprusi traders,[4] who made up at least a third of the total in 1964–5. The next largest group in 1964–5 consisted of the Wala[5] (69 bringers) and the Frafra[6] and Kusasi (60 bringers).

[1] The element of estimation in the figures (see p. 111, n. 2) should be constantly borne in mind.
[2] There was no duplication in this list. Any bringer who failed to buy more than 30 cattle *in any one centre* was not included in the list—which was compiled by totalling purchases in all centres by 'large bringers' who bought more than 30 in any one centre.
[3] Bringers are classified in Table 5.13 according to the manner in which they classified themselves at Kumasi market—or, perhaps, in some instances, as others classified them. As is well known, the label by which a man is addressed when travelling may not be one which he would dream of using when at home.
[4] Dagomba certainly greatly outnumbered Mamprusi bringers, perhaps in the ratio of about 5 to 1.
[5] 'Wala' is almost meaningless as the name of an ethnic group, but at least it connotes some connexion with the Wa area—where the population is ethnically very mixed.
[6] The Tallensi and other neighbouring ethnic groups, tend to designate themselves 'Frafra' when away from home.

TABLE 5.13. *Ethnic classification of bringers of cattle to Kumasi*

| | Numbers of bringers whose ethnic group was stated | | Estimated addition[a] | | Total | |
|---|---|---|---|---|---|---|
| | 1962–3 | 1964–5 | 1962–3 | 1964–5 | 1962–3 | 1964–5 |
| **E. and W. Dagomba and Mamprusi** | | | | | | |
| Dagomba | 54 | 96 | } 51 | } 98 | } 124 | } 215 |
| Mamprusi | 19 | 21 | | | | |
| **North-west** | | | | | | |
| Wala | 31 | 45 | 16 | 24 | 47 | 69 |
| Dagarti | 6 | 6 | — | — | 6 | 6 |
| Sissala | 10 | 7 | — | — | 10 | 7 |
| Grunshi | 3 | 7 | — | — | 3 | 7 |
| Wangara | 3 | 2 | — | — | 3 | 2 |
| | | | | | 69 | 91 |
| **North-east** | | | | | | |
| Builsa | 10 | 6 | 15 | 8 | 25 | 14 |
| Frafra, Kusasi | 12 | 36 | 63 | 24 | 75 | 60 |
| 'Kassena-Nankani'[b] | — | — | 19 | 10 | 19 | 10 |
| Busanga | 1 | 2 | — | — | 1 | 2 |
| Gruma[c] | 3 | — | — | — | 3 | — |
| Tallensi | — | 1 | — | — | — | 1 |
| | | | | | 123 | 87 |
| **Gonja** | | | | | | |
| Gonja | 10 | 8 | — | — | 10 | 8 |
| **Brong-Ahafo** | | | | | | |
| Banda | 5 | 19 | — | — | 5 | 19 |
| **Non-Ghanaian[d]** | | | | | | |
| Mossi | 16 | 9 | — | — | 16 | 9 |
| Fulani | 14 | 45 | — | — | 14 | 45 |
| Gao | 1 | 1 | — | — | 1 | 1 |
| Zabrama | 1 | 8 | — | — | 1 | 8 |
| Hausa | 10 | 12 | — | — | 10 | 12 |
| 'Lagos'[e] | — | 13 | — | — | — | 13 |
| Kotokoli | — | 1 | — | — | — | 1 |
| | | | | | 42 | 89 |
| Total of above | 209 | 345 | 164 | 164 | 373 | 509 |
| Not known | | | | | 75 | 98 |
| Grand Total | | | | | 448 | 607 |

NOTES

*General*—See p. 116, n. 3.

a These additions relate solely to those few buying centres where it was quite clear from the names that most of the bringers were of local origin; it there seemed reasonable to regard all those whose origin was not stated as being local, given that strangers, such as Fulani, always liked to state their ethnic origin.

b Natives of Kassena-Nankani, whose ethnic group is unknown.

c Not necessarily natives of the North-east, though included here as they bought the cattle in that area.

d Some of these men are likely to be Ghanaian citizens even though they chose to denote themselves as Hausa, etc.

e In Ghana 'Lagos' is a common name for Yoruba men, irrespective of their local town of origin.

The number of traders of non-Ghanaian origin had risen strikingly between the years—from (at least) 42 to 89; in the latter year nearly half of these men were designated in the records as 'Fulani'.

The list of the 22 largest bringers included 10 Dagomba, 4 Mamprusi and 4 Wala traders.

In some buying centres most of the traders belonged to the same ethnic group, being then usually local men, though not necessarily permanently resident in the cattle-buying centre; in others they formed a very mixed group ethnically, many of whom had, presumably, travelled to the centre to buy. The two most highly commercialized Sections, the North-west and Western Dagomba, provided an interesting contrast: in the former the bringers were drawn from many different ethnic groups and competition was, presumably, very strong: in the latter, most bringers were Dagomba while some were Mamprusi—although large bringers had been establishing an increasing hold on the trade (Tamale was one of the few centres where a substantial proportion of the large traders were the same men in the two years), there had still been much opportunity for the small man.

The Notes on Buying Centres (see the Appendix, p. 121) deal, in more detail, with the ethnic classification of bringers of cattle from different buying centres.

The North-east (the least commercialized Section) is seen to be different from other Sections in various ways. The number of bringers from the North-east (see Table 5.11) actually fell (from 183 to 145) between the two years, though the figures for all other Sections rose. Bringers from the North-east were, on average, smaller than those from elsewhere: the average bringer handled 15 cattle in the earlier year and 20 in the later—the corresponding figures for the North as a whole having been 20 and 27. Table 5.14 shows that at least two-thirds of all bringers were of North-eastern origin. It appeared that only 2 of the 22 largest bringers—those who handled 100 cattle or more—brought any cattle from the North-east: nearly all the wealthiest traders had concentrated on buying elsewhere.

To summarize, the changes that were associated with the increase in Northern Ghanaian exports to Kumasi from 9,146 cattle (in 1962–3) to 15,894 cattle (in 1964–5), were:

(i) A less than proportionate increase in the number of bringers involved;

(ii) A higher proportion of the trade having been handled by the large bringers (over 30 cattle each);

(iii) A very much higher proportion of the trade having been handled by the very large bringers (over 100 cattle each);

(iv) An increase in the number (and proportion) of traders of non-Ghanaian origin;

TABLE 5.14. *Ethnic classification of bringers of cattle to Kumasi from the North-east*

| | | (number of bringers) | |
|---|---|---|---|
| | | 1962–3 | 1964–5 |
| North-eastern origin | Frafra | 74 ⎫ | 55 ⎫ |
| | Builsa | 25 ⎪ | 14 ⎪ |
| | 'Kassena-Nankani' | 19 ⎬120 | 10 ⎬87 |
| | Busanga | 1 ⎪ | 2 ⎪ |
| | Grunshi | 1 ⎭ | 6 ⎭ |
| Other Northern Ghanaians | Dagomba and Mamprusi | 10 ⎫ | 19 ⎫ |
| | Gonja | 3 ⎪ | 2 ⎪ |
| | Sissala | 2 ⎬18 | 1 ⎬22 |
| | Dagarti and Wala | 2 ⎪ | — ⎪ |
| | Wangara | 1 ⎭ | — ⎭ |
| Non-Northern Ghanaians | Mossi | 10 ⎫ | 3 ⎫ |
| | Hausa | 4 ⎪ | — ⎪ |
| | 'Lagos' | — ⎬17 | 2 ⎬16 |
| | Fulani | — ⎪ | 6 ⎪ |
| | Other non-Northern Ghanaians | 3 ⎭ | 5 ⎭ |
| | Not known | 28 | 20 |
| | Total | 183 | 145 |

N.B. See notes on Table 5.13.

TABLE 5.15. *Ethnic classification of 'large bringers' of cattle to Kumasi from the North-east*

| | | Number of cattle brought (number of large bringers in parentheses) | |
|---|---|---|---|
| | Ethnic classification | 1962–3 | 1964–5 |
| North-east | Frafra | 334 (7) | 280 (7) |
| | Builsa | 192 (3) | 248 (3) |
| | 'Kassena-Nankani' | 43 (1) | — |
| | Mossi | 43 (1) | 38 (1) |
| | Sissala | — | 54 (1) |
| | Dagomba | — | 193 (4) |
| | Grunshi | — | 171 (2) |
| | Not known | 40 (1) | 243 (5) |
| | Total | 652 (13) | 1,225 (23) |

N.B. See notes on Table 5.13. (There is an element of estimation in the figures.)

(v) Preservation of the position of small bringers (making no more than one delivery of cattle annually) in all buying centres.

Perhaps the most important conclusion is that, at least so far as particular buying centres were concerned,[1] the cattle bringers *were a changing group as between the years*: outside Tamale, only 7 of the large bringers from any buying centre in 1964–5 had also been large bringers from that centre in the earlier year: in 1964–5 there were 13 large bringers of cattle from Wa, none of whom had been large bringers from that buying centre in 1962–3, and the same applied to the 6 large bringers from Bolgatanga in the later year.

The extreme seasonality of Northern Ghanaian exports to all destinations has already been examined in Section III; Northern Ghanaian exports to Kumasi market were even more seasonal, in the sense that they fell proportionately even lower in the 'off-season', especially in January to March— Tables 5.5 and 5.10 and Graphs 1 and 10, should be compared. In the three years 1962 to 1964 about four-fifths of all arrivals of Northern Ghanaian cattle were received in the five months May to September.

There is clearly a strong inverse relationship between arrivals of imported cattle at Kumasi market and arrivals of local (Northern Ghanaian) cattle— see Graph 10 and Table 5.10. Arrivals of imported cattle were far larger in quantity than those of Northern Ghanaian cattle—and proportionately even greater in value as Northern cattle usually weigh no more than 450–500 lb. As, in addition, the imported cattle (a high proportion of which came from as far away as Mali)[2] took much longer to arrive[3] from the place where they had been bought from rearers than did Northern Ghanaian cattle, nearly all of which came through quickly by lorry, and as such cattle *could not be brought down during the rainy season*, so arrivals of imported cattle were appropriately regarded as the short-term *given factor*, arrivals of local cattle then being the *variable*. In 1962 and 1963 arrivals of imports began to fall right off in March and remained low until October;[4] arrivals of Northern Ghanaian cattle in those years rose steeply after a lag of about 2 months. In 1964, arrivals of imported cattle reached their peak in April and the 'gap' which resulted from the fall in May was at once filled by arrivals of Northern Ghanaian animals. While fluctuations in total monthly arrivals (imports

---

[1] The extent to which cattle buyers at all centres taken together were a constantly changing group cannot be indicated: but it is clear from the records that many buyers who bought in the earlier year did not buy (at least for the Kumasi market) in the later year.

[2] In 1964 total recorded Ghanaian imports of cattle were 77,568, of which 41,236 were recorded as coming from Upper Volta and 30,257 from Mali: in that year, when imports from Nigeria were negligible owing to the closure of the Ghanaian frontier with Togo, most of the imported cattle passed through Kumasi market.

[3] Most of the cattle were *driven* as far as the Ghanaian frontier: those destined for Kumasi market then nearly all proceeded onwards by lorry. See Gould (7).

[4] The severe floods of September 1963 probably also affected the trade in October.

plus Northern Ghanaian cattle) were not eliminated by the Northern Ghanaian response to the demand created by the falling-off in arrivals of imports,[1] yet as Table 5.10 shows, average total arrivals for 1962, 1963 and 1964 in the peak month (December) were only about half as much again as in the lowest month (June)[2]—7,650 cattle (December), 4,877 cattle (June). An extraordinary responsiveness to demand in Kumasi is here revealed.

## APPENDIX

NOTES ON BUYING CENTRES FOR KUMASI MARKET: THE TWO YEARS (1962–3 AND 1964–5) COMPARED (Table 5.12)

BAWKU (N.E.). Bawku is in Kusasi, very near the north-eastern frontier. It is the place where most *imported* cattle are loaded on lorries for transport south to Kumasi. There was a slight drop (403 to 362) in 'local exports' to Kumasi between the two years and a large drop in the number of bringers concerned—from 33 to 20. The percentage of cattle handled by the large bringers nearly doubled. The bringers are ethnically a very mixed group indeed—as would be expected in a place so important as an international trade centre. However, more than one-third of the bringers in 1964–5 were Kusasi men—the remainder being Dagomba, Mamprusi, Mossi, Hausa, Fulani, Busanga (each one).

BOLE (Gonja). The increase in local exports from 150 to 384 was associated with an increase in the number of bringers from 14 to 31; most of these bringers made only one delivery to Kumasi and none bought as many as 30 cattle. They were of mixed ethnic origin—Banda (7), Gonja (6), Wala (5), Fulani (2), Zabrama (1), Sissala (1), not known (7). Presumably most of the bringers travelled to Bole in order to buy. Two of the Gonja traders bought in both years.

BOLGATANGA (N.E.). Purchase of cattle for the Kumasi Market fell somewhat (from 692 to 572), the number of bringers falling more than proportionately (43 to 25). In 1964–5 the 6 'large bringers' handled 49% of all the cattle: none of these 6 bringers was the same as any of the 4 large bringers in the earlier year. Seventeen out of the total of 25 bringers (1964–5) made one delivery only. Most of the bringers were probably local (Frafra) people; there were otherwise 4 Dagomba, 1 Hausa and 1 Mamprusi.

CHEREPONI (E. Dagomba). An increase in local exports to Kumasi from 48 to 182 was associated with an increase in the number of bringers from 2 to 10. In 1964–5 three of the bringers were Hausa: otherwise there were Fulani (1), Mossi (1), not known (5).

GAMBAGA (Mamprusi). The great increase in exports to Kumasi from 323 to 790 was associated with an increase in the number of bringers from 14 to 31. The cattle bringers were a different group in 1964–5 from that in 1962–3. Thus none

---

[1] There is no evidence of any great seasonality in the demand for meat at Kumasi, or at the other centres supplied by Kumasi—in 1962 and 1963 only about a quarter of all the cattle which passed through Kumasi market were for slaughter there.

[2] The September figure is omitted owing to the floods in that month in 1963.

of the 7 large bringers in 1964–5 (they handled 54% of the cattle) were large bringers in the Kumasi market in 1962–3: they were Mamprusi (2), Frafra (1), Dagomba (1), Fulani (1), not known (2). The total number of Mamprusi bringers in 1964–5 is not clear: otherwise there were 6 Fulani, 3 Frafra, 1 Hausa, 1 Tallensi, 1 Zabrama, 1 Wala and 1 Dagomba, none of whom had exported to Kumasi in the earlier year. Gambaga, being situated on the Great North Road, had begun to attract buyers away from other centres.

GUSHIEGO (E. Dagomba). The great increase in local exports to Kumasi (23 to 293 cattle) was associated with an increase in the number of bringers from 2 to 15. Most of the bringers were Dagomba.

KUMBUNGU (W. Dagomba). Local exports remained constant (169 to 182). The bringers were mainly Dagomba, presumably from nearby Tamale.

LAMBUSSIE (N.W.). The origin of the bringers was not known.

LAWRA (N.W.). Local exports to Kumasi rose from 853 to 936; the number of bringers, 37 to 47, rose more than in proportion. The 6 large bringers (1964–5) brought only 38% of the cattle—a lower percentage than in any other buying centre of comparable importance. In general, the statistics suggest a highly competitive situation: (*a*) only 2 of the 9 (known) Wala bringers in 1964–5 had sent cattle to Kumasi in the earlier year; (*b*) the bringers for the Kumasi Market were a very mixed ethnic group and were nearly all newcomers to the trade in Lawra—they were Wala (9), Banda (5), 'Lagos' (6), Fulani (6), Zabrama (2), Mossi (1), Wangara (1), Dagomba (1).

MOGONORI (N.E.). The reason for the great fall (404 to 70) in local exports to Kumasi from this town on the frontier, north of Bawku, is not known; it might be, for instance, that all available lorry transport was employed for imported animals, or that local cattle loaded at Mogonori went to some market other than Kumasi. It is probable that in 1962–3 most of the bringers were local men.

NANDOM (N.W.). Some special factor, such as the opening of a new office of the Animal Health Division, must have accounted for the sudden emergence of Nandom as a large exporting centre for the Kumasi market—exports to that market having risen from nil in 1962 to 903 in 1964–5. Clearly Nandom replaced neighbouring Lambussie (exports from which fell from 93 to nil) and it possibly took away some business from Tumu, further east, exports from which fell from 515 to 357. However this may be, a host of traders of very mixed ethnic origin surged in to Nandom to buy. Six of the 9 large bringers (who brought 48% of all the cattle) were Wala (there were 10 Wala bringers altogether): other bringers included Fulani (6), Dagomba (5), Banda (3), Mossi (2), Zabrama (2), 'Lagos' (2), Dagarti (1), not known (10). Twenty-four of the 41 bringers made only one delivery to Kumasi.

NAVRONGO (N.E.) Some special factor (as with Nandom) must have accounted, at least in part, for the increase in exports to Kumasi from 77 to 536. However, it is unlikely that, in this case, the growth was mainly accounted for by an insurge of stranger-traders, for a high proportion of the bringers were probably local—Grunshie and Frafra. Most of the 6 large bringers, who accounted for 65% of total purchases in 1964–5, were local.

PAGA (N.E.). Perhaps some of Paga's Kumasi trade, which fell from 287 to 204 cattle, was taken over by neighbouring Navrongo. The bringers were mainly local men. Five of the 14 bringers in the two years were the same men.

PONG-TAMALE (E. Dagomba). Pong-Tamale is on the Great North Road and started to develop as an additional loading point to Savelugu and Tamale, slightly further south.

PUSIGA (N.E.). Both in terms of the number of cattle and of the number of bringers, Pusiga's trade with Kumasi declined (328 to 210 cattle, 22 to 13 bringers). Pusiga is on the frontier near Bawku and transport difficulties may have accounted for the reduced trade—see Mogonori. The cattle bringers are an ethnically mixed group.

SANDEMA (N.E.). The cattle trade with Kumasi remained at a constant level. While more than half of the bringers were local men (Builsa and Frafra), there were also (1964–5), Hausa, Mossi, Lagos, Dagomba, Mamprusi, Gonja and Fulani bringers. Only 2 of the 10 Builsa bringers in 1962–3 also exported cattle to Kumasi in 1964–5: 2 of these were large bringers, one of whom exported 132 cattle to Kumasi. Eighteen of the 24 bringers in 1964–5 made only one delivery to Kumasi.

TAMALE (W. Dagomba). Exports to Kumasi from Tamale rose greatly from 1,928 to 3,164 head, the number of bringers rising nearly correspondingly (44 to 64). Three-quarters (76%) of all the exports to Kumasi were handled by the 23 large bringers in 1964–5, the corresponding percentage for the earlier year being 65. In 1962–3, only one bringer took more than 100 cattle to Kumasi, but in the later year there were 8 such bringers, the largest of whom exported 428 animals. Most of the traders were Dagomba, though this did not necessarily mean that they were mainly resident in Tamale: there was also a significant number of Mamprusi. Of the 15 large bringers in 1962–3, as many as 9 were again large bringers in 1964–5. However, there was still room for the small trader, or even the cattle rearer-exporter, in Tamale: in 1964–5 half of the bringers (32 out of 64) made a single delivery to Kumasi.

TUMU (N.W.). Exports to Kumasi fell from 515 to 357—see Nandom. This fall was associated with a drop in the number of bringers from 26 to 16; with a fall in the percentage handled by large bringers; and with the presence of fewer stranger-traders. Whether in 1964–5 most of the bringers were local men is not clear.

WA (N.W.). Exports to Kumasi rose from 1,031 to 1,724 and the number of bringers rose nearly correspondingly—45 to 63. At least a third of the bringers, in each year, was Wala. Of the 13 known Wala bringers in 1962–3, 7 again took cattle to Kumasi in 1964–5. The next largest ethnic group was the Fulani; 3 of the 9 Fulani bringers in 1962–3 were among the 7 Fulani bringers in 1964–5. Many traders clearly travelled to Wa to buy and they were an ethnically mixed group: apart from the Wala and Fulani (who were not all necessarily resident in Wa), there were (1964–5) Banda (4), Dagomba (4), Hausa (2), Wangara (1), Zabrama (1), Kokotoli (1), Gao (1) Sissala (1). That the Wa market was basically highly competitive (providing, in this respect, a contrast to Tamale) is shown by the fact that none of the 9 large bringers in 1962–3 was included in the list of 14 large bringers in 1964–5. There was much scope for the small bringer in Wa (as in Tamale): 37 out of the 63 bringers in 1964–5 made only one delivery to Kumasi.

WALEWALE (Mamprusi). Walewale is on the Great North Road so that it was to be expected that its exports would rise more than those of Gambaga, the other main Mamprusi cattle centre, which is not so situated. The number of bringers rose in the same proportion as exports. Probably most of the bringers were Mamprusi or Dagomba, but the 1964–5 list included 5 Fulani, 1 Hausa, 1 Wala and 1 'Lagos'. Three of the 7 large bringers in 1962–3 were also on the list for 1964–5.

YENDI (E. Dagomba). In 1964–5, when exports to Kumasi rose from 409 to 1,192, Yendi suddenly emerged as the centre where the highest percentage of the trade (84%) was in the hands of large bringers—2 of them, both Dagomba, buying respectively 444 and 389 cattle. (Yendi's trade had not formerly been to any significant extent with Kumasi and, as Table 5.11 shows, Eastern Dagomba's total local exports *to all markets* had risen proportionately less in this period than those from all other Sections except the North-east.) The Yendi trade was dominated by Dagomba bringers. Good opportunities remained for the small man, 14 out of 21 bringers having made a single delivery to Kumasi market.

ZEBILLA (N.E.). Exports rose from 12 to 298 cattle and bringers from 2 to 22. Nearly all the bringers in 1964–5 were local Kumasi or Frafra men, 15 out of 22 of whom made but a single delivery to Kumasi.

SECTION V

The seasonality of local exports: further consideration

But the Northern responsiveness to the strength of demand in Kumasi was not high in all areas. In particular it was not high in the North-east, although that Section sent as much as 66 % of its total local exports to Kumasi—compared with 71 % for Western Dagomba and 49 % for the North-west (Table 5.11). Table 5.16 shows that the seasonal patterns of local exports to Kumasi from some North-eastern buying centres were quite at variance with the seasonal pattern for Northern local exports to Kumasi from all sources. Thus, local exports from Bolgatanga to Kumasi were trivial in May, June and July (when demand was so great in Kumasi owing to the falling-off in imported supplies), and tended to be as high in November and December as in August. The figures for Navrongo showed a similar pattern. On the other hand, local exports from Sandema in 1964–5 (though not in 1962–3) were very responsive to the high Kumasi demand in May, June and July.

There are, therefore, two main questions:

(i) How did it come about that local exports from certain buying centres, such as Tamale, exhibited such an acute seasonality?

(ii) Why were local exports from the North-east generally (and from

TABLE 5.16. *Monthly arrivals at Kumasi cattle market from centres in the North-east*

(Number of cattle)

| Month of arrival at Kumasi | Mogonori 1962–3 | Navrongo 1964–5 | Sandema | | Bolgatanga | | Bawku | |
|---|---|---|---|---|---|---|---|---|
| | | | 1962–3 | 1964–5 | 1962–3 | 1964–5 | 1962–3 | 1964–5 |
| May | 21 | 2 | 15 | 127 | 13 | — | 5 | 7 |
| June | 24 | 16 | 44 | 203 | 5 | — | 5 | 63 |
| July | — | 49 | 189 | 98 | 50 | 15 | 76 | 16 |
| August | 143 | 54 | 215 | 56 | 151 | 101 | 66 | 112 |
| September | 74 | 92 | — | 6 | 49 | 96 | 84 | 26 |
| October | — | 98 | — | 22 | 49 | 81 | 55 | 53 |
| November | 19 | 24 | 24 | 12 | 155 | 74 | 21 | — |
| December | 40 | 163 | 48 | 22 | 182 | 67 | 53 | — |
| January | — | 10 | 35 | 12 | 6 | 50 | 37 | 1 |
| February | 21 | 16 | — | 7 | 16 | 24 | — | 85[a] |
| March | 14 | — | 14 | — | — | 18 | 1 | — |
| April | 48 | 12 | — | — | 6 | 46 | — | — |
| | 404 | 536 | 584 | 565 | 682 | 572 | 403 | 362 |

[a] 80 cattle were brought to Kumasi market by one trader on one day.

certain buying centres in particular) neither acutely seasonal nor conformable to the usual seasonal pattern?

Before attempting to deal with these questions, I shall deal with two related matters—seasonality in local slaughter of cattle and in local exports of small livestock (sheep and goats).

While I was unable, in the time available, to collect comprehensive monthly statistics relating to official slaughter of cattle for meat, such statistics as were made available showed that the rate of slaughter was not notably seasonal—quarterly figures for 1964 for Western Dagomba (and for Tamale within that Section) are shown in Table 5.17, and monthly figures (1964) for the North-west Section are shown in Table 5.18.[1]

Local exports of sheep and goats from Northern Ghana were not nearly as seasonal as exports of cattle, as Table 5.20 and Graph 11 show.[2] This is remarkable, as Ghanaian imports of sheep and goats were even more seasonal

[1] The number of cattle slaughtered at licensed slaughterhouses in the North rose from 8,441 in 1950, to 10,925 in 1955, to 13,718 in 1960, to 20,170 in 1963 (Sources, files at Pong-Tamale and *Ghana Statistical Yearbook, 1961*, Central Office of Statistics, 1962). Meat consumption per head, on the basis of the official figures, rose from 14 cattle per 1,000 of the human population in 1962 to 16 per 1,000 in 1963—see Table 5.19. Meat consumption, according to these figures, was highest in Western Dagomba and lowest in the North-east and Gonja: but there was much more unofficial slaughter by butchers in some areas than in others, and the official figures for sparsely populated Gonja were probably the most defective of all.

[2] Whether statistics of local exports of sheep and goats were as reliable as the corresponding data for cattle, one does not know—though one presumes they were not.

TABLE 5.17. *Local exports and official slaughter of cattle, 1964*

(Number of cattle)

| | W. Dagomba/Mamprusi (Total) | | | Tamale (W. Dagomba) | | |
|---|---|---|---|---|---|---|
| | Local exports | Slaughter | Local exports and slaughter | Local exports | Slaughter | Local exports and slaughter |
| January to March | 355 | 1,212 | 1,567 | 48 | 1,130 | 1,178 |
| April to June | 4,183 | 1,512 | 5,695 | 2,204 | 1,446 | 3,650 |
| July to September | 3 592 | 1,752 | 5,344 | 1,617 | 1,616 | 3,233 |
| October to December | 1,132 | 2,052 | 3,184 | 793 | 1,845 | 2,638 |
| Total | 9,262 | 6,528 | 15,790 | 4,662 | 6,037 | 10,699 |

N.B. The total figures for W. Dagomba/Mamprusi include Tamale.

TABLE 5.18. *Monthly cattle slaughter at licensed slaughterhouses, North-west Veterinary Section*

(Number of cattle)

| 1964 | | 1964 | |
|---|---|---|---|
| January | 434 | July | 251 |
| February | 377 | August | 257 |
| March | 412 | September | 247 |
| April | 797 | October | 412 |
| May | 425 | November | 264 |
| June | 416 | December | 232 |
| | | Total | 4,524 |

TABLE 5.19. *Licensed cattle slaughter and meat consumption*

| | Number of cattle | | Human popu-lation 000's | Annual meat consump-tion per thousand persons (No. of cattle) | |
|---|---|---|---|---|---|
| | 1962 (1) | 1963 (2) | 1960 (3) | 1962 (1)/(3) | 1963 (2)/(3) |
| Veterinary Section | | | | | |
| North-east | 3,614 | 5,909 | 469 | 8 | 13 |
| North-west | 6,263 | 4,464 | 289 | 22 | 15 |
| Eastern Dagomba | 2,199 | 2,844 | 168 | 13 | 17 |
| Western Dagomba | 5,066 | 5,523 | 245 | 21 | 23 |
| Gonja | 1,405 | 1,430 | 118 | 12 | 12 |
| Total: Northern Ghana | 18,547 | 20,170 | 1,289 | 14 | 16 |

TABLE 5.20. *Monthly local exports of sheep and goats, N. Ghana*

| | Sheep | | Goats | |
|---|---|---|---|---|
| | 1962 | 1963 | 1962 | 1963 |
| January | 3,366 | 3,464 | 3,106 | 3,196 |
| February | 2,652 | 2,871 | 2,565 | 2,678 |
| March | 2,912 | 3,821 | 2,500 | 3,240 |
| April | 4,027 | 5,392 | 2,934 | 3,772 |
| May | 4,300 | 3,564 | 2,958 | 4,252 |
| June | 2,842 | 4,092 | 3,373 | 4,939 |
| July | 1,286 | 3,740 | 2,741 | 4,868 |
| August | 3,350 | 4,165 | 2,367 | 3,859 |
| September | 13,927[a] | 1,864 | 1,526 | 1,374 |
| October | 1,880 | 2,342 | 1,101 | 600 |
| November | 2,015 | 2,088 | 1,258 | 2,187 |
| December | 4,152 | 5,193 | 3,397 | 4,790 |
| Total: | 46,709 | 42,596 | 29,826 | 39,755 |

[a] Reference to Table 5.21 shows that these exports must have been mainly from the North-east. Was there a famine that year? If so, why were cattle exports in that month much lower than in August? Perhaps the figure is erroneous.

TABLE 5.21. *Local exports, official slaughter and take-off of sheep and goats*

(Number of animals)

| | 1962 | | | 1963 | | |
|---|---|---|---|---|---|---|
| | Local export (1) | Official slaughter (2) | Take-off (1)+(2) | Local export (4) | Official slaughter (5) | Take-off (4)+(5) |
| Veterinary Section | Sheep | | | Sheep | | |
| North-east | 35,588 | 2,669 | 38,257 | 30,292 | 1,289 | 31,581 |
| North-west | 3,320 | 956 | 4,276 | 5,241 | 5,146 | 10,387 |
| Gonja | 132 | 540 | 672 | 464 | 446 | 910 |
| E. Dagomba | 6,814 | 1,670 | 8,484 | 4,480 | 2,105 | 6,585 |
| W. Dagomba/Mamprusi | 855 | 6,720 | 7,575 | 2,119 | 7,285 | 9,404 |
| Total: Northern Ghana | 46,709 | 12,555 | 59,264 | 42,596 | 16,271 | 58,867 |
| | Goats | | | Goats | | |
| North-east | 19,859 | 14,963 | 34,822 | 23,071 | 8,569 | 31,640 |
| North-west | 5,152 | 9,968 | 15,120 | 10,089 | 16,761 | 26,850 |
| Gonja | 545 | 1,521 | 2,066 | 1,695 | 1,329 | 3,024 |
| E. Dagomba | 3,750 | 6,740 | 10,490 | 3,141 | 6,470 | 9,611 |
| W. Dagomba/Mamprusi | 520 | 10,857 | 11,377 | 1,759 | 12,223 | 13,982 |
| Total: Northern Ghana | 29,826 | 44,049 | 73,875 | 39,755 | 45,352 | 85,107 |

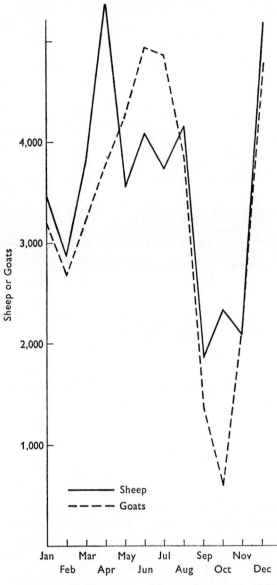

11  Monthly local exports of sheep and goats, 1963. Table 5.20

than imports of cattle:[1] sheep imports (which were much more valuable than goat imports, the animals being far larger) reached their monthly peak in April in each of the three years 1962 to 1964, to the degree that 23% of *all* the sheep imported in those years were imported in the month of April. Imports fell off most abruptly in May and did not pick up again until the later months of the year.[2]

Official slaughter figures for sheep and goats are given in Table 5.21: unfortunately, unofficial slaughter of sheep and goats for meat plus ceremonial slaughter is likely to be so high in relation to slaughter at official slaughter-houses, especially in some localities, as to make these figures of little value.

The strong association between the degree of commercialization of cattle rearing and the degree of seasonality of local exports has already been emphasized. An important cause of the acute seasonality has been shown to be the increased demand for cattle at Kumasi in the middle months of the year, consequent upon a falling-off in imported supplies. Presumably, Northern Ghanaian cattle command a better price during these months than at other times of the year, when total supplies at Kumasi are greater. Therefore, it may be argued, both rearers and traders would prefer, other things being equal, to do business at that time.

Certainly, also, there are other factors which facilitate such a sudden response to the increased Kumasi demand in April and May. Except in the far North the first rains are apt to come as early as March, so that by the end of April much of the weight that was lost by the cattle during the dry season may have been regained, with a consequent rise in value of the stock.[3] Secondly, those rearers who were in such urgent need of cash during the dry season that they were obliged to sell lean animals would often find the local butchers prepared to buy, since (as we have seen) the local demand for meat continues strongly throughout the year—such rearers would not have to resort to exporting during the off-season. (There is also sometimes the possibility of selling to traders who buy animals for fattening.[4]) Thirdly, the

[1] Local exports of sheep from Northern Ghana in 1962 and 1963 amounted to about two-thirds of the total quantity imported by Ghana from other countries—but much less than two-thirds in value; the corresponding proportion for the quantity of sheep was less than a half. Annual imports of sheep averaged about 63,000 in 1962–4, the corresponding figure for goats being about 87,000. (Both in Ghana and Nigeria the importance of sheep and goats as a source of meat, skins and manure has been grossly neglected in the literature—see Oppong (15).)

[2] Statistics of arrivals of sheep and goats at Kumasi sheep market were not available to me; but as there was only one other sheep market of any importance in Ghana (that at Accra, which handled, I think, far fewer animals than that at Kumasi), seasonality of total imports was bound to be reflected in seasonality of arrivals at Kumasi.

[3] West African cattle very seldom receive any supplementary feed (other than salt or natron), being entirely dependent on grazing.

[4] The suddenness of the rise in local exports suggests that this might have been fairly common practice among richer traders.

increased Kumasi demand comes at the very time when farmers are apt to experience an increased need for cash both because their food stores are becoming exhausted and because they require finance for farming—and perhaps some of them realize their cattle-capital to finance their current expenditure.

This third point, which might seem the most obvious of all, has been carefully expressed, so as to read almost hypothetically. If poverty were indeed an important cause of acute seasonality, then it would have been expected that local exports from the North-east, where the average standard of living was presumably lower than elsewhere,[1] would have been more, not less, seasonal than from the North as a whole.

But account should be taken here of the pattern of seasonality. Sheer poverty—as distinct from the need for cash to finance farming—grows as the farming season progresses, so the volume of poverty-relieving cattle selling would be expected to be greater in the weeks immediately preceding the early millet harvest—say in June or July. But our data show (Graph 5) that total local exports from the North-east often reached their peak later than this—though something of a tendency for exports to Kumasi to increase in the month of August is discernible from the erratically moving figures in Table 5.16.

Nor could local exports of sheep and goats from the North-east have been notably seasonal, as Table 5.21, read in conjunction with Table 5.20, shows. (About two-thirds of total Northern local exports of sheep and goats were from the North-east.)

In what other ways was the North-east known to be 'different'? The number of cattle per head of human population was slightly lower in the North-east than in Northern Ghana generally—but as the average showed as much variation within the North-east as within Northern Ghana generally, this was hardly a significant variable. Irrelevant, also, was the greater use of oxen-drawn ploughs in the North-east than elsewhere for the number of plough-oxen is insignificantly small in relation to the total cattle population. Where else should one look?

I suggest, as a hypothesis, that one reason why North-eastern exports (even to Kumasi) were less acutely seasonal than Northern exports generally was that the bringers of cattle from that Section were less efficient, and lacking in finance. We have already seen (p. 118) that bringers of cattle from the North-east to Kumasi were 'smaller' than average bringers and that an unusually high proportion of them were resident in the buying centres, and did not travel in from elsewhere to buy. I suggest that it is possible that many of these local traders lacked the finance to achieve a sudden rapid increase in

[1] At any rate in the areas of high population density in the extreme North-east.

the rate of purchase in the middle months of the year before the harvest and that, being non-specialists, many of them were tied by their own farming work until July or later. The same may have been true of Northern traders in sheep and goats—and hence their failure to fill the gap in supplies of small livestock resulting from the falling-off of imports in May.

Cattle-traders, as has been noted, usually pay full cash to cattle rearers at the time of purchase[1] and a trader who had bought a lorry-load of some 10 beasts would require capital of at least £200—£300. (As for the costs of transport, lorry-owners are often prepared to receive payment after sale of the loads.) Given that the buying process might take several weeks and that traders might have to wait about in Kumasi for full payment, it might have been that there were few resident North-eastern traders with adequate money *and* time to finance this trade until after the harvest was over.

It has already been noted that there is a tendency for take-off from the herds to be rather uniform within any District, even in those which, like localities in the North-west, are ethnically very diverse. This suggests that some general factor, such as the efficiency of cattle-traders, is of greater influence than the attitude of the owner towards selling his stock. Another piece of evidence would lead to the same conclusion: it is that there is no reason to believe that the owners of large herds are any more inclined to sell their animals than the owners of small herds.[2] Therefore, even if herds in the North-east were, on average, smaller than elsewhere, this is unlikely to have affected take-off.

But, of course, it must not be assumed that the penuriousness of North-eastern traders[3] was the only factor responsible for the curious timing of North-eastern exports to Kumasi market. In Tallensi country[4] October marks the beginning of the 'marriage season' and December the height of the 'ritual season' when there are many ceremonies: perhaps North-eastern peoples spend relatively more at these seasons than do other Northern peoples—but the ethnic diversity of the North-east is so great as to suggest

---

[1] This is what I invariably learnt in Kumasi, Prang, Western Dagomba, Wa and on the Accra Plains—and the same applied to sales by rearers to butchers. While, in general, farmers and other producers are much less willing to supply their goods on credit than are those primarily concerned with the distributive trade (thus, cattle-traders who supply butchers often do so on credit terms), this unwillingness might break down in the case of transactions involving kin, or if the buyers are well-known local residents who may then be regarded as selling 'on behalf of' the producer. It is not, therefore, beyond the bounds of possibility (though it *is* unlikely) that North-eastern cattle-traders were 'different', sometimes buying on terms involving full, or partial credit.

[2] In the Wa Division in the North-west and in the Kumbungu Division of Western Dagomba, where I examined some of the detailed cattle-census statistics, the ratio of male animals in the herds appeared not to be correlated with herd-size—see p. 136 for definition of 'herd'.

[3] Throughout this discussion I have been rather begging the question of whether most of the bringers from the North-east were, in fact, traders: perhaps more of them were rearers than in other parts of the North?

[4] See 'Food in the Domestic Economy of the Tallensi' by M. and S. L. Fortes, 1937 (4).

the inappropriateness of such an explanation.[1] Speculate as one may, it is certain that the traditional belief that Northern Ghanaian cattle rearers only sell when in dire extremity has been torn in shreds by this statistical analysis—as much in the North-east as elsewhere.

SECTION VI

Postscript: *some notes on the Northern Ghanaian cattle population and on cattle ownership*

The first census of livestock in the (then) Northern Territories was made in 1914 when only 16,000 cattle were counted: 'There was then only one Veterinary Officer on the establishment and during the war years he was on active service.'[2] The next census was in 1921 when the cattle population was given as 69,000. Between 1921 and 1931 active measures were taken to control rinderpest and contagious bovine pleuro-pneumonia, and the cattle population was recorded as rising to about 111,000. From 1930, when the first mass immunization campaign against rinderpest was started, the cattle population increased rapidly and in 1941 as many as 170,000 cattle were counted. During 1950 'a census and survey of all livestock' in the Northern Territories was made and cattle numbered 310,000.

It is probable that the 1952 livestock census was the first for which statistics by District were made available—see Table 5.22.

In 1958 the Chief Veterinary Officer announced that no comprehensive livestock census had been carried out since 1951–2[3] and that it was, therefore, time for another: this was not, in fact, conducted until 1959–60 on the basis of the statistical forms, classifying cattle by sex and maturity which are still in general use—see p. 90. Between 1954–5 and some date after 1959 no Annual Reports of the Veterinary Department were written and the results of the 1959–60 census were not available in the Pong-Tamale files[4]—the

---

[1] In this connexion, I am grateful to Mr Keith Hart for suggesting that the conventional shape of the Sandema (Builsa) graph of local exports (see Graph 9 and p. 102) may be associated with the fact that the Builsa have no bride-price, whereas with the Kusasi, Frafra and Kassena-Nankani the payment of bride-price undoubtedly influences the attitude to cattle—as, of course, it may likewise do in some localities outside the North-east. I am also grateful to Dr E. N. W. Oppong for pointing out that some of the local exports from the North-east (as well as from Gambaga) might have been imported cattle bought by traders there: this could partially account for the pronounced peak in local exports at Christmas, when imports are at full flood.

[2] From an unsigned minute dated 1950, in the files at Pong-Tamale. Although the figure of 16,000 is, presumably, hopelessly inaccurate, it at least suggests that the cattle population was very small.

[3] But in *Economic Survey, 1954* there was reference, p. 27, to the 'figure 1953 census' which had recorded the total cattle population as 421,000: perhaps this figure was an estimate.

[4] As the Ghanaian Veterinary headquarters had not, at that time, moved back from Pong-Tamale to Accra, it was not thought likely that the Accra files would fill the gap. (Accra had been the headquarters for about 5 years up to 1954 and again from 1960: the frequent transfers resulted in loss of files.)

TABLE 5.22. *Cattle census statistics*

(Number of cattle)

| | 1931[a] (1) | 1952 (2) | 1961–2[b] (3) | 1963[c] (4) | 1964 (5) | (5) as percentage of (3) |
|---|---|---|---|---|---|---|
| **Veterinary Sections and Districts** | | | | | | |
| **North-east** | | | | | | |
| Frafra | 12,000 | 35,000 | 21,105 | 31,251 | 30,878 | 146 |
| Kassena-Nankani | } 23,000 | 30,743 | 27,617 | 27,480 | 27,824 | 101 |
| Builsa | | 22,391 | 21,249 | 20,791 | 22,133 | 104 |
| Kusasi | 15,000 | 38,363 | 32,836 | 38,657 | 43,375 | 132 |
| | 50,000 | 126,497 | 102,807 | 118,179 | 124,210 | 121 |
| | | | | | | |
| **North-west** | | | | | | |
| Tumu | } 26,000 | 8,384 | 11,863 | | 12,129 | 102 |
| Lawra | | 39,366 | 50,525 | | 11,555 | } |
| Jirapa | | | | | 10,963 | } 71 |
| Nandom | | | | | 7,208 | } |
| Lambussie | } 11,000 | | | | 6,042 | |
| Nadawli | | } 35,506 | 39,139 | | 20,847 | } 132 |
| Wa | | | | | 30,812 | } |
| | 37,000 | 83,256 | 101,527 | | 99,556 | 98 |
| | | | | | | |
| **W. Dagomba/Mamprusi** | | | | | | |
| Tamale (W. Dagomba) | 11,000 | 26,490 | 42,371 | | 53,147 | 125 |
| Gambaga (Mamprusi) | } 2,000 | 21,198 | 31,605 | | 21,785 | } 112 |
| Walewale (Mamprusi) | | | | | 13,491 | |
| | 13,000 | 47,688 | 73,976 | | 88,423 | 119 |
| | | | | | | |
| **Eastern Dagomba/Nanumba** | | | | | | |
| Yendi | | 40,071 | 26,296 | | 10,047 | |
| Zabzugu | | | | | 5,181 | |
| Saboba | | | | | 11,838 | } 141 |
| Gushiegu | 10,000 | | | | 10,043 | |
| Chereponi | | | 9,897 | | 9,670 | 98 |
| Bimbilla (Nanumba) | | 5,918 | 10,677 | | 16,561 | 155 |
| | 10,000 | 45,989 | 46,870 | | 63,340 | 135 |
| | | | | | | |
| **Gonja** | | | | | | |
| Damongo | } 500 | 7,235 | 6,882 | | 7,206 | 105 |
| Bole | | | 13,491 | | 12,006 | 89 |
| Salaga | 500 | 4,229 | 3,833 | | 4,114 | 107 |
| | 1,000 | 11,464 | 24,206 | | 23,326 | 96 |
| Grand total | 111,000 | 314,894 | 349,386 | 389,202 | 398,855 | 114 |

[a] Estimates from *The Gold Coast, 1931*, by A. W. Cardinall, p. 102: it was stated (p. 101) that the Principal Veterinary Officer considered the estimates to be 'fairly accurate'. (The Districts are not necessarily entirely comparable with those for later years.)

[b] This census was presumably carried out over a period, but the dates were not stated in the files.

[c] Only the figures for the North-east Veterinary Section were extracted from the files at Pong-Tamale.

NOTE. The gaps in cols. (1)–(3) result from the tabulation of Districts as they were in 1964, though not earlier—see note on Table 5.3.

Ghana *Economic Survey 1960* stated (p. 28) that the total Ghanaian cattle population in 1960 was 480,000, but no regional breakdowns were published.

In 1962, 1963 and 1964 annual censuses were conducted and the cattle population showed further growth from about 350,000 in 1962 to about 400,000 in 1964.

The above account does little to inspire one with much confidence in the reliability of the censuses before the 1960s—though that of 1952 might have been of reasonable accuracy.

If any reliability is to be attached to the 1931 estimates (see Table 5.22), then the varying rates of growth up to 1964 in different Veterinary Sections are noteworthy. The North-east showed least growth—but then it accounted for nearly half the total Northern cattle population in 1931. Between 1962 and 1964 the high rate of growth (35%) in Eastern Dagomba is to be noted; the slight decline in the population in the North-west (and the large decline in the Wa District) could be accounted for by the increase in local exports.

When the 1960 human population is related to the 1964 cattle population it is found (see Table 5.23), that there is remarkably little variation in the ratio as between Veterinary Sections—the two extremes were 2·7 people per head of cattle in Eastern Dagomba and 5·1 in Gonja. (Rather surprisingly, there is as much variation in the ratio *within* the North-east—Builsa 2·3, Frafra 4·9—as within the North as a whole.) In order to allow for the varying rates of male migration from different Districts, an inverse ratio based on adult males (over 20 years) was calculated—see Table 5.24, column (7)— and the results were found to be generally similar: for 9 out of 13 Districts the average *number of cattle per man over 20 years* lay within the range 1·3 to ·55.

That the ratio of the human to the cattle population varied within such narrow limits was surprising considering the greater variation in cattle population per square mile—see Table 5.24, column (6): this ratio varied between 43 and 26 for the 4 Districts in the North-east and 2·2 and 0·8 in Western and Eastern Gonja. One has no idea of the extent to which the North-east is *over-grazed*, in the sense that the annual take-off expressed in terms of the weight of the cattle would have been greater had the cattle population been reduced,[1] but the carrying capacity of the land must certainly have been the factor limiting total cattle ownership in some parts of the North-east as well as in parts of Lawra and Western Dagomba.[2]

[1] There is also, of course, the question of the balance between the cattle population and food production.
[2] Though it would not then follow that individual owners with money would necessarily be prevented from building up herds, they might have done so at the community's expense.

TABLE 5.23. *Ratio of human and cattle population by Veterinary Section*

| | Cattle population (000's) 1964 (1) | Human population (000's) 1960 (2) | Humans per head of cattle (2)/(1) |
|---|---|---|---|
| Veterinary Section | | | |
| North-east | 124 | 469 | 3·8 |
| North-west | 100 | 289 | 2·9 |
| W. Dagomba/Mamprusi | 88 | 245 | 2·8 |
| E. Dagomba/Nanumba | 63 | 168 | 2·7 |
| Gonja | 23 | 118 | 5·1 |
| Total | 398 | 1,289 | 3·2 |
| North-east | | | |
| Frafra | 30·9 | 150 | 4·9 |
| Kassena-Nankani | 27·8 | 93 | 3·3 |
| Builsa | 22·1 | 51 | 2·3 |
| Kusasi | 43·3 | 174 | 4·0 |

TABLE 5.24. *Cattle population per square mile and per adult man*

| | Total human population 1960 (1) | Population of men (20 years and over) (2) | Population density per sq. mile (3) | Area in sq. miles (approx.) (4) (1)/(3) | Cattle population 1964 (000's) (5) | Cattle population per sq. mile (approx.) (6) (5)/(4) | Cattle per adult man (7) |
|---|---|---|---|---|---|---|---|
| **Veterinary Sections and Local Authority areas, 1960** | | | | | | | |
| North-east | | | | | | | |
| Builsa | 50,922 | 13,069 | 59 | 860 | 22·1 | 26 | 1·6 |
| Kassena-Nankani | 93,397 | 22,867 | 147 | 640 | 27·8 | 43 | 1·2 |
| Frafra | 150,028 | 36,230 | 204 | 730 | 30·9 | 42 | ·58 |
| Kusasi | 174,291 | 45,535 | 147 | 1,190 | 43·4 | 36 | ·72 |
| North-west | | | | | | | |
| Wala | 130,973 | 28,427 | 39 | 3,360 | 51·7 | 15 | 1·2 |
| Lawra | 114,193 | 21,496 | 105 | 1,100 | 35·8 | 33 | 1·8 |
| Tumu | 43,540 | 8,789 | 16 | 2,720 | 12·1 | 4·4 | ·95 |
| W. Dagomba/Mamprusi | | | | | | | |
| Tamale | 58,183 | 18,902 | 626 | 100 } 53·1 | | 25 | ·98a |
| W. Dagomba | 82,288 | 15,090 | 41 | 2,010 } | | | |
| Mamprusi | 104,463 | 24,211 | 35 | 2,990 | 35·3 | 12 | ·88 |
| E. Dagomba/Nanumba | | | | | | | |
| E. Dagomba | 122,473 | 30,418 | 20 | 6,240 | 46·7 | 7·5 | 1·3 |
| Nanumba | 45,937 | 10,789 | 31 | 1,480 | 16·6 | 11 | ·55 |
| Gonja | | | | | | | |
| W. Gonja | 62,431 | 16,064 | 7 | 8,920 | 19·2 | 2·2 | ·45 |
| E. Gonja | 55,792 | 13,412 | 11 | 5,070 | 4·1 | 0·8 | ·32 |

N.B. Column (3): statistics from the Ghana Census Report. Column (7): column (2) in Table 5.22 divided by column (2) in this table, except for the N.E. Veterinary Section for which statistics in column (3) of table 5.22 have been used.

a The effective male population (of 20 years and over) has been reduced to 27,000 in calculating this figure to allow for the presence of non-cattle-owning strangers in Tamale town.

On the basis of interviews with 61 cattle owners[1] in Western Dagomba and in Wa in the North-west, and of scrutiny of certain detailed cattle census returns in these localities, some attempt was made to judge the size-distribution of the herds and the means by which individuals set about developing their herds.

Statistically there was no choice but to define a *herd* as a group of cattle registered, in the official livestock census, against the name of a single owner, even though most herds, especially those of any size, included cattle owned by persons other than the herd-owner.[2] A statement such as that most herds in Western Dagomba and Wa were 'small', implies that the groups of animals actually owned by individual registered herd-owners were even smaller. Most herds in those areas were, in various senses, relatively small: they were not, for instance, large enough to justify the employment of a Fulani herdsman,[3] this being in great contrast to the situation on the Accra Plains. Throughout the North, so far as the evidence goes, cattle are invariably herded by young boys, if no Fulani is in charge.

The statement that the herds are, in some senses, 'small', is not based on the sample of herd-owners I interviewed, as I deliberately sought out the larger owners, whose experience was likely to have been especially interesting. In Western Dagomba 20 of the herd-owners interviewed had recently had 979 cattle in their herds,[4] and in Wa—where there were a few very large

[1] I am very grateful to the officials of the Animal Health Division who introduced me to the cattle owners: being in such good company, I was immediately trusted.
[2] Many registered herd-owners said that they were prepared to look after cattle on behalf of others (both kin and non-kin) and especially when a Fulani herdsman was employed. There was always the possibility that the proportion owned by the registered herd-owner might be quite small. Cattle owners were no more prepared to discuss herd-ownership in detail than were those on the Accra Plains.
[3] In Western Dagomba the employment of Fulani as herdsmen was very rare: thus I was told that in the Kumbungu Division (where, in 1964, there were 182 registered cattle owners, with 3,695 cattle in their herds) there were only 5 such herdsmen. The 1960 population census recorded only 390 persons of Fulani origin in the whole of Western Dagomba: as many of them would have been in non-cattle work and as women and children were included, the conclusion which had been derived from the fieldwork, that the employment of Fulani herdsmen was unusual, must clearly have been correct. The same applied, in general, to the Wa area, where the presence of 720 Fulani was recorded in 1960: in general, only the very largest cattle owners, or men whose main occupation was something other than farming, employed Fulani, except in the Nadawli district where it was a little more common. The Fulani herdsmen in the North were badly off compared with those on the Accra Plains. They were in charge of fewer animals; the price at which they could sell milk was lower; and there were fewer opportunities of building up a special relationship with outside owners who remunerated them directly. Consequently, few of them could afford to employ assistants. In the Wa area there was a practice of giving the Fulani a lump sum in cash during the dry season—sums of £10, £13 and £15 were mentioned. Alternatively, some Wa owners gave their Fulani a fixed sum per animal per year, this being usually as little as 1s. or 2s. (say £3 or £6 for a herd of 60), though one informant mentioned that he, like his father before him, paid 6d. a head a *month*—he had a herd of 116 animals, so this was nearly £3 monthly.
[4] The largest herd, that of 157 head, had greatly diminished in size since the census, many animals having been sold or slaughtered as a consequence of the owner's death.

herds—32 interviewed herd-owners had had as many as 2,277 cattle in their herds.[1]

Inspection of the census figures for Gukpegu or Tamale (1963), Kumbungu (1964) and Savelugu (1964) Divisions showed that about half of the 18,715 cattle enumerated were in herds containing fewer than 30 animals, that about a quarter were in herds of 30 to 64 animals and that most of the remainder were in herds with less than 100 animals.[2]

The impression was formed that in Western Dagomba the ownership of cattle by women was very rare.[3] So it seems interesting to relate the number of registered herd-owners to the estimated male population aged 20 and over. If the three Divisions for which cattle census figures were analysed are regarded as representative, then the number of registered cattle owners in Western Dagomba in 1964 might be estimated at about 2,100.[4] As the estimated male population aged 20 and over of Western Dagomba (exclusive of non-cattle-owning strangers living in Tamale) was about 27,000 in 1960, it seemed that only about one adult man in 13 was a registered herd-owner.

When this ratio was related to average herd-size (25 head), it was at once apparent that there were many adult males in Western Dagomba who owned no cattle—the average registered owner was certainly not looking after cattle for as many as 12 other owners. As fathers reportedly seldom gave cattle to their sons and as those who had been able to acquire a few cattle for themselves were seldom in charge of their own animals, the number of registered owners was perhaps appropriately related to the male population aged 40 and over—which, according to the 1960 census, was about half the total adult male population. Such a calculation would have made the ratio of registered cattle owners among men aged 40 and over about 1 in 7— clearly there were many older men who did not own cattle.

Turning to the North-west Section, cattle census figures showed that the Wa Division (based on Wa town) had an exceptionally high proportion of large herds, many of them having been owned by cattle-traders and others not primarily engaged in farming; nearly one-third of the cattle there were in herds containing 100 head or more, and (as in the Gukpegu Division) there was also a substantial number of owners with herds in the size-group 65 to 99 head. But nearly a half of all owners had fewer than 30 animals in their herds.

---

[1] Census figures were extracted for 52 of the herd-owners interviewed (20 in W. Dagomba, 32 in Wa).

[2] There were a few cases where cattle owned by two or more persons were amalgamated in one large herd—at least for registration purposes—so that the number of herds which contained 100 animals or more is not worth recording here.

[3] Women seldom inherited cattle and they received few gifts from their husbands or others. (Women took no interest in cattle husbandry and never milked the animals.)

[4] Based on an average herd of 25 head and a cattle population of 53,147.

In the Wechiau Division of the Wa District, where the population was predominantly Lobi, all save one of the 18 cattle owners with herds of 30 or more animals belonged to that ethnic group.[1] About 30% of the total of 3,561 cattle enumerated in that Division in 1964 were in the herds containing 30 or more—the corresponding proportion for the Wa Division having been 13%.

It was not to be expected that either the Wa or the Wechiau Divisions would have been typical of the North-west Section as a whole, which is ethnically heterogeneous,[2] so I draw no general conclusions about the distribution of cattle ownership in that Section. (But, as already noted, this ethnic heterogeneity had no relevance to the rate of take-off from the herds, which was everywhere high.)

The cattle populations of Western Dagomba and of Wa (including Nadawli) grew fast between 1952 and 1964—that of Western Dagomba roughly doubled and that of Wa rose by nearly 50% (Table 5.22). Whether this growth was associated rather with an increase in the average size of herds than with an increase in their number we do not know.

The fieldwork showed that the picture of 'net growth' had many aspects. Many herds were clearly the creation of their owners, who had not inherited any significant number of cattle. Many had grown out of a herd that had been inherited from father or grandfather. Many herds had 'vanished' as a result of outbreaks of disease, or because of sales resulting from death, poverty, food shortage, or a desire to invest in some other asset, for instance a pilgrimage to Mecca, or education for children.

Most of those who had themselves created (or greatly expanded) their herds claimed to have done so on the proceeds of farming. Often the herd had been built up very slowly indeed, starting with an initial investment in one or two heifers.[3] Occasionally, huge herds had been built up very rapidly indeed—an example being a Grunshi farmer in Wa whose herd included 256 cattle. A significant class of owner consisted of cattle (or general) traders or butchers who had invested their profits in cattle.

Five Fulani cattle owners were interviewed, 4 of them in the Nadawli area of the North-west. It appeared that few of the Lobi cattle owners in the North-west had brought any animals with them on their migration into

---

[1] Nearly all the Lobi interviewed in the Wechiau Division had migrated from Upper Volta within the previous 10 to 20 years.

[2] Including Dagarti, Sissala, Wala and Lobi people. (Although each of these was regarded as a 'tribe' for the purposes of the 1960 census, none is an ethnic group in any conventional sense.)

[3] Informants often emphasized the difficulty they had had in buying their first heifer at a reasonable price—this being a serious difficulty considering the rarity of organized cattle markets.

Ghana from west of the river Volta. These people are very active food traders with a strong ambition to invest their profits in cattle.[1]

As there is such a serious lack of ethnographic data bearing on the inheritance of cattle among Western Dagomba and North-western peoples, I think it is worth recording that neither in Western Dagomba nor among the Wala was there any evidence that herds, as such, were apt to be divided among the sons at death—though the cattle are sometimes sold and the proceeds divided.[2] At the same time there was no concept of a 'family herd', such that any distinction was made between self-acquired and inherited cattle. In Wa, where there are so many active Muslims, there was no evidence that the Muslim rules regarding division of property among sons applied to cattle.

With some Dagarti,[3] on the other hand, a strict distinction was sometimes made between inherited animals (which together with their progeny make up the family herd) and self-acquired stock. It was emphasized that when a man bought cattle for himself it was necessary for him to inform his relatives of this, so that his freedom to deal as he wished with these animals (and their progeny) would be recognized. To avoid confusion with family property, a man who bought stock for himself might prefer to ask a maternal relative to buy on his behalf. The practical conclusion was that individual Dagarti are less free than Wala or Dagomba to sell animals from their herds without consulting their relatives. There was no evidence of herds being divided on death.

With the Dagomba and the Wala, bride-wealth either did not exist or was so small as to be irrelevant in this context. It was said that with the Dagarti no actual cattle were included in bride-wealth, though it might be necessary for a beast to be sold so that the required cowries,[4] say 30,000 to 60,000 of

[1] The rural markets in the Wechiau Division were predominantly 'populated' by Lobi women traders, many of whom still affected the traditional huge lip-disc and most of whom (unlike their menfolk) disdained clothing.

[2] This is particularly likely to occur on the death of a chief—or other office-holder—which is one reason why the common practice of seeking information exclusively from such people is apt to be so misleading.

[3] This relates only to Dagarti in the Wa area.

[4] In some markets in the North-west, mainly those frequented by Lobi women sellers, cowry shells were still in use in 1965 as a genuine medium of exchange, circulating parallel to Ghanaian notes and coin. Cowries were also used as a store of value, principally by the Lobi but also by the Dagarti, whose bride-wealth was apt to include cowries. In Wechiau Market, south-west of Wa, there was evidence of a preference for cowries on the part of some Lobi sellers, those who paid cowries receiving more produce than corresponded to the 'official rate' of 10 cowries to a penny— thus a buyer who paid 10 cowries for *pito* (guinea-corn beer) received a fuller calabash than one who proferred a penny coin. One informant reported having bought a bag of 55,000 cowries in Kumasi for £23—almost exactly 10 a penny. (Ethnographers will not be surprised to learn that one man volunteered that a bag of cowries 'happened' to be equal in value to a mature cow.) Such was the apparent demand for cowries in some North-western frontier districts that it was

them, might be acquired by the man's father—being payable to the woman's father.

As for inheritance among the Lobi of Wechiau Division, I can only record that although, in 1932, R. S. Rattray thought that a change was imminent in the rule that 'inheritance of property is still through the sister's son',[1] there was no evidence that, some 35 years later, such a change had occurred.[2] It still seemed that 'all the cows go to the matrilineal nephew' (*ibid.* p. 435), unless the deceased had a surviving brother.[3] Perhaps that nephew still removed the cattle gradually, 'not leaving the son destitute all at once' (*ibid.* p. 445)—'he may leave some with the son even for ten years'. The only practical conclusion of which is that, with the migrant Lobi of Wechiau, there is no 'evidence' that 'the cow is the enemy of matriliny'.[4]

tempting to wonder whether, in these days of exchange control, it was not appropriate that they should stage a comeback as an international currency—tempting, until one saw 'French' and Ghanaian notes openly displayed as 'wares' on a market stall.

[1] *The Tribes of the Ashanti Hinterland*, R. S. Rattray (1932) (17), p. 432.

[2] None of the earlier forecasts which were made by observers in Ghana, that matriliny was on the way out, for instance with the Akan, seemed to have been borne out by events.

[3] See *Les Tribus du Rameau Lobi*, H. Labouret (1931) (12), p. 254.

[4] See 'A model of African Indigenous Economy and Society', H. K. Schneider (18), p. 51, the citation being words of D. Aberle drawn from *Matrilineal Kinship*, ed. D. Schneider and K. Gough, p. 680.

# CHAPTER 6

# NOTES ON THE HISTORY OF THE NORTHERN KATSINA TOBACCO TRADE[1]

## INTRODUCTION

Tobacco (*taba*) was grown as an *export crop* in northern Katsina in the nineteenth century. The trade was mainly conducted by farmers, resident in dispersed hamlets, who stored the tobacco for a price-rise and later transported it north. It is my hope that these brief notes will do a little to dispel the prevailing urban bias, which would have it that most significant economic enterprise in West Africa generally, and in Hausaland in particular, is city-based.

In the insignificant dispersed hamlets of Kabakawa there are, today, at least a dozen men, known locally as 'tobacco Alhajis', whose pilgrimage to Mecca derived from the magic weed. Their trade is now mainly conducted at a number of important market-places situated on the Niger frontier. Although some Kabakawa farmer-traders still proceed directly to Zinder by donkey, and although many go by lorry to Agadez, with which they retain very close links, the direct tobacco trade with Niger is now increasingly falling into the hands of Niger traders who travel to Kabakawa (and to other more rapidly developing Nigerian tobacco-growing areas) to buy for themselves.

[I am most grateful to Mr M. S. Nuhu for obtaining additional valuable information from Abubakr Labo (see p. 143, n. 1) in 1968.]

The historical importance of the northerly long-distance trade in tobacco grown in northern Katsina appears to have been overlooked. Important for its own sake, this trade also had great pump-priming significance, for it directly enabled the farmers to adventure southwards on *fatauci* (long-distance trading), as far as Lagos. At the end of the nineteenth century the trading stereotype was as follows. In the middle of the rainy (or farming) season the tobacco farmer-traders from northern Katsina set out for Damagaram (Zinder) (and also to other destinations, including Agadez, 250 miles north) with donkey-loads of tobacco, which they had deliberately stored for a

[1] Reprinted, with amendments and additional material, from the *Journal of the Historical Society of Nigeria* (October 1968).

price-rise for some six to nine months. With the cowries received for the tobacco they bought livestock in Damagaram and natron (*kanwa*) at neighbouring Muriya, then returned home to complete their harvest and to fatten the animals. A few weeks later they proceeded southward, again in donkey caravan, with the natron and livestock, which they sold in such places as Ilorin, Ibadan, Abeokuta. With the proceeds they bought imported kola at Lagos, which they carried home with them, the trading cycle being then complete.

Partly because many features of this tobacco trade remain unchanged today, historical information is readily obtained from participants. My own informants were some half-dozen elderly men who live in the adjoining hamlets of Kabakawa, Morawa and Kaukai, which are situated in Mallamawa District, some 5 to 10 miles south and south-east of Katsina city.[1] None of these hamlets is on a road or a map—Kabakawa and Kaukai are areas of dispersed settlement[2] and Morawa, though compact,[3] is very small. I here refer to this neighbourhood, generally, as 'Kabakawa'.

Kabakawa, I venture to suggest, was the most renowned tobacco-growing centre in north-central Hausaland in the late nineteenth century. Although my informants could say no more than that they had inherited this trade from their 'fathers', that unrivalled observer of the rural scene, Henry Barth, who slept the night in Kabakawa (proper) on 21 March 1853, wrote this account of his southward journey the following day:

beyond the village of Doka [a hamlet south of Batagarawa] the dorawa [locust bean tree], which is the principal tree of the provinces of Katsena and Zariya, again came prominently forward...The country was populous and well cultivated, and extensive tobacco-grounds and large fields of yams or gwaza [i.e. cocoyams, not yams proper] were seen, both objects being almost a new sight to me; for tobacco, which I had been so much surprised to see cultivated to such an extent in the country of the pagan Musgu,[4] is scarcely grown at all in Bornu, with the exception of Zinder, and I had first observed it largely cultivated near the town of Katsena... Numerous herds of cattle were seen dotting the landscape, and contributed largely to the interest of the scenery.[5]

Although Barth makes no mention of the long-distance tobacco trade in this region, the likelihood is, then, that such trade with the north was already

[1] I am grateful to Alhaji Nuhu, Arabic teacher of Batagarawa school, for the necessary introductions.
[2] The 'centre' of Kabakawa is now so small that it is reported that a surveyor arrived there recently asking where the renowned village could possibly be. Some of the inhabitants of Kaukai have recently removed to a small settlement near the road.
[3] So compact, that in 1966 nearly every house and granary was damaged by an accidental fire, much tobacco being destroyed.     [4] Where farms generally were much manured.
[5] *Travels and Discoveries in North and Central Africa, 1849–1855*, by H. Barth (1), citation from vol. III of the American edition published in 1859, pp. 89–90.

well established at Kabakawa in the mid-nineteenth century—that, indeed, tobacco was being grown on the 'extensive grounds' as an 'export crop'.

I now proceed to provide a few details of the structure of the tobacco trade with Damagaram at about the end[1] of the nineteenth century, as related by informants. Prices in Damagaram were higher than they were locally, partly because the people there were much given to chewing tobacco (mixed with natron).

The Kabakawa farmer-traders who were involved in the Damagaram trade were all sufficiently secure, financially, to store the tobacco for a price-rise for some six to nine months and were, also, those who could leave the responsibility for their farming in the hands of slaves and/or sons when they set out on their journey, at about the time of the second-weeding of their farms, when the tobacco price in Damagaram was known to reach its peak. Although all the traders were themselves tobacco farmers, some of them bought, and stored, tobacco grown by others.

If tobacco were properly processed and stored it would keep for years. At a time when quality control of export crops bound for overseas markets is achieved mainly through official organizations such as Marketing Boards,[2] it may be worth while recording, in rough outline, the various processes which were necessary to secure a good-quality export crop seventy years ago.

1   The tobacco was picked, between December and early February, four different grades of leaf (according to the position on the stalks) being treated separately —certain of them were unsuitable for 'export'.

2   The leaves were stored for two days, in a well-ventilated room, until they went brown.

3   The leaves were then tied in fan-shaped bundles (*sanka*, pl. *sankaye*) and sun-dried for several days. (At that stage the leaves were brittle and were not touched.)

4   The bundles were then sprayed with water at intervals of some hours, until they had lost their brittleness.

5   A hole was then completely lined with *kalgo* (*kargo*) leaves (from a tree which commonly grows on uncultivated land), and the bundles, which had also been wrapped in these leaves and then blanketed in an ash-coloured mat made from palm-leaves (*malfa*), were gently placed inside the hole.

6   Heavy stones were then placed on the tobacco for one day.

7   The leaves and mats having been removed, the bundles were then placed on a floor, or rock, for a short time, each bundle being turned over and over again until it was perfectly dry and well aerated.

[1]   The earliest trading expeditions of my main informant, Abubakr Labo of Kaukai, to whom I am greatly indebted, can be precisely dated, since as a youth he was in Damagaram with his father (nicknamed Geshe), a famous *madugu* (caravan-leader), during the reign of Sarki Ahmadu, who ruled from 1893 to 1899, when he was forced to flee—Geshe had been there much earlier, regarding the place as a second home.

[2]   As is necessary, since the growers are not the ultimate sellers of the produce.

8 The bundles were then placed in corn-stalk huts for final drying.

9 When completely dry, the bundles were removed to a clean, dry, safe place and left there until the advent of the rains.

10 The bundles were then stored in an ordinary clay granary (*rumbu*), which had been lined, on the floor and walls, with 3 to 5 layers of mat, which were bent and rolled at the mouth of the bin, covering the tobacco completely. The granary was then closed with a thatch.

11 When the time came for selling the tobacco (perhaps in June or July), the bundles (which may have been stored for more than a year) were removed from the granary, sprayed with water, and baled to protect them from the rains, using mats and a network of rope (*taitai*).

12 The bales, which were then loaded on donkeys for transport, required no further attention until Damagaram was reached.

The price of native (as distinct from commercial) tobacco exhibits great seasonal variation today. At the end of the nineteenth century it seems that a rough doubling in price, during the six to nine months the traders held off the market, was quite common. Obviously, the traders would not have set out on their journey at a time of maximum inconvenience, during the muddy rains and active farming season, had prospects of higher profits not motivated them.

For the purposes of their journey to Damagaram, which was about 100 miles distant, the individual traders, some of whom rode oxen, formed themselves into small groups; many of them were accompanied by sons or servants, who often walked separately with the donkeys, which were loaded with skin water-bottles (*salka*) as well as with tobacco. On arrival at their destination each trader lodged with his *mai gida* (lit. house-owner), the 'landlord' whose function it was to store his tobacco and arrange for its sale.[1] The *mai gida* was rewarded in kind with a proportionate share of the bundles traded—say 5 out of every 100 *sankaye*—and his wife, or servants, might receive part of the tobacco dust (*gari*). The traders sold little of their tobacco in Damagaram market-place and any kola or locust-bean cakes (*daddawa*),[2] which they also happened to be trading,[3] was likewise mainly sold outside markets.

Payments for the tobacco were in cowries. Too little has been made in

---

[1] For a general account of the 'landlord' system of house-trade see 'Landlords and Brokers: A West African Trading System', by the present author (3). See also 'The Social Organisation of Credit in a West African Cattle Market', by Abner Cohen (2), for a detailed description of the workings of the Hausa landlord system in Ibadan cattle market.

[2] *Daddawa* is another neglected product of importance in long-distance trade. Near Zakka, southwest of Katsina city, Barth noted the arrival of 'a troop of about 100 fataki [traders] with asses laden entirely with the famous dodowa [*daddawa*] cakes' (*op. cit.* (1), p. 95).

[3] Informants were agreed that these goods were of minor importance compared with tobacco. (Most of the kola brought back from the south on the previous expedition had been sold before the traders set forth again.)

the literature of the extreme inconvenience of the cowry currency in the latter years of the nineteenth century, when cowry values were so inflated. It was nothing unusual for the weight of the cowries to be greater than that of the merchandise for which they were exchanged, so that the traders lacked the transport to return home with the cowries, even had they been inclined to load nothing else save water, on to their donkeys.[1] The traders were therefore obliged to spend their cowries either wholly on goods less weighty than the equivalent currency or, partly, on ambulatory purchases—livestock or slaves. Furthermore, the risks and inconvenience of openly counting huge piles of cowries in a market-place were such as to favour house-trade.

The Kabakawa traders mainly invested their cowries in livestock (cattle, sheep and goats) bought in Damagaram and in natron[2] (*kanwa*) bought in the market-place at Muriya a few miles east of Damagaram. At Muriya, also, there were lodging-houses for traders, owned by *fatoma*, the Kanuri word for landlord. Occasionally a Kabakawa trader would buy a slave, the price of which could have been up to 100,000 cowries—a weight of shells which might require 3 to 5 donkeys for its transport.[3] Thus it was that, in Abubakr Labo's words, 'you went with your capital, and you returned with your capital'; and after waiting for a few weeks at Kabakawa, perhaps until the bean (*wake*) harvest had been completed, off you went southwards with your capital again.

[1] I am indebted to Mrs Marion Johnson for reminding me of the following citation: 'The trouble is that we cannot sell it [a dying horse] as its value in cowries would require fifteen porters to carry, to whom we should have to pay all the money they carried and a great deal more besides; there is in fact nothing we could get in exchange for it which it would pay to carry with us.' *Hausaland*, by C. H. Robinson (5).

[2] Natron is still widely consumed, by both humans and livestock, as condiment and medicine.

[3] Although this estimate is based on long discussion with Abubakr Labo, much uncertainty remains owing to variations in the proportions of small (Maldive) cowries and (the much heavier) large cowries. Mrs Marion Johnson tells me that 20,000 of the Maldive cowries weighed about 50 lb., being a conventional man's load—see also *Baba of Karo* by Mary Smith (6), p. 81; she adds that some authorities—including P. L. Monteil (4), p. 282, who was in Hausaland in the early 1890s—regarded 50,000 cowries as a conventional donkey-load. On donkey-back the cowries were carried in *birgami* (*burgami*), defined in Bargery's *Hausa Dictionary* as being 'a dressed goat-skin made into a wide-mouthed bag, the shape of the animal being retained'.

CHAPTER 7

# FARMS AND FARMERS IN A HAUSA VILLAGE (NORTHERN NIGERIA)

---

INTRODUCTION

This brief study provides an introduction to a few aspects of my forthcoming publications relating to farms and farmers in Nigerian Hausaland, with special reference to a village called Batagarawa in northern Katsina Emirate, where I lived for nearly six months in 1967. Owing to the farmers' preference for a system of annual cultivation of manured farms with no fallow, farming may be considered as relatively capital-intensive and, for this and other reasons, some of the ideas about West African rural capitalism, which had been developed in other contexts, were found relevant here.

As this is merely a brief introductory study, references have been reduced to a minimum.

Batagarawa is the seat of the District Head of Mallamawa. I wish to express my deep gratitude to Mallamawa personally for welcoming me to Batagarawa as an *uwar gida* (lit. 'mother of a house'—woman head of a house) and to the many friends I made in the village. My first introduction to Batagarawa came in 1966 through Muhammed Sabiu Nuhu, then a student at Ahmadu Bello University, whose father Alhaji Nuhu is teacher of Arabic in the Batagarawa primary school: Mr M. S. Nuhu worked as my assistant for ten months and my gratitude to him, for his efficiency, intelligent work and kindness, knows no bounds. When in Northern Nigeria in 1966 and 1967 I was so fortunate as to be appointed Visiting Senior Research Fellow of the Nigerian Institute of Social and Economic Research (NISER), University of Ibadan. I am much indebted to members of the Institute for their efficient helpfulness.

This study is mainly concerned with certain aspects of the socio-economic life of farmers in a Hausa village in Northern Nigeria which might seem unexpected, even surprising, to anyone with some knowledge of rural West Africa, but little or none of rural Hausaland. I start with some background information on the village, which is (I think) an ordinary—not especially

146

atypical—village of north central Hausaland. (I hasten to add that I am only too well aware that the state of our ignorance of rural Hausaland is such that any notion of typicality could be regarded as a reckless contradiction in terms.)

Batagarawa lies six miles south of the ancient walled city Katsina, near a minor road. The total population of the hamlet (*unguwa*) of Batagarawa in 1967 was about 1,400, of whom about 1,160 lived in a small compact 'town' (*gari*)—a 'miniature city' with clay-walled streets and compounds—the remainder in dispersed farmhouses nearby. The excellent primary school was founded as long ago as 1946—there are many much larger Hausa towns with no school today—and many young Batagarawa men are in higher education. In 1967 there was no market in the town; the latest of many attempts to establish one occurred in 1968.[1]

Farming is much the most important occupation in Batagarawa. Grains (millet and guinea corn) and groundnuts (mainly for export) are the chief crops, and numerous other crops including beans (*wake*) and native (not commercial) tobacco are also grown. It is nothing but misleading to refer to cash and subsistence 'sectors': any crop might happen to be sold by the grower for cash and there are few crops, other than tobacco, which are not apt to be self-consumed. Nor does the economist's word 'surplus' have any useful meaning: the better-off people aim at buying grain when it is cheap (just because it is cheap) and at selling it when it is dear, the worse-off people are often obliged to do exactly the opposite. As seasonal price fluctuations of farm produce are very marked, it is, as we shall see, the timing of grain selling, not its occurrence or non-occurrence, which is significant.

Virtually all the women of child-bearing age in the *gari* (but not in the dispersed farmhouses) are in full Muslim seclusion, to the extent that they seldom emerge from their husband's compounds; however, mainly through the medium of children, many of them are active traders,[2] and most have a gainful occupation. Polygyny is an ideal, but only about a quarter of all married men have more than one wife—this degree of unbalance between the sexes being achieved by means of men marrying later than women. Divorce is very common.

The norms of domestic organization are easily described, the nucleus of most households (or compounds) being a simple family consisting of a man and his wives and children. For economic purposes it is not the household but the group which I here call the 'farming-unit' which is significant—a 'farming-unit' consisting of the men who work together on a set of farms, together with their dependants. When a son marries he usually continues to work mainly on his father's farms (though as his family grows, he may move

---

[1] See 'Hidden Trade in Hausaland', by Polly Hill (12)        [2] *Ibid.* (12).

into a separate section of his father's house, or into another house), in return for which his father provides him with foodstuffs and/or cooked food, pays his tax, and assists him in numerous other ways; he is then spoken of as being in *gandu*[1] with his father. *Gandu* is a voluntary contract which, like marriage, may be broken by either party or by mutual consent: a father may ask his son to leave *gandu* (he may even dismiss him), or a son may decide to abandon his father. But in Batagarawa many sons (other than those who migrate)[2] stay with their father until he dies. The father has an obligation (which he usually honours if he can) to give his son a farm for his personal use (this, then, being outside the inheritance system) and many sons in *gandu* acquire farms for themselves—indeed some sons in *gandu* are larger farmers than their fathers. Although only about a quarter of all farming units consist of *gandu*, this is not due to the weakness of *gandu* as an institution, but rather to such factors as high mortality among middle-aged men (so that many young men are household heads) and the migration of sons—in Batagarawa there are altogether only two fathers *all* of whose *resident* sons have left *gandu*.

There is no doubt but that this *paternal gandu* is a strong institution in many parts of Nigerian Hausaland[3] though it has many variable features. On the other hand *fraternal gandu*, under which brothers work together under the authority of the eldest of them, on their late father's farms, is becoming rather uncommon in some areas—in Batagarawa and neighbouring hamlets it seldom exists unless the father died when some of his sons were very young, the eldest son then stepping into his father's position, and elderly informants are quite emphatic that a once flourishing institution is now dying.

When a father dies, then, his manured farms (see below) are usually divided between his sons[4]—in a rather rough-and-ready way, as is shown by our farm maps, which are based on air-photographs,[5] as well as on ground inspection.

[1] The main source on *gandu* in Muslim Hausaland is *The Economy of Hausa Communities of Zaria* by M. G. Smith (22); otherwise the literature is astonishingly slight. Those who write on rural land tenure ignore it completely and the system of community taxation takes no cognizance of it, sons in *gandu* not being listed together with their father.

[2] Most migration is either for farming, or for government employment, teaching, higher education or work as servants—there is only a small drift to Katsina city. The subsequent history of three whole classes of Batagarawa boys who had been at school in 1954 and 1955 was examined—a half of them were still farming in Batagarawa.

[3] Smith noted it in rural Zaria; I have observed it in Gwandu Emirate (Sokoto Province) as well as in Katsina; Greenberg (7) recorded its existence among non-Muslim Hausa in Kano; I am grateful to members of the Rural Economy Research Unit, Institute for Agricultural Research, Ahmadu Bello University, for informing me of its existence elsewhere, e.g. in heavily populated areas near Sokoto city. See also (1). It also exists, in a very different form (as women are not there in Muslim seclusion) among the Hausa of Niger (See (17), (18), (19)).

[4] In so far as daughters receive shares, they often proceed to sell them to a brother.

[5] Our air-photographs were enlarged copies of a print kindly lent by the Survey Department, Kaduna.

148

Lip-service only is paid to the rules of Muslim inheritance, and hardly any land cases reach the alkali's court in Katsina city.

The sale of manured farms is very common indeed, involving close kin (fathers, sons, brothers) as well as non-kin; so little formality attends a transaction that farms are often sold on impulse—though only by the most poverty-stricken, there being many steady farmers, some not at all well off, who never sell farms. In Batagarawa the last effective remnant of chiefly control over the farm rights of the citizenry[1] was abolished a few years ago, when migrating farmers were no longer required to pass their farms to the District Head on their departure, but were free to sell them to any citizen, though etiquette demands that they should give their brothers the right of first refusal. This informality over farm-selling is associated with the lack of any concept of lineage land, or (if one prefers to put it this way) with the lack of lineages:[2] to avoid begging all awkward questions, one may simply assert that there is no concept of 'rural land tenure', only a practice of 'farm tenure'.

Farms are of two types.[3] In a zone of variable depth (roughly $\frac{3}{4}$ to $1\frac{1}{2}$ miles) around the *gari*, and also around the dispersed farmhouses, nearly all the farms are manured and cultivated every year—only the poverty-stricken fail to manure their farms in this zone. Known to the farmers as *gonar karakara*,[4] the farms in this zone comprise most of those which are involved in trans-actions—being bought, sold, inherited, pledged and so forth. Most of the farm produce grown by the Batagarawa farmers comes from these farms,[5] which have an area of roughly 2 square miles. The other type of farm is the bush-farm (unmanured), or *gonar daji*, which is cultivated for a few years (there is no standard practice) and then allowed to go fallow; these farms are seldom involved in transactions, they are very seldom formally inherited, but they are sometimes rented (*aro*); they are most of them situated between about $1\frac{1}{2}$ to 4 miles of the *gari*, where there is much land which may be freely[6] cultivated—they are dotted about in the bush as the air-photographs show.

[1] A citizen is not, however, free to sell a farm to a stranger without at least mentioning the matter to the hamlet head.       [2] See M. G. Smith, *op. cit.* (22).

[3] A third type, consisting of farms on swampy ground (known as *fadama*), is much more important in some localities than in Batagarawa, where the acreage is relatively small.

[4] The meaning of *karakara* (*karkara*) according to Bargery's *Hausa Dictionary* is 'land, near a city, which is covered with hamlets and farms': thus, a farm which happens not to be manured though it falls inside the zone of continuous cultivation, is denoted as *gonar karakara*. (To avoid pedantry, all Hausa words are used in their singular form throughout.)

[5] Although it was unfortunately not possible to map the dispersed bush-farms (many of which would in any case have been under fallow in March 1966 when our air-photograph was taken), statistics relating to the extent to which certain labourers were employed on the two types of farm indicated the relative unimportance of the bush-farm.

[6] Much of this land is in the hamlet (*unguwa*) of Batagarawa; as for land in other hamlets, the farmer who cultivates it may give a few bundles of grain to the hamlet head at harvest.

The prices of manured farms appear usually to be very low in relation to potential net yield. This price represents the amenity value of the farm (mainly in terms of its proximity to the village) plus something representing the value of unutilized manure—the actual quality of Batagarawa land is said to vary very little.

Evidence is fast growing that the farmers' preference for the annual cultivation of manured farms is widespread in Hausaland, sometimes even in hamlets which are surrounded by oceans of uncultivated bush. Contrary to general belief, this practice is not Malthusian—the farmers *prefer* to keep all their farms within a mile or two of their residences under continuous cultivation every rainy season, irrespective of the supply of land outside this zone. In the Kano Close Settled Zone,[1] where population densities may be as high as 600 per square mile or more, and also in a large heavily populated zone around Sokoto city[2] there is, on the contrary, no element of choice—if the farmers did not cultivate their land every year they would either starve or be driven to migrate. But elsewhere in Nigerian Hausaland continuous (or permanent) cultivation is commonly the preferred system.[3]

In West Africa generally, continuous cultivation is very rare, except with permanent tree crops, although it is probably quite old in Hausaland. In particular, it does not exist in West Africa's other major groundnut-exporting region, the 'groundnut basin' of Senegal even where population densities are very high, as sometimes with the Serer.[4] Nor does it exist in Bornu[5]—or among the Hausa of the Niger Republic.[6] The usual agronomic system in the savannah involves special crops only being grown on the manured 'gardens' round the house—the bulk of the grains, for instance, being produced on farms which are cultivated under rotational systems involving fallow: in Batagarawa *all* the early millet, the most humdrum of all crops, is grown on the manured farms, only later varieties of millet, known as *maiwa* or *dauro*, being grown on bush-farms.

Whenever an observer encounters annual cultivation in West Africa he is apt to regard it as unique. Thus the Kabre of North Togo are said to 'practise an intensive agriculture, unique in West Africa, based on permanent cultiva-

---

[1] See *Land and People in the Kano Close-Settled Zone* by M. J. Mortimore and J. Wilson (14).
[2] Oral information from Mr D. Goddard of the Rural Economy Research Unit—see p. 148, n. 3.
[3] Except, perhaps, in those southern areas where the high incidence of trypanosomiasis prevents cattle rearing. See the Appendix for further discussion of the general question.
[4] See *Les paysans du Sénégal* by P. Pelissier (20).
[5] Oral information from Dr Ronald Cohen of Northwestern University.
[6] The valuable and extensive work of Dr G. Nicolas (which is unfortunately published only in the form of cyclostyled reports (three of which are (17), (18), and (19)) establishes that the socio-economic organization of *rural* Hausa in the Niger Republic is in striking contrast, in many ways, to that of the Nigerian Hausa just over the frontier.

tion in conjunction with stock-rearing'.[1] The explorer Henry Barth was astonished when, in the middle of last century, he observed that the Musgu, who live south of lake Chad, manured their fields.[2] But Dr R. McC. Netting makes no such claim with regard to the type of intensive agriculture[3] pursued by the Kofyar of the Jos Plateau in Northern Nigeria, and Dr J. M. Hunter is quite matter-of-fact in his assertion that the Nangodi of N.E. Ghana grow 'the bulk of their foodstuffs on manured farms round their houses'.[4]

I am not now concerned to speculate about the reasons for the Nigerian Hausa having a 'different' agronomic system from those of most West African savannah peoples. I will only observe firstly that it is a system which accords very well with the 'rules' formulated by locational geographers regarding rural settlement and land-holding;[5] secondly, that Netting's suggestion that 'the typical nuclear or small independent family household...is peculiarly adapted to the labour needs of intensive agriculture'[6] should be examined in relation to the Hausa; and thirdly that continuous cultivation is a relatively capital-intensive system, at least with the Hausa— a matter which might be associated (as I shall now consider) with a high degree of economic inequality among farmers as well as with acute poverty, including landlessness.

Although the general standard of living in Batagarawa is low (when compared for instance with that of certain migrant cocoa-farmers of southern Ghana),[7] a considerable proportion of farmers is sufficiently well organized

---

[1] W. Hetzel, 'Est-Mono: die Kabre und ihr neues Siedlungsgebiet in Mitteltogo' (10). The citation is from *African Abstracts*, XVIII (1967), abstr. no. 161.

[2] The land was so carefully cultivated 'that even manure had been put upon the fields in a regular manner, being spread over the ground to a great extent', *op. cit.* (2), vol. II, p. 382.

[3] See 'Household Organisation and Intensive Agriculture: the Kofyar case', by R. McC. Netting (16).    [4] See 'The Clans of Nangodi' (13), p. 393.

[5] Dr Michael Chisholm notes 'the frequency with which the same orders of magnitude keep on recurring among peoples of widely different technical achievements and inhabiting areas with markedly different physical characteristics...Over much of the world, the present spontaneous tendency is to modify the patterns of rural settlement and land-holding in such a manner that the distance separating the farmstead from the lands cultivated is reduced to something in the order of 1 or 2 kilometres, if the farmstead is not actually on the farm...At a distance of 3–4 kilometres the costs of cultivation necessitate a radical modification of the system of cultivation or settlement—for example by the establishment of subsidiary settlements—though adjustments are apparent before this point is reached.' *Rural Settlement and Land Use*, by Michael Chisholm (4), p. 148. See p. 157 of the Appendix.

[6] Netting, *op. cit.* (16), p. 422.

[7] Thus, no one owns any motorized transport; there are about 12 bicycles, 10 sewing machines, 15 imported metal ploughs and about the same number of groundnut decorticators—there is little other 'machinery', apart from a few radios; all dwellings are clay-roofed or thatched; there is no dispensary and most of those who die have received no modern medical attention. (It should be added that the water supply is excellent: the water-table is high and there are many wells, both privately and publicly owned.)

to withstand the usual vicissitudes of economic life, including very late, as well as very poor, harvests. We found that the farming-units which we came to regard as the 'top 10%' (this group, which excluded members of the ruling class, had initially been defined as those who in the weeks preceding the early millet harvest of September 1967 were actively helping others who were hungry)[1] owned about a third of the total acreage of manured farms, their average holding per farming-unit being about 20 acres compared with about 5 acres for the rest of the population. Whatever economic indicator one sought to measure a farming-unit's living standard (and we were in search of indicators since we lacked the staff to undertake a survey of income and expenditure, which in this type of seasonal economy is useless unless carried out for a full year), the 'top 10%' as a group always excelled. They grew much more of the basic food crops per working man or per head of the population; they owned most of the capital equipment used in farming, such as ploughs and decorticators; their *gandu* were exceptionally well organized; nearly all of them had reasonably lucrative non-farming occupations, mainly craft (notably tailoring) and local trading in grains and groundnuts.

At the other end of the scale were as many as 41 farming-units (nearly a quarter of the whole) which, after examining their circumstances as fully as possible,[2] we classified as the 'hopelessly poverty-stricken'—farmers caught up in a vicious circle of helpless poverty. Some of these farming-units had no manured farms—they or their fathers having sold the lot; many of them cultivated their bush-farms very poorly, or had none at all; many of them could be regarded as having 'no time to farm'—at the beginning of the farming season their granaries were empty (if there had ever been anything in them), so that they were obliged to earn their daily bread every day, by collecting and selling firewood, working as labourers for others, eking out a living as best they might; some of the households had abandoned cooking, buying all their food from others; many were considered such hopelessly bad risks that no one would lend to them—a serious situation in a society where a man can expect little help from close kin (other than a father or son) and where Muslim alms do not fill the gap.

In this community the only people who deliberately contract out of farming are a few of those who attach themselves as 'servants' to the ruling class—a group which includes courtiers, drummers, flatterers, etc., as well as house and farm servants: they are, most of them, illpaid but, unlike the 41

---

[1] The list was compiled on the basis of subjective judgments made by four well-informed farmers, each reporting separately: the statistics of acreages owned, numbers of working men, etc. were not computed until later. See 'The Myth of the Amorphous Peasantry', by the present writer (11).

[2] The procedure of selection in this case was different from that adopted with the 'top 10%'—see n. 1 (above): a tentative list was compiled using all the statistical and other information available to us and then opinions were sought from third-parties.

down-and-outs, they enjoy a minimum of security during all seasons. All those who enjoy high prestige in the community (and this goes as much for Koranic scholars as for others) are reasonably large-scale farmers, although they are not necessarily self-sufficient in foodstuffs. A failed farmer must, therefore, be regarded as a general failure.

An examination of the very narrow range of non-farming occupations pursued by the failed farmers indicates their plight. None of them works as a skilled craftsman; none is a trader in grains or groundnuts. Most of them are dependent on the sale or manufacture of 'free goods' (grass, twigs, cornstalks, palm leaves, wood, etc. from which mats, rope, thatches, beds, etc. are made for sale in Batagarawa) or on farm or general labouring.

In considering why some farmers are 'successes' others 'failures', I must first dispose of any idea that certain 'primal causes' *necessarily* determine a man's economic standard. In particular I must insist that Western notions of class stratification are quite inapplicable in this society. The proportion of the 'top 10%' who are of 'slave-descent'[1]—defined as those whose fathers were descended from male slaves—is perhaps about one-third (35%); the corresponding proportion for the poverty-stricken being one-third also (33%). Accidents of birth do not predetermine a man's success as a farmer.[2] Even if the 'top 10%' as a group had inherited greater acreages than the poverty-stricken (figures which cannot be computed owing to farm-sales by the latter), some members of the group were very ill endowed, two of them having inherited no farms at all. Then, some of the poverty-stricken had had fathers who had both been notable successes as farmers and had had few sons to share their property on their death.

Nor, in terms of a farming unit's *present circumstances* is there any evidence of the existence of primal causes of 'success' or 'failure'. It is particularly interesting that the ratio of the number of working males to the total weighted population (children being counted as 'half-adults') is about equal for the upper and lower crusts. I suggest that explanations should be sought in terms of a *conjunction* of favourable, or unfavourable, circumstances working together at a given time and involving individuals in short-term spirals of 'relative affluence' or poverty.

The kinds of factors which, *several of them working together*, produce relative affluence include: exceptionally good organizational powers as a farmer; inherited advantages (such as a father who had large farms and few

[1] This information was again sought from well-informed, reliable, third-parties—see p. 152, n. 1: obviously it could not have been obtained directly from informants. So many definitional and practical difficulties are encountered in making estimates of this kind, that they would seem to have very little use except for comparative purposes such as this one.
[2] Thus some of the 'failed-farmers' were at one time quite well off and some of the sons of 'failed-farmers' are clearly seen to be climbing out of the morass.

sons); personal good luck (such as having many sons); wise lending of money or farm produce; training as a craftsman; exceptional ability in non-farming enterprise; fame as a Koranic teacher; trustworthiness, so that people will lend to you in adversity; a great capacity for hard work; and so on and so forth.

The kinds of factors which, *several of them working together*, produce great poverty include: bad health; poor organizational powers as a farmer; failure in non-farming enterprise; inherited disadvantages (such as a father who sold all his manured farms); personal calamity (the death of a young father or of wives); cruel consequences of debt (such as the confiscation of a farm); no sons; impulsive or unavoidable selling of farms (although nearly all the poverty-stricken have sold farms, many others have done so too); and so on and so forth.

So much for the causes of *individual* 'success' or 'poverty'. I conclude by noting a few of the reasons why this system of rural capitalism tends to help those who help themselves—and *vice versa*. First of all, there is the question of manure: the farms of the better-off are much more productive per acre than those of the worse-off, as they can afford to manure them so much more adequately. (The main kinds of manure—apart from imported modern fertilizer, the popularity[1] of which is growing extremely fast—include compound sweepings, droppings of small livestock and donkeys, cattle manure—most of the cattle being owned by pastoral Fulani who are paid when they bring them to eat the stubble on the farms after harvest—and even latrine-manure; all kinds of manure command a price and one of the most fatal temptations to which the worse-off are subject is that of selling their compound sweepings.) Then, take output per man-day: the figures show that the 'top 10%' farm a much greater acreage (of more productive land) per working man than the average farming unit: if, for instance, no plough is owned, a member of the group can usually afford to hire[2] one. The manpower available to the 'top 10%' is much better organized than the average (their *gandu* organizations being really effective), and as, in addition, the better-off farmers often employ farm-labourers,[3] and own nearly all the ploughs and oxen, the possibilities of carefully timing their farming

---

[1] Supplies are restricted owing to Nigeria's current balance of payments difficulties.

[2] In Batagarawa virtually all plough owners hire out their ploughs: this makes nonsense of many discussions of 'mixed farming' which seriously consider the minimum acreage required by the plough owner: presumably one reason hiring is ignored in the literature is that it is (or was) prohibited by the loan-granting Native Authorities who regarded it as usurious—of course the farmers have always ignored the prohibition.

[3] More of them dependants than heads of farming-units. Nearly all employment is on a daily basis, the rate of pay for a long morning's work having been 2s. 6d. (plus porridge) in 1967, and 2s. in 1968; although some farmers are very much dependent on labourers, the volume of hired labour is fairly small relative to family labour; with rare exceptions, all heads of households, who are neither ill, decrepit, nor hopelessly poverty-stricken, work hard as farmers.

operations so as to take advantage of inter-cropping techniques, and successive planting of crops on the same land, are better exploited by them.

Seasonal price fluctuations are very severe in Batagarawa—they may, fortunately, be measured quite accurately owing to the universal use of a standard container called a *tiya*.[1] Although it seems that prices often (roughly) double between harvest and pre-harvest, there is a strong element of unpredictability, resulting mainly from varying crop-sizes and dates of harvest.[2] The better-off farmer aims at deploying his capital, and grain and groundnut storage-capacity, so as to buy cheaply and sell dearly; a poverty-stricken man, who is obliged to meet his debts by selling at harvest-time when prices are lowest, buys grain at a much higher average price, taking the year as a whole, than his better-off counterpart. The better-off are, effectively, paid by the poverty-stricken in their capacity as grain-storers.

It seems likely that everywhere in Hausaland where groundnuts are grown for export a large proportion of the farmers retain no groundnut seed at harvest,[3] and it is to be presumed that it is generally true, as in Batagarawa, that it is the richer farmers who store.[4] The poorer farmers are obliged to buy or borrow their seed when prices are highest, and given the extent and timing of price fluctuations it is not unreasonable that they should often be required to repay, from their harvest, twice the quantity of groundnuts borrowed. The better-off lender will be insured against the possibility of a negative interest-rate by his option of holding the repaid groundnuts for a later price-rise.

It is commonly said that interest-rates are so high in Hausaland because of the Muslim pretence that interest-taking is usurious: although there may be some truth in this, it is surely more appropriate to associate high apparent (though not necessarily actual) rates with great seasonal price fluctuations and capital shortage. At the village level there are so many devices enabling anyone to escape the Muslim 'prohibitions' (for instance by lending produce and receiving cash in return or *vice versa*) and so much overt interest-taking, that any better-off, versatile lender, who spreads his risk by lending to those he can trust in numerous different ways, is bound both to make a large profit and to enhance his prestige in the community as one who 'helps people'.

[1] This enamel bowl, which holds 5 to 6 lbs. of grains or shelled groundnuts, was originally introduced by the Katsina Native Authority: it cannot be forged and is a genuine standard.

[2] In 1967 the first (planting) rains came 6 weeks later than in 1966 and 1968.

[3] In a paper (in the Government Archives at Kaduna) on the supply and storage of groundnut seed, by Mr K. D. S. Baldwin (1957), it was estimated that roughly three-quarters of the farmers of Kano, Katsina and Sokoto Provinces sold all their groundnuts to the Marketing Board.

[4] There is some storage (by women as well as men) of nuts for making groundnut oil for local consumption.

The dice being weighted so heavily in favour of the better-off, how can one simultaneously argue that Batagarawa is not 'class-stratified'[1] in any conventional sense—that the spirals of individual economic involvement are apt to be *short-term*? I think this may best be expressed in terms of the ephemeral nature of the *gandu* institution which exists only during the (usually rather short) phase of a man's life when he has adult sons: on his death the *gandu* nearly always breaks abruptly—the 'farming business' collapses on the death of the founder, just like so many other types of West African business enterprise. The father's property is divided between his sons, some of whom may be in those peculiarly vulnerable phases of having no working sons, or incurring marriage expenses. Rich fathers own large acreages: but, owing to polygyny, they are also apt to have a more than average number of sons to share the property.

In general, the absence of 'class stratification' in West African rural life is associated with polygyny (among other factors). 'Rich' old men in Batagarawa (as elsewhere) are apt to have wives of various ages, so that when they die their sons may range in age from (say) 50 to infants. The older sons will have had an opportunity (which they may or may not have taken) of establishing themselves independently while under their father's wing—sons in *gandu* always have time to pursue serious non-farming occupations; but the future of the youngest sons will depend mainly on whom their widowed mothers marry—even if, ultimately, they do inherit a few acres of manured farmland, this will be no larger an area than many farms inherited by the sole sons of poorer farmers.

In an authoritarian Muslim society like Hausaland, it is all too easy to fall victim to the prevailing view that the status and standard of living of the individual farmer tend to reflect the position of his forebears. Assuming that Batagarawa is an 'ordinary Hausa village' I suggest that, on the contrary, historico-political factors have created the sort of sensitive rural economy in which a farmer's standard of living is mainly determined by his response to the opportunities offered.

### APPENDIX

My assertion that evidence is now fast increasing that continuous cultivation is common in Hausaland is so contrary to common belief, which would have it that the system has developed chiefly in the vicinity of the bigger towns—see *Land and People in Nigeria* by K. M. Buchanan and J. C. Pugh (3)—or where rural population densities otherwise exceed a critical figure (see below), that it is necessary to make some attempt to consider the circumstances in which the system (defined

[1] This discussion is not concerned with the possibility of the emergence of an élite group based on higher education, nor with the position of the very small ruling class—the *sarauta*

as one under which the bulk of crops is grown on manured land) may be expected to occur. This surmising is made necessary both by the extreme scantiness of reliable reports on this subject—most of the few investigators of Hausa rural economies have either neglected it (as did M. G. Smith), or dealt with it rather casually, or tended to take it for granted (as did A. T. Grove)—and by the unrepresentativeness of the single small hamlet for which detailed statistics of farm areas existed, before the Rural Economy Research Unit at Ahmadu Bello University started their work, this being Gata, in Zaria Province (see below).

The ability of any group of farmers to pursue this method of farming depends of course on their having sufficient manure, the main variables in this connexion (apart from the means to pay for imported fertilizer) being the size of the local cattle population (including visiting Fulani-owned cattle) and the possibility of 'importing' refuse etc. (as manure) from neighbouring cities, as is the practice in parts of the Kano Close Settled Zone (Mortimore and Wilson (14) report that $1\frac{1}{2}$ tons per acre of Kano city manure is applied to the farms in one area studied) but not in Batagarawa despite its proximity to Katsina city. Where there is no large city in the neighbourhood and where the visiting and resident cattle population is low—how low can never be generally estimated owing to the importance of other local forms of manure, especially the droppings of small livestock and donkeys, and also human excreta, which in some localities, including Batagarawa, is a saleable commodity traded by latrine diggers—then the farmers may be prevented from practising continuous cultivation on a large scale by progressive declines in yield which, it is important to note, do not *necessarily* occur (as 'common sense' so often suggests), even if continuous cultivation has been pursued for many decades, as is most certainly the case around Kano and Sokoto cities. Presumably the position has been stabilized around these big cities and there is not necessarily much outward migration of farmers (see (14)): where it cannot be stabilized there is, presumably, a strong tendency for farmers to migrate, much of Hausaland being very sparsely populated.

Then, the greater the number of ploughs per head of population, the greater the likelihood (other things being equal) that the farmers will favour continuous cultivation, owing to the convenience of stumpless, weedless, sandy land.

Clearly it is in accordance with the rules of the locational geographers (see p. 151, n. 5) that, within certain ranges, the farmers' preference for continuous cultivation increases with settlement size. A continuously cultivated zone of a radius of $1\frac{1}{2}$ miles could support a population of about 1,500 people, *on the basis of 2 acres of farmland per head of the population,*[1] an allowance of some 30% being made for the area taken up by houses, small grazing areas, stony or other infertile ground, streams, cattle-tracks, etc.—no account being taken of the yield of bush-farms outside this zone. The corresponding population for a zone with a radius of one mile would be about 700, and most farmers might well concentrate most of their farming within this zone. With smaller settlement sizes the farmers, considered as a group or as individuals, would have a greater range of rational choice—

---

[1] This was about half the acreage of *manured* farmland per head in Batagarawa: it equalled the approximate acreage of *cultivated* farmland per head in Gata (see below) and in the three localities studied in detail by A. T. Grove—see p. 159, n. 1.

as individuals, the richer farmers might still prefer to manure a large proportion of their acreage, the poorer farmers concentrating rather on nearby bush-fallow.

Farmers living in small hamlets, or wholly dispersedly, may practise continuous cultivation—as I have observed for myself in various localities in Katsina Emirate where there is no shortage of land for bush-farms. A glance at air-photographs may be sufficient to establish this—our investigations showed that, provided these photographs had been taken in the dry season, the weedless *gonar karakara* are white in contrast to the greyness of farms fallowed for only a single season.[1] But if the farmers are newcomers, then the proportion of farms under continuous cultivation is likely to be low, as the farmers require time to clear and stump their land completely and to build up their 'stock' of manure in the ground.

Mr D. R. Buxton who, in 1938–9, made an excellent map of the farmlands of the hamlet of Gata (pop. 180), which was published much later in *The Anchau Rural Development and Settlement Scheme* by T. A. M. Nash (15), now tells me that, so far as his memory goes, it is quite probable that the farmer Auta (see p. 8) who had an exceptionally large area under continuous cultivation, was (himself or his father) the hamlet founder. It is even noted that a farmer who had hardly any manured farmland, but had cleared a huge farm of 30 acres a mile away from the hamlet, was a newcomer. One may surmise that the proportion of Gata farmland which is now under continuous cultivation is bound to be much higher than it was thirty years ago (when it was a quarter of all land actually under cultivation), especially if ploughs have meanwhile been introduced—manure supplies should not be a serious problem as Gata is on an important cattle-route.

The difficulty with any approach to this question which is based on the general density of population is that of great local variations in this density, except of course in the very heavily settled zones around cities. When asked, in this connexion, about the population density in the Batagarawa area, I prefer to evade the question by pointing out that a great part of the land falling under the 'jurisdiction' of the Batagarawa hamlet head is uncultivated bush which may be freely cultivated. (There are never any maps of hamlet land, and in this case there is much doubt about certain boundaries—but anyway it would help little to relate the Batagarawa population to the Batagarawa hamlet area, as Batagarawa farmers often make bush-farms in other hamlet areas.)

The only other relevant source is Dr R. M. Prothero's work on land use at Soba in Zaria Province (21). Prothero did not map individual farms or holdings, and the population of Soba village is not known, owing to the unfortunate practice in the 1952 Nigerian census of including outlying hamlets in enumeration areas based on towns of all sizes. The fact that the zone of permanent cultivation at Soba had a depth of no more than $\frac{1}{2}$ to $\frac{3}{4}$ of a mile might very well have been explained by the

---

[1] Mr A. T. Grove has kindly shown me his collection of air-photographs covering large areas of Katsina Emirate, which establish that, irrespective of the general density of population, a high proportion of cropped land is under continuous cultivation. It is proposed to use the Print Laydowns, on the scale of 1:50,000, issued by the Directorate of Overseas Surveys, for further study of the position elsewhere.

impossibility of rearing cattle there owing to trypanosomiasis, with a consequent shortage of manure.

Although one may follow Mr A. T. Grove—'Population Densities and Agriculture in Northern Nigeria' (9), p. 125—in postulating a 'critical figure of population density', such that 'the outermost zone of bush-fallow farming is eliminated from the land-use pattern', he has been kind enough to explain to me personally that this means that there will necessarily come into existence at this critical density (which is only very tentatively put at 150 to 200 persons per square mile, owing to great variations in the quality of soil), a continuously cultivated zone between villages with islands of bush.[1] He goes so far as to add that he has always taken for granted that, irrespective of population density, continuous cultivation is very common in Hausaland: population density (provided it is below the critical figure) has little influence on the *proportion of crops* grown on manured farmland, as distinct from the *proportion of land* which is permanently cultivated: the kinds of generalization one makes on the latter point depend on the scale of the map with which one is concerned. So far as any particular village is concerned, the general density may have little influence on the proportion of crops grown on manured farmland. The really critical density is such that there are no bush-farms at all, as in the vicinity of Kano and Sokoto cities. Unless this density is reached, the size of the settlement is one of the crucial variables determining the proportion of farmland under continuous cultivation.

[1] The population density in the three localities of Dan Yusufu District which were studied in detail by Mr Grove—see (8)—exceeded the critical figure: in these localities about 90% of cropland was under cultivation in any year (pp. 56–7).

# REFERENCES AND BIBLIOGRAPHIES

REFERENCES TO CHAPTER 1

1   Allan, W., *The African Husbandman*, London, 1965.
2   Bohannan, P. and Dalton, G., eds., *Markets in Africa*, Northwestern University Press, 1962.
3   Dupire, Marguerite, 'Planteurs autochtones et étrangers en Basse-Côte d'Ivoire orientale', Études Éburnéennes, VIII, 1960, Abidjan.
4   Fallers, L. A., 'Are African Cultivators to be called "Peasants"?', *Current Anthropology*, April 1961.
5   Farnsworth, Helen C., 'Defects, Uses and Abuses of National Consumption Data', *Food Research Institute Studies* (Stanford University), II, No. 3, 1961.
6   Hill, Polly, 'Some Characteristics of Indigenous West African Economic Enterprise', *The Economic Bulletin* (Ghana), VI, No. 1, 1962, and in *Proceedings* of the Conference held in March, 1962 by NISER (Nigerian Institute of Social and Economic Research), University of Ibadan, 1963.
7   Hill, Polly, *The Migrant Cocoa-Farmers of Southern Ghana*, Cambridge, 1963.
8   Lewis, W. A., *Report of Industrialisation and the Gold Coast*, Government Printer, Accra, 1953.
9   Lloyd, P. C., *Yoruba Land Law*, Oxford, 1962.
10  Polanyi, K. *et al.*, eds., *Trade and Markets in the Early Empires*, 1957, chapter by W. C. Neale: 'The Market in Theory and History'.
11  Raeburn, J. R., in *Proceedings of the Ninth International Conference of Agricultural Economists*, 1956.
12  Reddaway, W. B., 'The Economics of Under-Developed Countries', *Economic Journal*, March 1963.
13  Schultz, T. W., *Transforming Traditional Agriculture*, Yale University Press, 1964.
14  Wallerstein, I., 'The Search for National Identity in West Africa', *Présence Africaine* (English edition), VI/VII, 1961.
15  Webb, Beatrice, *My Apprenticeship*, Longmans, London, 1926.


REFERENCES TO CHAPTER 2

1   Beckett, W. H., *Akokoaso: A Survey of a Gold Coast Village*, London School of Economics, Monographs on Social Anthropology, No. 10, 1944.
2   Brokensha, D. W., *Social Change at Larteh, Ghana*, Oxford, 1966.
3   Hill, Polly, *The Migrant Cocoa-Farmers of Southern Ghana*, Cambridge, 1963.

4  Hill, Polly, 'Three Types of Southern Ghanaian Cocoa-Farmer', in *African Agrarian Systems*, ed. D. Biebuyck, Oxford, 1963.

5  Johnson, Marion, 'Migrants' Progress', Parts I and II, *The Bulletin of the Ghana Geographical Association*, x, Nos. 1 and 2, 1964, 1965.

6  Green, R. H. and Hymer, S. H., 'Cocoa in the Gold Coast: a study in the relations between African farmers and agricultural experts', *The Journal of Economic History*, xxvi, No. 3, September 1966.


BIBLIOGRAPHY TO CHAPTER 3

1  Barbot, J., *A Description of the coasts of North and South Guinea*, London, 1746.
   Brown, A. P., see (14)

2  Firth, Raymond, *Malay Fishermen: Their Peasant Economy*, London, 1946.

3  Fisheries Division, Ghana, *Report* for 1959, Government Printer, Accra.

4  FAO, *The Economics of Fisheries*, ed. R. Turvey and J. Wiseman, 1957. (Proceedings of a Round Table organized by the International Economic Association.)

5  FAO, *Fish Marketing in Ghana*, Report No. 1300, Rome, 1961.

6  Grove, Jean M., 'Some Aspects of the Economy of the Volta Delta (Ghana)', *Bulletin de l'IFAN*, January to April 1966.

7  Gruvel, A., *Les pêcheries de côtes du Sénégal*, Paris, 1908.

8  Gruvel, A., *L'industrie des pêches sur la côte occidentale d'Afrique*. Paris, 1913.

9  Härtter, Von G., 'Der Fischfang im Evheland', *Zeitschrift für Ethnologie*, 1906.

10  Hill, Polly, 'Some Characteristics of Indigenous West African Economic Enterprise' (Ghana) *Economic Bulletin*, vi, No. 1, 1962.

11  Hill, Polly, *Notes on the Socio-Economic Organisation of the Anloga Shallot-Growing Industry*, Institute of African Studies, University of Ghana, 1965 (cyclostyled).

12  Hill, Polly, 'Pan-African Fishermen', *West Africa*, 28 December 1963 and 4 January 1964.

13  International Fisheries Exhibition, 1883, *Fisheries Exhibition Literature*, v, London, 1884.

14  Irvine, F. R., including 'The Fishing Industry of the Labadi District' by A. P. Brown, *The Fishes and Fisheries of the Gold Coast*, Crown Agents, 1947.

15  Lawson, Rowena M., 'The Structure, Migration and Resettlement of Ewe Fishing Units', *African Studies*, xvii, 1958.

16  Manoukian, Madeline, *The Ewe-Speaking People of Togoland and the Gold Coast*, International African Institute, Ethnographic Survey of Africa: Western Africa, Part vi, 1952.

17  Nukunya, G. K., 'Kinship, Marriage and Family: A study of Contemporary Social Changes on an Ewe Tribe'; unpublished Ph.D. thesis, London University, 1964.

18  Singer, B. *Living Silver: An Impression of the British Fishing Industry*, London, 1957.

19   Spieth, J., *Die Ewe-Stamme*, Berlin, 1906.
20   Steven, G. A., *Report on the Sea Fisheries of Sierra Leone*, Crown Agents, 1947.
21   de Surgy, Albert, *Les pêcheurs de Cote d'Ivoire*; Tome I, *Les pêcheurs maritimes*; Fascicule I, *Les pêcheurs Anlo*, Fascicule 2, *Les pêcheurs Fanti*, Centre National de la Recherche Scientifique, distributed by IFAN, Paris, 1965 (cyclostyled).
22   de Surgy, Albert, *La pêche traditionnelle sur le littoral Evhé et Mina* (*De l'embouchure de la Volta au Dahomey*), Groupe de Chercheurs Africanistes, 44 Rue de Bellechasse, Paris 7ème, 1966 (cyclostyled).
23   Thomas, Rev. C. W., *Adventures and Observations on the West Coast of Africa and its Islands*, New York, 1860.
24   Volta River Project, *Appendices to the Report of the Preparatory Commission*, II, HMSO, 1965.
25   Ward, Barbara E., 'An example of the "Mixed" System of Descent and Inheritance', *Man*, January 1955.
26   Westermann, D., *Die Glidyi Ewe in Sud-Togo*, Berlin, 1935.


BIBLIOGRAPHY TO CHAPTER 4

1   Barbot, J., *A Description of the Coasts of North and South Guinea*. London, 1746.
2   de St Croix, F. W., *The Fulani of Northern Nigeria: Some General Notes*. Government Printer, Lagos, 1945.
3   Cardinall, A. W., *The Gold Coast, 1931*. Government Printer, Accra.
4   Dupire, Marguerite, *Peuls Nomades*, Institut d'Ethnologie, Université de Paris, 1962.
5   Edinburgh University, Centre of African Studies. *Markets and Marketing in West Africa* (Proceedings of a seminar held in April 1966), 1966.
    Ferguson, W., 'Nigerian Livestock Problem', inc. in (5).
6   Fulton, A., *Report on the Development of the Livestock Industry of the Eastern Province*. Gold Coast Sessional Paper No. 5, 1935.
7   *Gold Coast Gazette*, 'Findings delivered at Dodowa' by Mr Justice Jackson, Stool Lands Boundaries Settlement Orders, 24 March 1955.
    Hutchinson, R. A., 'Stock and Methods of Animal Husbandry' in Wills, J. B. (14).
8   Meredith, H. *An account of the Gold Coast of West Africa with a brief history of the African Company*, London, 1812.
9   Montsma, G., 'Sale of Milk and Rearing of Calves in Ghana', *The Ghana Farmer*, IV, No. 1, Feb. 1960.
10   Ollennu, N. A., *Principles of Customary Land Law in Ghana*, London, 1962.
11   Oppong, E. N. W., 'Bovine Brucellosis in Southern Ghana'. *Bulletin of Epizootic Diseases of Africa*, XIV, 1966.
    Rose Innes, R., 'Grasslands, Pasture and Fodder Production' in Wills, J. B. (14).
12   Stewart, J. L., 'The Cattle of the Gold Coast', *The Empire Journal of Experimental Agriculture*. January 1938.

13  White, H. P. 'Environment and Land Use in the South Eastern Savannas of the Gold Coast', *Proceedings of the Fifth Annual Conference* of the West African Institute of Social and Economic Research, 1956 (cyclostyled).

14  Wills, J. B., ed., *Agriculture and Land Use in Ghana*, Oxford, 1962.


BIBLIOGRAPHY TO CHAPTER 5

1   Bauer, P. T. and Yamey, B. S., *The Economics of Underdeveloped Countries*, Cambridge Economic Handbooks, 1957.

2   Cardinall, A. W., *The Gold Coast, 1931*, Government Printer, Accra.

3   Fortes, M., *The Web of Kinship among the Tallensi*, Oxford, 1949.

4   Fortes, M. and S. L., 'Food in the Domestic Economy of the Tallensi', *Africa*, 1937.

5   Ghana Census 1960, *Special Report 'E': Tribes in Ghana*, Government Printer, Accra.

6   Goody, J. R., *The Social Organisation of the LoWiili*, HMSO, Colonial Research Studies, No. 19, 1956 (2nd edition Oxford, 1967).

7   Gould, P. R., 'Man against his environment: a game-theoretic framework', *Annals of the Association of American Geographers*, 1963.

8   Gray, R. F. and Gulliver, P. H., eds., *The Family Estate in Africa*, London, 1964.

9   Grove, A. T., *Land and Population in Katsina Province*, Government Printer, Kaduna, 1957.

10  Hill, Polly, 'Landlords and Brokers: A West African Trading System', *Cahiers d'Études Africaines*, 1966.

11  Hunter, J. M., 'Population Pressure in a part of the West African Savannah': A study of Nangodi, Northeast Ghana', *Annals of the Association of American Geographers*, March 1967.

    Hutchinson, R. A., Chapter on 'Stock and Methods of Animal Husbandry, in (21).

12  Labouret, H., *Les Tribus du Rameau Lobi*, Paris, 1931.

13  Manoukian, M., *Tribes of the Northern Territories of the Gold Coast*, International African Institute, 1951.

14  Murdock, G. P., *Africa: its Peoples and their Culture History*, New York, 1959.

15  Oppong, E. N. W., 'A Note on Goats in Ghana with reference to the need to Develop Goat Husbandry to improve the Nation's Diet', *The Ghana Farmer*, IX, no. 4, Nov. 1965.

16  Pogucki, R. J. H., *Gold Coast Land Tenure*, I, *A Survey of Land Tenure in Customary Law of the Protectorate of the Northern Territories*, Government Printer, Accra, 1955.

17  Rattray, R. S., *The Tribes of the Ashanti Hinterland*, II, Oxford, 1932.

18  Schneider, H. K., 'A Model of African Indigenous Economy and Society', *Comparative Studies in Society and History*, October 1964.

19  Tait, D., 'On the Growth of some Konkomba Markets', *Report of Annual*

Conference—Sociology Section, West African Institute of Social and Economic Research, 1953.

20  Werhahn, H., Frick, W., *et al. The Cattle and Meat Industry in Northern Nigeria*, Frankfurt am Main, 1964 (cyclostyled).

21  Wills, J. B. ed., *Agriculture and Land Use in Ghana*, Oxford, 1962.

22  Wilson, A. S. B., 'A Regional Comparison of Human and some Meat Animal Populations', *Economic Bulletin of Ghana*, VII, no. 1, 1963.

23  University of Edinburgh, Centre of African Studies, *Markets and Marketing in West Africa*, 1966.


REFERENCES TO CHAPTER 6

1  Barth, H., *Travels and Discoveries in North and Central Africa, 1849–1855*, American edition, III, New York, 1859.

2  Cohen, A., 'The Social Organisation of Credit in a West African Cattle Market', *Africa*, 1965.

3  Hill, Polly, 'Landlords and Brokers: A West African Trading System', *Cahiers d'Études Africaines*, 1966.

4  Monteil, P. L., *De St Louis à Tripoli par lac Chad 1890–92*, Paris, 1895.

5  Robinson, C. H., *Hausaland*, London, 1896.

6  Smith, Mary, *Baba of Karo*, London, 1954.


REFERENCES TO CHAPTER 7

1  Ahmadu Bello University, Institute for Agricultural Research, *An Economic Study of Three Villages in Zaria Province: 1. Land and Labour Relationships*; *3. Maps*, by D. W. Norman, Samaru Miscellaneous Papers Nos. 19 and 23, Zaria, 1967.

2  Barth, H., *Travels and Discoveries in North and Central Africa, 1849–1855*, first British edition 1857, American edition 1859.

3  Buchanan, K. M. and Pugh, J. C., *Land and People in Nigeria*, London, 1955.

4  Chisholm, M., *Rural Settlement and Land Use*, London, 1962.

5  Cohen, Abner, *Custom and Politics in Urban Africa: A study of Hausa Migrants in Yoruba Towns*, London, 1969.

6  Cohen, R., *The Kanuri of Bornu*, New York, 1967.

7  Greenberg, J. H., 'The Influence of Islam on a Sudanese Religion', *Monographs of the American Ethnological Society*, 1946.

8  Grove, A. T., *Land and Population in Katsina Province*, Government Printer, Kaduna, n.d.

9  Grove, A. T., 'Population Densities and Agriculture in Northern Nigeria', in *Essays on African Population*, ed. K. M. Barbour *et al.*, London, 1961.

10  Hetzel, W., 'Est-Mono: die Kabre und ihr neues Siedlungsgebiet in Mitteltogo', *Würzburge geog. Arbeiten*, XII, 1964.

11  Hill, Polly, 'The Myth of the Amorphous Peasantry: A Northern Nigerian Case Study', *Nigerian Journal of Economic and Social Studies*, July, 1968.

12  Hill, Polly, 'Hidden Trade in Hausaland', *Man*, iv, no. 3, September 1969.

13  Hunter, J. M., 'The Clans of Nangodi: A geographical study of the territorial basis of authority in a traditional state of the West African Savannah', *Africa*, October 1968.

14  Mortimore, M. J. and Wilson, J., *Land and People in the Kano Close-Settled Zone*, Department of Geography, Ahmadu Bello University, 1965.

15  Nash, T. A. M., *The Anchau Rural Development and Settlement Scheme*, HMSO, 1948.

16  Netting, R. McC., 'Household Organization and Intensive Agriculture: the Kofyar case', *Africa*, Oct. 1965.

17  Nicolas, G., *Problèmes agraires en Pays Haoussa—Canton de Kantché*, Rapport provisoire—Mission 1961–62, Centre National de la Recherche Scientifique (cyclostyled).

18  Nicolas, G., *Circulation des richesses et participation sociale dans une société Hausa du Niger—Canton de Kantché*, Bordeaux, 2nd edition, 1967 (cyclostyled).

19  Nicolas, G. and Mainet, G., *La Vallée du Gulbi de Maradi*, IFAN-CNRS, Documents des Études Nigériennes, no. 16, 1964 (cyclostyled).

20  Pelissier, P., *Les paysans du Sénégal*, Saint-Yrieix (Haute-Vienne), 1966.

21  Prothero, R. M., 'Land Use at Soba, Zaria Province, Northern Nigeria', *Economic Geography*, 1957.

22  Smith, M. G., *The Economy of Hausa Communities of Zaria*, HMSO, Colonial Research Studies, no. 16, 1955.

# INDEX

# Index

# Index

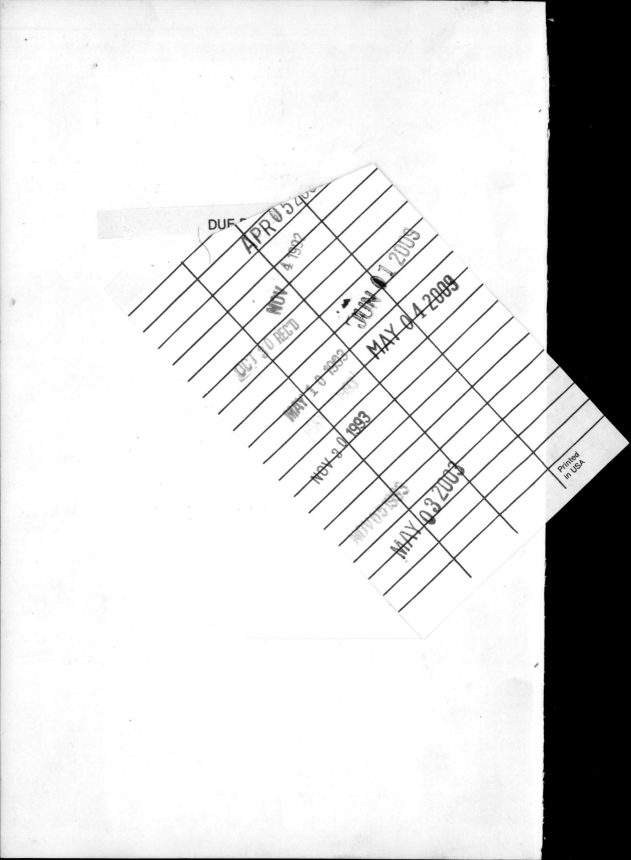